T5-ANV-736

The Role of the Legislature in Western Democracies

A Conference Sponsored by the
American Enterprise Institute for Public Policy Research,
the U.S. International Communication Agency,
the Konrad Adenauer Stiftung, and
the British-American Parliamentary Group

The Role of the Legislature in Western Democracies

Edited by Norman J. Ornstein

American Enterprise Institute for Public Policy Research
Washington and London

The complex business of putting together this multinational conference was aided greatly by the work of Robert Pranger, Austin Ranney, and Iris Volkman of AEI, Peter Wolcott of ICA, Doug Wilson and Janet Sherrard of the U.S. Embassy in London, and Manfred von Nordheim of the Konrad Adenauer Stiftung. The editor also thanks the Center for Advanced Study in the Behavioral Sciences in Stanford, California, for both assistance in preparing this volume and an idyllic setting for editing transcripts and essays.

Library of Congress Cataloging in Publication Data

Main entry under title:

The Role of the legislature in Western democracies.

(AEI symposia ; 81F)
Proceedings of a conference held at Selsdon Park Hotel, Surrey, England, June 8–10, 1979, and sponsored by the American Enterprise Institute for Public Policy Research.
1. Legislative bodies—Congresses. 2. Democracy—Congresses.
I. Ornstein, Norman J. II. American Enterprise Institute for Public Policy Research. III. Series.
JF511.R63 328′.3 81-7923

ISBN 0-8447-2214-6 AACR2
ISBN 0-8447-2215-4 (pbk.)

AEI Symposia 81F

Printed in the United States of America

The American Enterprise Institute for Public Policy Research, established in 1943, is a publicly supported, nonpartisan, research and educational organization. Its purpose is to assist policy makers, scholars, businessmen, the press, and the public by providing objective analysis of national and international issues. Views expressed in the institute's publications are those of the authors and do not necessarily reflect the views of the staff, advisory panels, officers, or trustees of AEI.

Participants

American Participants

Burnett Anderson
Minister for Information, U.S. Embassy, London

Roger H. Davidson
Professor of Political Science, University of California, Santa Barbara

Butler Derrick
United States Representative (Democrat, South Carolina)

Bob Eckhardt
United States Representative (Democrat, Texas)

Richard F. Fenno, Jr.
Professor of Political Science, University of Rochester

Thomas Foley
United States Representative (Democrat, Washington)

Robert Griffin
Former United States Senator (Republican, Michigan)

Clifford Hackett
Staff Aide to Senator Paul Sarbanes

Henry Hubbard
Congressional Correspondent, *Newsweek*

Charles O. Jones
Professor of Political Science, University of Pittsburgh

Jeane Kirkpatrick
Resident Scholar, American Enterprise Institute
and Georgetown University

Michael Malbin
Resident Fellow, American Enterprise Institute
Contributing Editor, *National Journal*

Norman J. Ornstein
Professor of Politics, Catholic University
and American Enterprise Institute

Valerie Pinson
Office of Congressional Liaison, The White House

Nelson Polsby
Professor of Political Science, University of California, Berkeley

Austin Ranney
Resident Scholar, American Enterprise Institute

Charles Rose
United States Representative (Democrat, North Carolina)

Christopher Snow
Cultural Affairs Officer, U.S. Embassy, London

Iris Volkman
Administrative Assistant, American Enterprise Institute

Charles Whalen
Former United States Representative (Republican, Ohio)

Douglas Wilson
Assistant Cultural Affairs Officer, U.S. Embassy, London

BRITISH PARTICIPANTS

David Alton
Member of Parliament (Liberal)

David Adams
Director, David Bruce Centre for American Studies, University of Keele

Kenneth Baker
Member of Parliament (Conservative)
Chairman of the Hansard Society

Clifford Boulton
Clerk of Overseas Office, House of Commons

Kenneth Bradshaw
Principal Clerk, Table Office, House of Commons

David Butler
Fellow, Nuffield College, Oxford

Lord Crowther-Hunt
Fellow and Lecturer, Exeter College, Oxford

George Cunningham
Member of Parliament (Labour)

Bernard Donoughue
Senior Policy Adviser to former Prime Minister James Callaghan

Michael English
Member of Parliament (Labour)

Philip Goodhart
Member of Parliament (Conservative)

Sydney Irving
Former Member of Parliament (Labour)

Douglas Jay
Member of Parliament (Labour)

Peter Jenkins
Policy Editor and Columnist, *The Guardian*

Anthony King
Department of Government, University of Essex

Clive Landa
Political Director, Tory Reform Group

John Lees
Department of American Studies, University of Keele

James Lester
Member of Parliament, Parliamentary
Under Secretary of State, Department of Employment

Robert McKenzie
Professor of Sociology with special reference to politics
London School of Economics

Tom McNally
Member of Parliament (Labour)

David Marquand
Department of Sociological and Political Studies, University of Salford

Charles Morris
Member of Parliament (Labour)

Roger Moate
Member of Parliament (Conservative)
Hon. Sec. British-American Parliamentary Group

Christopher Price
Member of Parliament (Labour)

Francis Pym
Member of Parliament, Secretary of State for Defence

Giles Radice
Member of Parliament (Labour)

Lisanne Radice
Lecturer, Department of Government, Brunel University

Tim Rathbone
Member of Parliament (Conservative)

Peter G. Richards
Professor of Political Science, University of Southampton

Malcolm Rutherford
Political Editor, *Financial Times*

Michael Ryle
Clerk of the Select Committees, House of Commons

Geoffrey Smith
Leader Writer, *The Times*

Janet Sherrard
Cultural Affairs Assistant, U.S. Embassy, London

Leslie Stone
Assistant Head of Central Current Affairs and Talks
BBC World Service

Shirley Williams
Former Secretary of State for Education and Science

Ian Wrigglesworth
Member of Parliament (Labour)

Esmond Wright
Director, Institute of United States Studies,
University of London

German Participants

Werner Blischke
Bundestag Legislative Staff

Klaus Daweke
Member of Bundestag (Christian Democratic Union)

Michael Hereth
Armed Forces Academy, Hamburg

Ludolf Herrmann
Editor-in-Chief, *Deutsche Zeitung*, Bonn

Rudolf Kabel
Bundestag Legislative Staff

Gerhard Kunz
Member of Bundestag and Parliamentary Leader (Christian Democrats)

Heinrich Oberreuter
Free University, Berlin

Manfred Schulte
Member of Bundestag (Social Democratic Party)

Winfried Steffani
Professor of Political Science, University of Hamburg

Uwe Thaysen
Professor of Political Science, University of Hamburg

Josef Theysing
Director, Office of External Relations, Konrad Adenauer Stiftung

Hans-Joachim Veen
Deputy Director, Social Science Research Institute
Konrad Adenauer Stiftung

Manfred von Nordheim
Washington Research Office, Konrad Adenauer Stiftung

Spanish Participants

Julien Guimon
Member of Cortés (Christian Democrats)

Javier Ruperez
Member of Cortés (Christian Democrats)

Nigerian Participants

Omobola Onajide
Special Assistant, Political Department Cabinet Office

Tunji Olagunju
Deputy Secretary, Political Department Cabinet Office

Canadian Participant

Mark MacGuigan
Member of Parliament (Liberal)

This conference was held
at Selsdon Park, Surrey, England,
June 8–10, 1979

Contents

Preface

For many decades, it has been an article of faith among political scientists and politicians that dramatic differences exist between the parliamentary system of government displayed in Britain and elsewhere and the presidential system of government that was created in the United States. Nowhere is this difference more stark than in the legislature—the parliament versus the congress. The difference begins with the names. As James Q. Wilson has pointed out, "parliament" derives from the French *parler*, "to talk," while "congress" comes from a Latin term meaning "a coming together."[1] Wilson notes that the principal daily work of a parliament is debate, while a congress engages first and foremost in representation and action, especially lawmaking.

There are also other differences, ranging from the legislature's relationship with the executive to the selection of individual members to the internal legislative structures. A main focus of scholars has been the difference in voting patterns—a parliament, such as the British, has party discipline; a congress (at least, the American Congress) does not.

Legislatures, of course, are still legislatures and thus have much in common, but it has been the differences between Congress and various parliaments that have characterized most of the analysis and comparison over the years.

In recent years, however, changes have been occurring in most western legislatures that suggest important, common trends. The U.S. Congress, in the 1970s, decentralized power and perquisites to rank-and-file "backbench" members; expanded resources, particularly staffs and information processing equipment, to all legislators and committees; and opened proceedings and actions to outside interests, the public and the mass media. All these changes occurred before a backdrop of growing mutual distrust and animosity between Congress and the executive. By the end of the decade, however, many in Congress who had precipitated these reforms were having second thoughts and were talking

[1] James Q. Wilson, *American Government* (Lexington, Mass.: D.C. Heath, 1980), p. 254.

about the need to recentralize and to bring more coherence to the policy process and more responsibility to the congressional parties.

Legislatures as diverse as those of Canada, Germany, Britain, Australia, France, and Israel, in the late 1970s saw similar, though less sweeping trends of reform. Committee systems, long meaningless in most parliaments, began to expand and to increase in importance in many assemblies. The backbench legislator, long forgotten, began to rise up and demand attention and significance—and achieved some measure of success. The meager staff resources available to many parliaments began to increase. Parliaments in Canada and elsewhere opened their proceedings to the television cameras. And in many of these legislatures, the members saw a growing gulf between the legislative branch and the executive branch, that is, between the parliament and the government. By the end of the decade serious debate had developed over how much further to expand the role of parliaments and their individual members.

Western parliaments started out far behind the United States in terms of committees, perquisites, and staffs even before the developments of the 1970s; since then, they have not appreciably closed the gap in quantitative terms. But these common themes of discussion and points of debate at the end of the 1970s indicated some convergence in attitudes and some coming together in institutional direction.

Americans, after overdecentralization, overdemocratization, and overstaffing, looked ever more longingly at the coherence, accountability, and efficiency of the parliamentary model (without, of course, an accompanying willingness to give up any of their staff or perquisites). Parliamentarians, after countless decades of totally centralized authority and a dictatorship-by-executive, looked ever more longingly at the offices, computers, chairmanships, and staff aides of each rank-and-file congressman (without, of course, their accompanying willingness to accept the messiness, deadlock, and indecisiveness of Congress).

It was in this context, as many legislatures in western democracies were beginning in concert to rethink their roles, structures, and resources, that a conference was convened in June 1979 at Selsdon Park, Surrey, England. The United States, Canada, Great Britain, and the Federal Republic of Germany were the principal focal points, with discussion groups composed of legislators, staff, journalists, and academics from these four countries, along with several observers from Nigeria and Spain.

The conference, sponsored by the American Enterprise Institute, the U.S. International Communication Agency, the Konrad Adenauer Stiftung, and the British-American Parliamentary Group commissioned six papers, which are published in the first part of this volume. The second part is the edited, transcribed record of the four sessions that made up the bulk of the conference.

The legislatures discussed in the sessions have continued to evolve since this conference was held on June 8–10, 1979. At that time, the British House of Commons was poised to debate the recommendations of its Select Committee on Procedure, to expand and enhance select committees in the House. Subsequently, a modified version of the Select Committee report was adopted. Some two years later, the full effect of the changes was being felt; a comment in the June 20, 1981, *Economist* notes,

> After the events of the past few months, nobody will be disposed any longer to write off the British House of Commons as a moribund institution. In March, a report by the treasury and civil service select committee did much to undermine the credibility of the Thatcher Government's monetary policy; in May, a threatened backbench revolt forced ministers to cut by half an increase in the duty on diesel fuel.

A change in legislative roles has not been confined to Britain. Members of the German Bundestag have been making life increasingly difficult for the government of Chancellor Schmidt, and the U.S. Congress has displayed far more party unity and has been far more attentive and responsive to President Reagan than has any recent Congress to any of his predecessors.

The debate presented in this volume sheds some comparative light on these contemporary developments. More important, by examining several different legislatures from the perspective of their counterparts, the conference discussion helps us understand the operations and development of each of these important institutions as they continue to move through the 1980s.

Norman J. Ornstein
Washington, D.C.

The Role of the Legislature in Western Democracies

Papers

The Two Congresses and How They Are Changing

Roger H. Davidson

The U.S. Congress has a persistent image problem. The other branches of government have nothing quite comparable to the comic-strip figure of Senator Snort, the overblown and incompetent windbag. Pundits and humorists find Congress an inexhaustible source of raw material. Seemingly, the public shares this disdain toward the institution. Since the mid-1960s, public approval of congressional performance has been notoriously low, surging upward only briefly at the time of President Nixon's 1974 resignation. In a recent nationwide opinion survey, three times as many citizens gave Congress a negative rating as gave it positive marks.[1]

The view of Congress held by serious commentators—seasoned journalists and scholars—is often scarcely more flattering than the public image of Congress. The currently fashionable textbook portrait of Congress, for example, is of a collection of politicians obsessed by reelection fears and surrounded with staff and facilities for constituency errand running (not a wholly erroneous picture, to be sure, but a caricature nonetheless). Legislators themselves often contribute to their shabby image by portraying themselves to their constituents as gallant warriors against the dragons back on Capitol Hill; as political scientist Richard F. Fenno, Jr., notes, they "run *for* Congress by running *against* Congress."[2]

The Two Congresses

Fenno's observations is a reminder that the U.S. Congress has a uniquely dual character: it is both a "deliberative assembly of one nation" and a "congress of ambassadors"—to use Edmund Burke's words to describe a most un-Burkean institution. It is not extravagant to observe that there is not one Congress but two. They are analytically and even physically distinct, yet they are inextricably bound together. What affects the one sooner or later affects the workings of the other.

[1] Associated Press/NBC News Poll, November 1978.

[2] Richard F. Fenno, Jr., *Home Style: House Members in Their Districts* (Boston: Little, Brown, 1978), p. 168.

One of these two entities is Congress as an institution. It is Congress, the lawmaking and policy-determining body. It is Congress acting as a collegial body, performing its constitutional duties and deliberating legislative issues. Of course, as a large institution with a demanding workload, Congress functions more often in subgroups than as a single body; yet its many work groups—there are now more than ever before—are attending to public business, and the outcomes, whatever form they take, affect the public as a whole.

There is a second Congress, however, every bit as important as the Congress of the textbooks. This is the Congress of 535 (actually 539) individual senators and representatives. They possess diverse backgrounds and follow varied paths to win office. Their electoral fortunes depend not upon what Congress produces as an institution but upon the support and goodwill of voters hundreds or thousands of miles away. As the noted journalist Richard Rovere once noted, Congress as an institution is perceived mainly as a legislative body. It is evaluated largely on the basis of citizens' generalized attitudes about policies and the state of the union: Do people like the way things are going, or do they not? By contrast, citizens view their own representatives as agents of local interests, evaluating them on the basis of such factors as their ability to serve the district materially, their communication with constituents, and their "home style."

Significantly, citizens profess to be far happier with the performance of their individual legislators than with the performance of Congress as a whole. This is the source of the observation that Americans love their congressmen but denigrate their Congress and explains why incumbents can be overwhelmingly returned to office while Congress itself remains low in the public's esteem.[3]

Notwithstanding a reputation for inertia, Congress—in both its manifestations—is now arguably the most dramatically altered of the three governmental branches. The changes have rendered obsolete much of what scholars and journalists used to write about the House and Senate. They have touched virtually every nook and cranny on Capitol Hill—membership, structures, procedures, folkways, and staffs. Some changes resulted from pressures built up over many years; others occurred suddenly and almost casually. Some have been well chronicled by journalists and scholars; others are little known and even less well understood.

In cataloging the major forces for change and analyzing their consequences, it is useful to continue the metaphor of the two congresses. What forces have affected Congress-as-institution? What forces

[3] Glenn R. Parker and Roger H. Davidson, "Why Do Americans Love Their Congressmen So Much More than Their Congress?" *Legislative Studies Quarterly* 4 (February 1979): 53-61.

have affected Congress-as-career-entrepreneurs? What innovations have these forces produced, and what new generation of problems have these innovations created?

Congress as Institution

If ours is an antiparliamentary age, it is surely because of profound ever-shifting challenges emanating from the larger economic, social, and political environment. These may take the form of pressing national problems, rising public expectations, fast-moving events, competing institutions, or simply a burgeoning agenda. Like most of the world's legislative bodies, the U.S. Congress faces a prolonged crisis of adaptation to this larger environment. On this point most analysts are agreed, although they differ over the exact causes and outlines of the crisis. Whatever its origins, the crisis is acutely felt on Capitol Hill and stretches legislative structures and procedures to their limits and sometimes beyond. Contributing to this state of affairs are several salient features in Congress's external environment.

Forces for Change. First, the government—and Congress in turn—continues to be asked to resolve all manner of problems. House and Senate workloads, in absolute terms, are enormous and rapidly growing. In recent sessions, approximately five thousand measures have been introduced in the Senate and nearly twenty thousand in the House. Even if measures decline in number in the future, review of ongoing programs is a continuing, time-consuming challenge.

Second, relative to these policy demands, resources for resolving them in politically attractive ways have probably contracted. The United States is undergoing a painful transition from a growth-oriented society with cheap resources to a steady-state society of ever-more-costly resources. Rather than distributing benefits, politicians find themselves having to assign costs. In political scientists' terminology, this represents a shift from distributive to redistributive politics—an uncomfortable predicament for politicians, and comparatively novel for those in America.

Third, contemporary problems do not come in familiar packages or submit to traditional solutions. Many of them transcend traditional categories and jurisdictions, not to mention the two-year legislative timetable. President Carter's 1977 energy package embraced some 113 separate pieces of legislation, referred to half a dozen committees in each house. What is true of energy is equally true of other broad-gauged issues: the 1,806 health bills introduced in the House during the first five months of 1977, for example, were referred to no less than eighteen of the twenty-two standing committees.

Fourth, challenges from the executive establishment cause acute stresses on Capitol Hill. On the one hand, legislators have grown accustomed to White House leadership and grumble when it is not forthcoming; on the other hand, they chafe under vigorous leadership, sensing a threat to legislative prerogatives. The Nixon period represented a recent zenith in the constitutional struggle between White House and Capitol Hill, with presidential incursions in impoundment, executive privilege, war powers, dismantling of federal programs, and even abuse of the pocket veto. The weaker post-Nixon presidency confronts a Congress determined to protect its prerogatives; but the relationship is by no means free of tension.

A final impetus for change—external in the sense that it emanates from electoral decisions—is the nation's shifting partisan and factional structure. The Democratic party remains dominant in Washington, but within both parties regional variations have become muted. Partisan and ideological ties—never compelling in the American system—have been further diluted. Interest groups are flooding into the vacuum left by the political parties' decline—not just the few traditionally powerful lobbies but rather a bewildering and shifting profusion of groups organized around all manner of issues and programs.

Institutional Innovations. In the wake of these shifts in its external environment, Congress has adopted a variety of innovations. Several of these are noteworthy: workload adjustments; committee and subcommittee proliferation; "democratization" of the two houses in reaction to the seniority system; and the growth of staff bureaucracies.

Workload adjustments. From all accounts, the House and Senate are working more diligently than ever before. Within the past decade Congress has gone to virtually a year-long schedule. In the twenty years ending in 1976, House and Senate committee and subcommittee meetings doubled in number; in the same period, the number of recorded floor votes tripled in the Senate and increased sixfold in the House. The average senator or representative puts in an eleven-hour day when in the nation's capital, according to surveys made in 1977.[4]

Congress has adapted to its burgeoning workload by manipulating its structure: concentrating on fewer but more complex issues; delegating many decisions to executive agents; and shifting its own role to

[4] U.S. Congress, House of Representatives, Commission on Administrative Review, *Administrative Reorganization and Legislative Management,* H. Doc. 95-232, 95th Congress, 1st session, 1977, 2: 20-22; Allen Schick, "Complex Policymaking in the United States Senate," in U.S. Congress, Senate, Commission on the Operation of the Senate, *Policy Analysis on Major Issues,* Committee Print, 94th Congress, 2nd session, 1977, p. 6.

one of monitor, vetoer, and overseer. Although introduced measures are more numerous and more wordy than ever before, fewer of them are reported by committees, considered in the House and Senate chambers, or passed into law.[5] Typically, legislation delegates vast powers but directs executives to report and recommend, oftentimes subjecting their actions to a legislative veto of one or both chambers or even a committee.

Reliance upon executive agents carries its own costs. Sometimes, as in the 1973 War Powers Act or the 1974 Budget and Impoundment Control Act, legislative innovation lends formal recognition to de facto shifts in the constitutional blend of powers. To recover power they sense is slipping away, legislators grasp for new instruments of control. In the wake of the Watergate and Vietnam crises, and propelled by an antigovernment mood, legislators of all persuasions proclaim their fealty to the concept of oversight. Predictably, cries of congressional "meddling" are heard from the White House, and some of the more ambitious oversight techniques will prove to be cumbersome and time-consuming.

Work group proliferation. Perhaps the most significant organizational phenomenon on Capitol Hill is the profusion of work groups. In the Eighty-eighth Congress, the House of Representatives had 156 committees and subcommittees, with the average member holding down 4.3 committee and subcommittee seats. By the Ninety-fifth Congress the number of House work groups had risen to 184 (actually, the number constantly changes), with the average member serving on 6.1 of them. Early in the Ninety-fifth Congress, the Senate succeeded in paring its 175 subcommitees to about 120. This was achieved by coupling the consolidation with limits on the number of subcommittee assignments and chairmanships each senator could hold, thus assuring a more equitable distribution of committee posts.[6] The average number of assignments per senator was cut from approximately eighteen (four committees, fourteen subcommittees) to approximately ten (three committees and seven subcommittees).

Still, Congress boasts an impressive number of work groups, and only someone unfamiliar with the ways of the Hill would expect the number to remain stable. Senators and representatives are spread very thinly. Virtually any day the houses are in session, a large majority of legislators face meeting conflicts. Members are tempted to committee-hop, quorums are hard to maintain, and deliberation suffers. Com-

[5] Schick, "Complex Policymaking," p. 7.

[6] See U.S. Congress, Senate, Committee on Rules and Administration, *Committee Systems Reorganization of 1977,* S. Rept. 95-2, 95th Congress, 1st session, 1977.

mittee specialization and apprenticeship norms have been diluted, casting doubt on the committees' continued ability to give in-depth consideration to detailed measures that come before them.

Jurisdictional competition among committees is the order of the day, resulting in member complaints about the need for tighter scheduling and coordination. Attractive issues often cause an unseemly scramble for advantage—sometimes breaking into open conflict, more frequently simply escalating decision-making costs by necessitating complicated informal agreements or awkward partitioning of issues.

The "democratization" of Congress. Democracy is in full flower in the House and Senate. Formal positions of power still remain, as do inequalities of influence. But the Senate boasts nothing to match its bipartisan, conservative "inner club" of the 1950s, which so vexed the little band of liberal Democrats. Over on the House side, the old committee barons have been replaced by a horde of committee and subcommittee baronets. Decision-making processes have been opened up and are no longer monopolized by the committees having jurisdiction on a given subject.

The war over the "seniority system" has been fully recounted, both in academic studies and in the mass media.[7] One attribute of seniority was that it recorded past electoral triumphs, rewarding a party's centers of strengths as they existed in an earlier generation. When a party's factional balance shifted, the seniority system distorted its leadership ranks, causing a generational gap between leaders and backbenchers. Such a gap—in region, district type, ideology, and even age—lay at the heart of the Democrats' seniority struggles. By the late 1960s, internal contradictions within the congressional party were too glaring to continue and were resolved, inevitably, in favor of youth and liberalism. In the House, the revolts were spasmodic and occasionally bloody, punctuated by a series of intracommittee revolts against recalcitrant chairmen, dispersion of power into the subcommittees (1971 and 1973), and, finally, overthrow of several unpopular committee chairmen (1975). Since then, no committee chairmen have been removed by the caucus, although several subcommittee chairmanships have been contested in committee caucuses—a clue, perhaps, to the current locus of power within the committee system.

In the Senate the transformation was more gradual and peaceful,

[7] Two reliable accounts of aspects of the change are: Norman J. Ornstein, "Causes and Consequences of Congressional Change: Subcommittee Reforms in the House of Representatives, 1970-73," in Norman J. Ornstein, ed., *Congress in Change* (New York: Praeger, 1975), pp. 88-114; and David W. Rohde, "Committee Reform in the House of Representatives and the Subcommittee Bill of Rights," *Annals of the American Academy of Political and Social Sciences* 411 (January 1974): 39-47.

hastened by caucus and chamber rules that dispersed desirable committee assignments, not to mention the permissive leadership of Majority Leader Mike Mansfield (1961–1976).

Republicans experienced similar tensions, although they were more generational than ideological. For the GOP, however, seniority was never the burning issue it was among Democrats. Because of the GOP's prolonged minority status, its seniority posts were simply less valuable than those of the Democrats. Moreover, lacking the incentive of chairmanships, senior GOP members were more willing to retire, thus producing more rapid generational turnover.

Reforms have by no means eliminated seniority. As H. Douglas Price has remarked, "Seniority, like monarchy, may be preserved by being deprived of most of its power."[8] The benefits of seniority, moreover, have been extended to far more members. At the latest count, 57 Democratic senators and 156 representatives were committee or subcommittee chairmen. That adds up to 92 percent of all Senate Democrats and 54 percent of House Democrats. Thus, there are more seniority leaders in the House and Senate than ever before. If Woodrow Wilson were around to revise his classic book, *Congressional Government,* he would no doubt be led to observe that "Congressional government is subcommittee government."

The growth of staff bureaucracies. To help cope with escalating workloads, proliferating work groups, and executive-branch challenges, Congress has created a rapidly growing staff apparatus. No visitor to the Hill these days can fail to be impressed by the hordes of people who work there. More than thirteen thousand staff aides now work for members and committees, and some twenty-five thousand more are in congressional support agencies like the Congressional Research Service, the Office of Technology Assessment, and the Congressional Budget Office.[9] Simply housing them is a major, unsolved logistical problem.

The Capitol Hill bureaucracy has grown in ways betraying the character of Congress as a decentralized, nonhierarchical institution. Congress has begot not one bureaucracy but many, clustered about centers of power and in one sense defining those centers. Efforts to impose a common framework on the staff apparatus have thus far been stoutly resisted.

The Future Agenda. Post–World War II shifts in congressional organization and procedures—shifts that came to a head in the early 1970s—

[8] H. Douglas Price, "Congress and the Evolution of Legislative 'Professionalism,'" in Ornstein, *Congress in Change,* p. 19.

[9] Harrison W. Fox, Jr., and Susan Webb Hammond, *Congressional Staffs* (New York: Free Press, 1977), pp. 168, 171.

have reinforced the historic decentralization in the House and Senate. Congressional history is a struggle of the general versus the particular, in which the particular seems the most powerful force. This particularism—so characteristic of Congress from its beginnings, and with rare exceptions ever since—is underscored by recent developments.

These changes have made the House and Senate more democratic bodies, and they have given members more channels for participating. What the past generation of reform has not solved, however, is how to orchestrate the work of the separate, semiautonomous work groups into something resembling a coherent whole. Indeed, the advent of subcommittee government compounds the dilemmas of congressional leadership. The next generation of reform politics will have to direct its energies to unifying what the last generation of reforms has dispersed.

Two related problems of coordination will form the pivots for tomorrow's innovative efforts. These are strengthening the central leadership and realigning the committee system.

Central leadership. Congressional leadership embodies a paradox. Today's leaders are stronger on paper than any of their recent predecessors, and it is hard to imagine leaders more skilled in employing their powers than House Speaker Thomas P. O'Neill and Senate Majority Leader Robert Byrd. Yet congressional leadership is extremely precarious, perhaps more so than at any time since the overthrow of Speaker Cannon in 1910.

The Speaker of the House has significant powers conferred upon him by the Democratic caucus. He chairs the Democratic Steering and Policy Committee and appoints nearly half its members. He now nominates all Democratic members of the Committee on Rules, subject to ratification by the caucus. For the first time since the days of Speaker Cannon, the Rules Committee serves as a veritable leadership arm in regulating access to the House floor.[10]

The Speaker also exercises crucial new powers under the House rules. He may now make joint, split, or sequential referrals of bills to two or more committees with jurisdictional claims—options that are invoked hundreds of times each session. In sequential referrals, he may lay down time limits upon the committees' deliberations. He is also empowered to create ad hoc legislative committees to handle bills claimed by two or more committees. Lacking the power to create a new committee with appropriate jurisdiction, Speaker O'Neill created an ad hoc body in 1977 to process the Carter energy package and coordinate the standing committees' deliberations. He selected its members from

[10] See Spark M. Matsunaga and Ping Chen, *Rulemakers of the House* (Urbana: University of Illinois Press, 1976), pp. 52-54, 60 ff., et passim.

loyalists, placed a deadline on the standing committees' work, and controlled floor deliberation through a carefully constructed "rule" governing floor debate. Yet the ad hoc committee was, as its name implies, a temporary expedient, cumbersome and not to be invoked every time coordination is required.

Over in the Senate, although leadership trends have been less clear, there are signs of new vigor. That tireless mechanic of Senate procedure, Senator Robert Byrd (Democrat, West Virginia), has employed his mastery of procedures and meticulous attention to detail to direct floor procedure. New limits on amendments after cloture has been invoked should give the majority leader and the presiding officer potent weapons in combating dilatory tactics.

Still, central leadership is suspect, and for the time being decentralizing forces predominate. The next few years will see the reform battle lines forming around leadership prerogatives. Because a majority of members in both houses now have immediate stakes in preserving the present decentralized structure, efforts to centralize leadership will be hazardous. Moreover, party discipline is at a low point. Every legislator, it seems, is intent upon forging a unique voting record; blocs of members cluster not around the parties but around special-purpose caucuses—to exchange information, develop legislative stands, and even operate whip systems. According to a recent estimate, at least forty-five of these groups are presently in operation.[11]

Leaders, for their part, seem not to know which way to turn. Oftentimes they seem reluctant to accept new prerogatives, preferring to rely on informal powers; yet they sense that, although publicly held responsible for congressional performance, they lack the power to coordinate or schedule the legislative program. That is why virtually every leader since House Speaker Sam Rayburn (1940–1947; 1949–1953; 1955–1961) has supported reforms that promised to increase his leverage upon the legislative process.

Committee realignment. Reorganization efforts have thus far failed to recast House or Senate committees to dovetail with contemporary categories of public problems. A wide-ranging House committee realignment proposed by a House select committee in 1974 fell victim to intense lobbying by committee leaders who opposed curbs on their jurisdictions and by allied lobbyists who feared that structural shifts would unwire their mutually beneficial alliances. The reorganization plan was defeated by a reverse-lobbying process, in which committee

[11] Daniel F. Mulhollan and Arthur G. Stevens, "Congressional Liaison and the Rise of Informal Groups in Congress" (Paper presented at the annual meeting of the Western Political Science Association, March 1979).

members and staffs, seeking to preserve their positions, mobilized support from groups that had previously benefited from committee decisions.[12] An effort to revive committee reorganization three years later was struck down summarily, partly because of the same forces. A new committee reorganization effort was launched in 1979, though by the narrowest of floor votes and with a severely limited mandate.

The Senate was reasonably successful when a 1977 realignment package was adopted, with modifications. This realignment left jurisdictional lines pretty much untouched, concentrating instead on consolidating several obsolete committees. The scheme was accepted because, by limiting assignments and leadership posts, it succeeded in spreading the workload more equitably among the Senate's more junior members.

Committee-system modernization is politically the most difficult reorganization challenge. It severely upsets the institution's internal balance, for it threatens not only individual legislators' committee careers but also their mutually supportive relationships with potent outside clientele groups.

Still, senators and representatives profess profound dissatisfaction with the present committee system. In a survey of 101 House and Senate members conducted during the 93rd Congress, a foreign policy commission discovered that 81 per cent of the legislators were dissatisfied with "committee jurisdictions and the way they are defined in Congress." Only 1 percent of the legislators were "very satisfied" with the jurisdictional situation, and 13 percent were "very dissatisfied."[13] In a House study conducted in 1977, committee structure was the most frequently mentioned "obstacle" preventing the House from doing its job. "Scheduling" and "institutional inertia" were next in line.[14] In short, legislators are fully aware of the committee system's disarray, although as yet they have not brought themselves to pay the price for remedying the problem. Meanwhile, costs of living with the present structure are escalating, and more will certainly be heard of the question.

Reputedly slow and tradition-bound, Congress has launched a surprisingly large number of major reorganization efforts in the past generation. There have been two joint committee investigations (1945, 1965), three major committee reform efforts (1973–1974 and 1979–1980 in the House, 1976–1977 in the Senate), two administrative

[12] Roger H. Davidson and Walter J. Oleszek, *Congress against Itself* (Bloomington: Indiana University Press, 1977).

[13] Commission on the Organization of the Government for the Conduct of Foreign Policy, *Report,* app. vol. 5 (1975), app. M.

[14] U.S. Congress, House of Representatives, Commission on Administrative Review, *Final Report,* H. Doc. 95-272, 95th Congress, 1st session, 1977, 2: 868-69.

review bodies (one for each house), and a major budgetary reform. Still, the agenda of innovations is lengthy, and pressures for further institutional innovation are going to persist. This is the most eloquent testimony to the continuing nature of Congress's crisis of adaptation.

Congress as Career Entrepreneurs

A second set of pressures for a change emanates from individual members of Congress—their careers, activities, and goals. Senators and representatives make their own claims on the institution—claims that must in some measure be satisfied if Congress is to attract talented men and women, provide a workplace where this talent can be utilized, and command loyalty from its members.

Individual legislators have a variety of goals.[15] All members, or virtually all of them, want to be reelected; some members have no other interest. But men and women—even politicians—do not live for reelection alone. They seek opportunities to make a contribution, to shape public policy, to see their ideas become reality, to influence others, and to work in dignity. In a body of 535 politicians, this jostling of individual goals and careers inevitably causes friction. No less than the institution of Congress itself, the careers of individual senators and representatives are beset by stresses and strains.

First, of all the factors affecting today's politicians in the United States, the most conspicuous is the long-term decline of political party organizations. In only a minority of areas do party organizations still serve as sponsors and anchors for political careers; nor do voters rely as heavily as they once did upon party labels to guide their choices. Hence, politicians are thrust into the role of individual entrepreneurs, relying upon their own resources for building and nurturing supportive constituencies. This yields an electoral politics comprising a series of cottage industries—a situation strikingly parallel to the fragmentation of interest groups, in which the traditional bloc-group system is dissolving into a fluid system of narrow-purpose groupings. Second, congressional careerism is changing. Historically, the trend has been toward longer careers—a trend that reached its peak in the post–World War II era. Since the late 1960s, however, careerism seems to be on the wane. This phenomenon is not caused primarily by competition at the polls.

Third, rising constituency demands are inundating individual legislators and their staffs. The average state now numbers some 4 million people, the average House district close to a half-million. Educational

[15] Richard F. Fenno, Jr., *Congressmen in Committees* (Boston: Little, Brown, 1973), chap. 1.

levels have risen; communications and transportation are easier. Public opinion surveys show unmistakably that voters expect legislators to "bring home the bacon" in terms of federal services and to communicate frequently with the home folks. In 1976, the House post office logged 53 million pieces of incoming mail—three and a half times the 1970 figure. Surveys suggest that future constituency demands will not diminish.

Finally, citizens' traditional ambivalence toward politicians turned into overt cynicism in the 1970s. Politicians of all persuasions have felt a backlash from the Vietnam war, the Watergate scandal, and the perceived ineffectiveness of government domestic programs. A number of congressional careers were halted by scandal—perhaps because a "new morality" spotlighted practices that previously would have escaped censure.

The "Incumbency Party." At first glance, senators' and representatives' careers would seem to be thriving. Certainly incumbents generally do well at the polls. In the twelve elections held between 1956 and 1978, an average of 94 percent of the House members and 82 percent of the senators running in the general elections were successful.[16] In 1978, 95 percent of the House members and 68 percent of the senators who contested in the general elections were returned to office.

Partisan swings are less pronounced than they once were. What is more, electoral competition is relatively low—although the picture in the Senate is somewhat different. In any given election year, only about 15 percent of the congressional races are "marginal"—that is, won by a margin of 55 percent or less. Little wonder, then, that political observers have remarked that it is not the Democratic party or the Republican party but rather the "incumbency party" that controls Congress.

In an era of weak political parties, incumbency itself—with its attendant visibility and opportunities for ombudsman service—is probably the leading factor (though not the only factor) in the electoral picture. A 1977 survey found that 15 percent of all citizens (or members of their families) had requested help from a member of Congress. By better than a two-to-one margin (69 percent to 31 percent), the citizens were satisfied with the service they had received.[17] No less than two-thirds of all respondents claimed to have received some communication from their member of Congress. Half could correctly identify his or her name, and, as we have noted, constituents are more favorably disposed to their own representatives than to the Congress as a whole.

[16] Rhodes Cook, "Midterm Elections: Past Trends Indicate Small Democratic Loss," *Congressional Quarterly Weekly Report* 36 (March 25, 1978): 755.
[17] House, Commission on Administrative Review, *Final Report,* 2: 814-16, 830-31.

American legislators, especially House members, have always been expected to run errands for constituents. Yet in an era of limited government, there were few errands to run. At the turn of the century, for example, constituency mail was pretty much confined to rural mail routes, Spanish-American War pensions, free seed, and only occasionally a legislative matter. A single clerk sufficed to handle correspondence.

As Capitol Hill observers whose memories go back to the early 1960s can attest, this constituency service role has been transformed quantitatively and qualitatively. Senators and representatives now head veritable cottage industries for communicating with voters, responding to constituents' requests, and even generating these requests through newsletters, targeted mailings, and free telephone access. Staff and office allowances have grown, district offices have proliferated, and recesses are now called "district work periods." This apparatus extends the legislators' ability to reach their constituents, and it provides badly needed ombudsman services for citizens for whom coping with the federal bureaucracy is a bewildering prospect.

One estimate places the monetary value of this apparatus to the average representative at $567,000 annually—all provided by taxpayers.[18] This includes $388,000 in staff salaries and office space, $143,000 in communications (mostly franked mail) and travel, and $36,000 in miscellaneous benefits. The biennial advantage for an incumbent would thus exceed $1 million—and the figure would be even higher for a senator. Not included in this accounting are ancillary services such as reduced rates for radio and television recording studios and use of informational services such as the Congressional Research Service.

Role Conflicts. Which came first, the congressional apparatus for performing constituency service functions or the public's expectation that such functions should be performed? I believe it can be plausibly argued that legislators are reacting to what they interpret as strongly held and legitimate voter expectations. There is no question that voters expect accessibility and material service and that they give less attention to legislative stewardship in Washington. For their part, a large number of legislators evidence antipathy toward constituency chores—even while acknowledging they are essential aspects of the job, and ones that yield handsome dividends at the polls.

Indeed, legislative and constituency role conflicts are now at dangerously high levels because of heavy demands in both areas. Senators long ago relegated the bulk of their legislative work to staff aides; but in the House the transition has been more recent and, for many, not with-

[18] Cook, "Midterm Elections."

out a sense of loss. Even in the early 1960s, many representatives did their own research and preparation for committee meetings and floor debates. According to a 1965 study, the average House member devoted virtually one day a week to "legislative research and reading"; another 2.7 hours a week was spent writing speeches and articles.[19]

Today's representatives probably spend as much time in the chamber or in committee as did their predecessors of two decades ago—given the burgeoning committee meetings and floor votes. Qualitatively, however, legislative duties are quite differently performed. In 1977 the average representative reported spending twelve minutes a day preparing legislation or speeches and another eleven minutes reading.[20] With such schedules, reliance upon staff aides is essential.

Legislators are beset by these conflicting demands, and many of them want to spend more time on legislation than they do. In the 1977 survey, 154 House members were asked to identify the differences between what others expected them to do and what they thought they should be doing. The most frequently mentioned problem, mentioned by fully half of the members, was that "constituent demands detract from other functions." A second complaint, cited by 36 percent of the legislators, was that "scheduling problems and time pressures detract from the work of the House."[21]

Role conflict is not the only factor impinging upon the congressional career. The seeming intractability of public problems and the difficulty of gaining credit for domestic policy achievements have reduced the rewards of public life. So has the post-Watergate antigovernment sentiment. The press and the public have adopted a moralistic stance toward government and its agents, who are often regarded as guilty until proved otherwise. Stung by criticism, Congress has enacted stricter rules over campaign finance, financial disclosure, and ethics. The new codes in turn have exacted a price in legislators' morale and self-regard. Reactions in both houses have been embittered—accounting for the House's rejection of a reform package late in 1977 and the Senate's controversial delay of limitations on outside income in 1979. Several members have cited the codes in explaining retirement from public life.

Declining Careerism?

Whatever the reason, many senators and representatives evidence weariness and alienation from their jobs. In a survey of House members in

[19] From research completed by John S. Saloma and reported in Donald G. Tacheron and Morris K. Udall, *The Job of the Congressman* (Indianapolis, Ind.: Bobbs-Merrill, 1966), pp. 280-81.

[20] House, Commission on Administrative Review, *Administrative Reorganization,* 2: 18.

[21] House, Commission on Administrative Review, *Final Report,* 2: 875-76.

the mid-1960s, a generally high level of satisfaction with the institution's performance was discovered—an attitude characterized as "a vote of aye—with reservations."[22] A survey that was conducted a decade later and that focused on foreign policy uncovered widespread discontent among the members of both houses. Dissatisfaction was expressed by four-fifths of the legislators and extended to all groups and factions on Capitol Hill.[23]

In the 1977 survey of the House members, only 16 percent of the representatives thought the House was "very effective" in performing its principal functions. Discouragement has been especially acute among the GOP members, who for many years felt no realistic hope of controlling Congress and ascending to leadership posts.[24]

Comments from retired legislators, many of them sensitive, productive ex-members who departed in midcareer, are too numerous to ignore. James W. Symington (Democrat, Missouri, 1969–1977) said that leaving Congress is "a release from a kind of bondage." Thomas Rees (Democrat, California, 1965–1977) exulted that he no longer had "to listen to some hysterical person who calls me about an issue that I care nothing about."[25] Otis G. Pike (Democrat, New York, 1961–1979) said he retired because he was "tired of wasting time on drivel."

Nor are these isolated sentiments of disgruntled legislators. During the past decade, the long-term rise in congressional careerism has been halted. When the Ninety-sixth Congress convened in 1979, of the 535 members of the House and Senate, 7 out of 10 were first elected in this decade and more than half since Richard M. Nixon resigned as president in 1974.

This was the result of voluntary retirements, not voter discontent. In 1978, for instance, the total House turnover was 14 percent (sixty-two members). But three-quarters of these were voluntary retirements (thirty-eight members, or 9 percent). Only twenty-four retirements were involuntary, the result of defeat at the polls—five in primaries and nineteen in general elections. Thus the *electoral* turnover was only 5.5 percent. For the Senate, however, in 1978 the turnover rate was 20 percent, less than half of which was voluntary. And, considering that only a third of the Senate seats are contested in any given election year, the actual turnover rate was much higher. In surprising numbers (for

[22] Roger H. Davidson, David M. Kovenock, and Michael K. O'Leary, *Congress in Crisis* (Belmont, Calif.: Wadsworth, 1966), p. 76.

[23] Commission on the Organization of the Government for the Conduct of Foreign Policy, *Report,* app. M.

[24] House, Commission on Administrative Review, *Final Report,* 2: 869.

[25] Ann Cooper, "Ex-members of Congress: Some Go Home, Many Don't," *Congressional Quarterly Weekly Report* 35 (September 17, 1977): 1970-1971.

modern times), legislators are choosing to retire from Congress or seek other jobs.

Congressional retirements are by no means a bad thing. In fact, turnover during the past generation was uncommonly low; and in the absence of meaningful competition in many states and a large majority of House districts, voluntary retirement may be the chief avenue for achieving turnover. Nonetheless, the number of voluntary retirements suggests that congressional life may not be as satisfying as it once was. Indeed, with other careers becoming relatively more attractive, with leadership within Congress more easily and rapidly attained, with congressional life betraying new stresses and strains, tomorrow's critics could conceivably be talking about a problem no one would have taken seriously a few years ago: how to make certain that the jobs of senator and representative continue to attract talented individuals and that their loyalty is commanded once they are in Congress.

The heightened demands thrust upon the two congresses may well lie beyond the reach of normal men and women. Reflecting on the multiplicity of presidential duties, Woodrow Wilson once remarked that the United States might be forced to select its leaders from among "wise and prudent athletes"—a small class of people. The same might now be said of senators and representatives—and if the job specifications exceed reasonable dimensions, will reasonable human beings volunteer for the jobs?

Conclusions

Congress is essentially a reactive institution. For better or worse, it mirrors the nation's political life—its values, standards, and organizing principles. Today's Congress is little different: it is open, representative, egalitarian, and fragmented. It lacks consensus and leadership, and there is little of the ideological or partisan commitment of earlier eras.

The members of Congress are, by and large—and contrary to popular beliefs—a diligent and harried group of men and women. Although it has its share of poseurs and philanderers, Congress is populated mainly by earnest individuals who are so busy keeping appointments that they have little time for expertise or reflection. There pervades an atmosphere of frantic frustration: members are busier than ever, but the complexity of their tasks and the overextension of their schedules militate against meaningful involvement in any given issue. Members are torn by conflicting expectations from the Washington community and the home communities that form their electoral bases.

In the 1960s, critics worried about the representative character of Congress. Long careers and low turnover seemed to heighten the insular, small-town atmosphere of the Hill; newly active ethnic and racial groupings were ill represented; because of the seniority system, leaders were especially unrepresentative; all too often, decision making took place in closed circles behind closed doors. Few commentators would now fault Congress on these counts. Capitol Hill is a far more open, democratic place than it was a decade or so ago. The transformation of Congress is not unlike that which took place in the political parties during the same period.

Now the chief impression is of a buzzing confusion. The two houses of Congress lack organizing issues or lines of battle. In place of party labels there is a plethora of individual politicians in business for themselves. In place of identifiable, consistent voting blocs there is a multitude of floating, ever-changing coalitions around specific issues. Instead of a few leaders or checkpoints for legislation, there are now many.

No doubt Congress reflects the atomization of political life in the United States. This era is likely to prevail until the pressure of adaptive challenges becomes too strong to resist, or the galvanizing force of an issue or a political movement will once again change the face of the American political landscape.

Can Our Parties Survive Our Politics?

Charles O. Jones

What have been the effects on political parties of recent congressional reforms? The purpose of this essay is to address that question. I begin with a discussion of the general concept of political party in the American setting, concluding that factionalism continues to characterize our political system. That conclusion alone suggests the problems associated with analyzing the effect of reforms on political parties. But I pursue that goal anyway, classifying the reforms, citing conditions likely to strengthen party, and reporting on how other observers judge the present situation.

Democracy without Parties?

Political parties are thought to be synonymous with democratic politics. Their traditional functions are associated with the means of selecting a government and of organizing that government to do its work. They developed with the growth of representative institutions and the expansion of suffrage during the nineteenth century. "Political parties constitute a basic element of democratic institutional apparatus," according to V. O. Key, Jr. "They perform an essential function in the management of succession to power, as well as in the process of obtaining popular consent to the course of public policy." [1] Austin Ranney and Willmoore Kendall find it difficult to imagine democracy without parties.

> Few persons today would argue that American government would be more democratic with *no* party system at all than with the one it has; and few would quarrel with the proposition that the party system is one of the most powerful forces, if not *the* most powerful, operating to "democratize" our formal-governmental system, which, be it remembered, was not intended to be democratic and which, if permitted to operate in its "pure" form, would probably provide a far less democratic system of popular consultation and majority rule than that which we actually have.[2]

[1] V. O. Key, Jr., *Politics, Parties, and Pressure Groups,* 5th ed. (New York: Thomas Y. Crowell, 1964), p. 9.

[2] Austin Ranney and Willmoore Kendall, *Democracy and the American Party System* (New York: Harcourt, Brace, 1956), p. 524.

At the same time, no student of American political parties is prepared to argue that these organizations have an independent role. Although no doubt influencing democratic structure from time to time, political parties are seen as performing their functions within the context of what goes on elsewhere. Parties exist to facilitate the workings of other institutions. Joseph A. Schlesinger puts it this way:

> A revolutionary organization which rejects existing institutions, a social club, a debating society, a pressure or propaganda group with independent goals, can all be studied as discrete entities. *But political parties compete to control a process which they did not establish and which could go on without them.* . . . Everything of interest about a political party—its organization, its leaders, its policies, its income, and its capacity to attract voters—is affected by the structure of political opportunities within a given state.[3]

One surely would not go to the party headquarters in the city, state, or nation to determine what forces were presently moving politics. Scholars compile lists of party functions and activities—for example, "selecting candidates and contest elections . . . propagandize on behalf of a party ideology or program, . . . organize and attempt to guide the elected officeholders of government"[4]—but much of the analysis of political parties is devoted to the limited extent to which these goals are achieved.

One is, in fact, led to question whether American political parties constitute a discrete subject, the existence of college courses and textbooks to the contrary notwithstanding. Making them a separate topic tempts one to understate their dependencies, perhaps even to overstate their existence. This is not to say that political parties cannot be treated independently. The Burkean definition of party—"a body of men united, for promoting by their joint endeavors the national interest, upon some particular principle in which they are all agreed"—suggests an independent organization. But when Burke's standard has been applied in the American setting, the results have not been impressive. Either one is led to proposing reforms that probably cannot be implemented or to writing essays on the desperate state of American politics.

I am much taken by Giovanni Sartori's discussion of faction and party because it elucidates the predicament of the American party system. Following Burke, Sartori argues that "parties are not factions." He points out that parties are not necessarily evil, whereas factions have traditionally been so identified: "Factions are nothing but the expression of personal conflicts, of ego-regarding and public disregarding

[3] Joseph A. Schlesinger, "Political Parties," *International Encyclopedia of the Social Sciences* (New York: Macmillan, 1968), vol. 2, p. 340; my emphasis.

[4] Taken from Frank J. Sorauf, *Party Politics in America* (Boston: Little, Brown, 1972), p. 12.

behavior."[5] Presumably the maturing political system moves from factions to parties, or at least develops parties to channel the selfish interests of factions.[6] Political parties obviously do not change human nature, but they do represent an initial acknowledgment of the need to sacrifice self for a common good. Thus, they perform important translating and linkage functions.

> Parties are instrumental to collective benefits, to an end that is not merely the private benefit of the contestants. Parties link people to a government, while factions do not. Parties enhance a set of system capabilities, while factions do not. In short, parties are *functional* agencies—they serve purposes and fulfill roles—while factions are not. This is so, ultimately, because a party is a part of a whole attempting to serve the purposes of the whole, whereas a faction is only a part for itself.[7]

Sartori concludes that whereas parties perform both representative and expressive functions, it is as channels of expression that the parties are most important. They "can best be conceived as means of communication. . . . They transmit demands *backed by pressure*."[8]

If we apply Sartori's standards to American party politics, we are forced to conclude that we normally have *political parties in the making*. Rarely have we moved close to the type of party system he describes (possibly in 1910–1916). More commonly we have had factionalism with organizations of convenience (called political parties) designed to promote factional interests. These organizations do, indeed, perform a communication function but seldom is it more than as "upgoing transmission belts of claims and grievances," which, Sartori rightly argues, is not sufficient for realizing the expressive function. "The party throws its own weight into the demands it feels compelled to respond to."[9] But American parties are weightless. What they throw, if they throw, either splatters or goes "poof." In short, one must seriously question whether we ever moved from factions to parties and acknowledge that any ground taken is quickly lost. Parenthetically, it is worth observing the irony of James Madison's creating devices (separation of institutions, bicameralism, federalism) to control the evils of factions that

[5] Giovanni Sartori, *Parties and Party Systems: A Framework for Analysis* (Cambridge: Cambridge University Press, 1976), p. 25.

[6] Ibid.

[7] Ibid.

[8] Ibid., p. 28.

[9] Ibid.

themselves either contribute to factionalism or prevent the party solution thereto.

Professor Sartori has, then, provided a means for increasing our understanding of, if not our satisfaction with, the role of parties in the American political system. Our politics are primarily *factional,* not party, politics. Moves toward strengthening party are expected to be for the purpose of facilitating factional gains or, perhaps, to break the advantage of one faction or set of factions in the political system. We move from factionalism toward party occasionally, not the reverse. This perspective of factionalism will be adopted here for analyzing recent congressional reforms and is, of course, what is behind the query in the title: Can our parties survive our politics?

The Recent Record of Congressional Reform

Studying political reform has always been a rewarding endeavor, serving more or less as a window to the expectations and workings of a political institution. In this sense, the past decade is a particularly rich period of study for congressional scholars. At no time in our history has there been so much contemplation of Congress's place in national decision making. It may well be that more reforms were enacted during this time (1970–1979) than during the first 180 years of Congress's existence.

Table 1 displays the actions taken during the decade. After being impressed with the sheer volume of reform, one has to consider the diversity of the measures. The following categories suggest themselves:

- *Jurisdictional reforms:* directed to the basic authority of the institution (for example, the War Powers Act of 1973 and Congressional Budget and Impoundment Control Act of 1974)
- *Electoral reforms:* directed to congressional campaign and election procedures (for example, the Federal Election Campaign Acts)
- *Procedural/organizational reforms:* directed to the rules and formal organization of Congress (for example, changes in the filibuster rule and other dilatory tactics, reorganization of the committee system, many of the changes in the Legislative Reorganization Act of 1970)
- *Political reforms:* directed to the means by which power is distributed and exercised (for example, modifications in the seniority system, increased authority for the Speaker, reactivation of the House Democratic Steering and Policy Committee)
- *Analytical reforms:* directed to improving congressional capacities for policy analysis (for example, the reorganization of the Legislative Reference Service into the Congressional Research Service, creation of the Office of Technology Assessment and the Congressional Budget Office, authorization of more program evaluation by the General Ac-

TABLE 1

CONGRESSIONAL REFORM, 1970–1979

Year	*Reform Approved*
1970	Legislative Reorganization Act (organizational and procedural changes)
	Provision for nonvoting delegate in House of Representatives, District of Columbia
1971	Seniority system modifications (House Democrats and Republicans)
	Authorization of computer services for House
1972	Federal Election Campaign Act
	Office of Technology Assessment (OTA)
	House electronic voting system approval
1973	War Powers Act
	Seniority system modifications (House Democrats, Senate Republicans)
	Steering and Policy Committee (House Democrats)
	House subcommittee bill of rights
	Open House committee meetings (markup sessions)
	Closed rule modification (House)
	House staff increases
1974	Federal Election Campaign Act
	Congressional Budget and Impoundment Control Act
	Congressional Budget Office (CBO)
	Steering and Policy Committee to assign committees (House Democrats)
	House Select Committee on Committees (Bolling committee)
	Adoption of Hansen Plan, House (organizational, leadership, party, committee changes)
	Nomination by Speaker of Democrats to House Committee on Rules
1975	Senate filibuster reform (three-fifths of Senate)
	Conference proceedings open to public
	Seniority system modifications (House and Senate Democrats)
	Open Senate committee meetings (markup sessions)
	Abolishment of House Committee on Internal Security
	House staff increases
	Open House party caucuses
	Commission on the Operation of the Senate
	Junior senators' staff assistance

Year	*Reform Approved*
1976	House Commission on Administrative Review (Obey commission)
	Senate Temporary Select Committee to Study the Senate Committee System (Stevenson committee)
	Revision of House perquisites
1977	Revision of Senate committee system (names, membership, appointments, limits on chairmanships, staffing)
	Adoption of ethics codes (House, Senate)
1978	Congressional approval of constitutional amendment giving the District of Columbia full representation in Congress (sent to states for ratification)
1979	Senate filibuster reform (postcloture)
	Reduction of dilatory floor votes (House)

SOURCE: Compiled from Congressional Quarterly, *Congress and the Nation,* vols. 3 and 4, and various issues of the *Congressional Quarterly Weekly Report,* 1977, 1978, 1979.

counting Office, increased committee and personal staff)

• *Ethical reforms:* directed to the personal conduct of members (for example, the ethics code for both houses).

Elsewhere I have made the observation that reforms enacted are not necessarily changes realized.[10] Changes may be of several types—in personnel, in authority, in process, and in actual product or output. It is possible to get a reform on the books without realizing much change at all. Or, it is also possible that the changes that do occur are unintended and unpredictable. Thus, what begins as an *analytical* reform may well have important *political* consequences; *ethical* reforms may have *electoral* and *political* effects, etc. It is at least in part because of this uncertainty regarding its eventual effect that reform is normally undertaken with such care, making the 1970s all the more remarkable for the number of changes made.

Having acknowledged the problem of ascertaining the direction and effect of congressional reform, I turn to precisely that task so as to say something about the role of faction and party in Congress. The first

[10] In my essays entitled "Will Reform Change Congress?" in Lawrence Dodd and Bruce Oppenheimer, eds., *Congress Reconsidered* (New York: Praeger, 1977), pp. 247-60; and "How Reform Changes Congress," in Susan Welch and John Peters, eds., *Legislative Reform and Public Policy* (New York: Praeger, 1977), pp. 11-29.

impression one gets in reviewing the record of the 1970s confirms that analyzing the effects of reforms is a difficult endeavor. Some actions appear on the surface to have decentralizing effects (for example, the subcommittee bill of rights, staffing increases, opening up of committee and subcommittee meetings, limits on chairmanships); others, to have centralizing effects (for example, budget reform, strengthening of the House Democratic Steering and Policy Committee and Caucus, increased authority for the Speaker, liberalizing of the filibuster rule). LeRoy Rieselbach refers to these contrasting, perhaps incompatible, reforms as emanating from two quite different pictures of Congress—one as a "responsible" institution, the other as a "responsive" institution.

> Because recent reform efforts have been inconsistent . . . reformers continue to project a future featuring one or another "pure" or abstract vision of Congress. . . . Those who put a high premium on prompt, efficient solutions to policy problems seek to move toward a more centralized legislature. They are prepared to sacrifice openness and multiple channels of communication—that is, responsiveness—in favor of effective resolution of policy issues—that is, responsibility. . . . They are prepared to rely on citizen-enforced accountability to keep the powerful executive in check. On the other side are those, equally committed to reform, who place the ultimate value on a free, open deliberative process. As a price for responsiveness they are prepared to endure a decentralized scheme of things, seemingly irresponsible, that reaches decisions slowly and only after considerable negotiation and compromise. . . . Although they do not oppose it, they rely less on accountability after the fact than on the ability of individual citizens or organized groups to present their views prior to policy formulation.[11]

Though the words are different, I believe Rieselbach and I are singing the same song. The pull toward his responsible Congress is a party-oriented effort; that toward his responsive Congress, a faction-oriented effort. And, of course, either characterization merely seeks to describe the classic representational problem of any freely elected legislature—namely, how to move from a collectivity of representatives to a community of legislators. Political party has traditionally been one important means for facilitating this advance.

Judging the Effect of Reform on Political Party

Saying that recent reforms have a two-directional pull is tantamount to saying that "it all depends." The potential for movement in either direc-

[11] LeRoy Rieselbach, *Congressional Reform in the Seventies* (Morristown, N.J.: General Learning Press, 1977), pp. 87-88.

tion is clearly there. On the one hand, a well-articulated subcommittee system could serve well the policy purposes of an active party organization. That is, decentralization of functions can contribute to centrally defined goals. On the other hand, strengthened party leadership may only facilitate the individual wants and needs of groups or factions, contributing little of "its own weight," to use Sartori's words.

What are the forces likely to drive the system in one direction or the other? Several possibilities come to mind:

- conditions facilitating presidential leadership (for example, party, previous congressional experience, electoral margin, personal capabilities)
- conditions facilitating congressional leadership (for example, party margin, president of same party, personal support, personal capabilities)
- the nature of major issues or crises
- demands for participation in decision making

Whether or not reforms result in a more party-oriented versus a more faction-oriented Congress, then, would seem to depend on these contextual variables (in what precise mixture, it is hard to say). When one reviews these conditions for the decade in question, the uncertain role of congressional parties is well illustrated.

Table 2 provides judgments about the four sets of conditions as applied to the three administrations during the decade. Presidential leadership has been relatively weak throughout the period. Nixon began

TABLE 2

CONDITIONS AFFECTING PARTY STRENGTH IN CONGRESS, 1970–1979

Year	*Presidential Leadership*	*Congressional Leadership*	*Major Issues*	*Demand for Participation*
1970–74 Nixon	Moderately weak to disastrously weak	Moderately weak	Vietnam Watergate	High
1974–77 Ford	Moderately weak to weak	Moderately weak	Energy Economy	Higher
1977–79 Carter	Moderately weak	Moderately strong	Energy Economy	Highest

SOURCE: Compiled by the author.

with the disadvantage of a Congress controlled by the other party and improved his own position by a spectacular victory in 1972, but his political advantage disappeared completely with Watergate. Ford had the ethical advantage of his comparison with Nixon, soon seriously compromised with the pardon, and his experience in Congress. Carter began with the advantage of a Democratic majority in Congress but suffered from the disadvantages of a small electoral margin, lack of previous congressional experience, and questions about his personal competence. Conclusion? There is little in the recent record of presidential leadership to turn congressional reforms toward a party advantage.

The situation in regard to congressional leadership is somewhat more encouraging for the strengthening of party. Carl Albert (Democrat, Oklahoma) as Speaker and Mike Mansfield (Democrat, Montana) as Senate majority leader were leaders in name only. Neither aspired to increasing personal authority or expanding the role of party in Congress. Of the four conditions facilitative of congressional leadership (party margin, president of the same party, personal support, and personal capabilities), Albert and Mansfield could fairly be said to depend on only one—party margin. A case might be made that they had support since each was returned to his position until he resigned, but I make a distinction between "acceptance" and "support" in their cases.

Thomas P. O'Neill (Democrat, Massachusetts) and Robert C. Byrd (Democrat, West Virginia), on the other hand, have been able to operate with all four advantages (though the president of the same party turned out to be less advantageous than might normally be expected). As a consequence they have been able to consolidate their leadership positions in each house despite other reforms that run counter to strong legislative leadership—increased resources for individual members (particularly staff), growth of congressional research agencies not directly responsible to them (Congressional Budget Office, Office of Technology Assessment), and increased subcommittee autonomy. Thus, the change in congressional leadership may be said to be incrementally in the direction of a stronger party role, particularly in the House.

The matter of issues and crises is obviously more complex than can be dealt with in depth here. The question is whether issues tend to be partisan in nature and whether there exists an overriding crisis that downplays partisanship. Many of the issues of the late 1960s and 1970s tended to blunt partisanship. Vietnam, energy shortages, government growth, and, in the end, even Watergate were highly visible and comprehensive issues that cut across party lines. Further, in the period after enactment of the Great Society, the issues before Congress and the president were more consolidative in nature; Congress and the president sought to develop and perfect means for implementing existing programs rather than initiating new ones. Therefore, the superficial evidence suggests that recent issues are an unlikely source of a stronger, more clearly articulated party system in Congress. Of course, the situation may change. For example, the movement to limit taxation and expenditures now enjoys bipartisan support (at least at the rhetorical level). Should limitations be widely imposed at the state and national levels of government one can imagine party differences emerging over how best to divide more limited resources. It is an interesting proposition that expanding government resources depress party differences; contracting resources accentuate party differences. We may soon be in a position to test those hypotheses.

The fourth condition cited above is that of the scope and diversity of participation in decision making. I recently spent a week on Capitol Hill to watch the comings and goings—to visit offices, attend hearings, listen to the debates, talk to journalists and congressional staff. Though I am an inveterate "Congress watcher," I had not spent a concentrated period on the Hill for several years. I came away somewhat in awe of the virtual quantum increase in activity there. One hardly fears for democracy by observing Congress—the place is crawling with petitioners.

A visit to the local polling booth leaves quite a different impression, however. Only three states had a voter turnout exceeding 50 percent of the voting-age population in 1978; the national turnout was 35.1 percent of the voting-age population.[12] Democracy seems in real trouble by this measure, particularly given the reduction in barriers to voting, the greater amount of information available on candidates, the voter participation drives, and the actual increase in the region that formerly depressed national turnout totals (the South).

In a recent article, Richard A. Brody takes note of this decline in voting but sees an increase in what he calls "politics one-on-one," that is, "the citizen pressing a personal case with the political system."[13] What I observed on Capitol Hill is related to Brody's "one-on-one," but it takes other forms too: politics "group-on-group," "group-on-one," "one-on-group," "groups-on-group." It begins to sound as though we are describing good old-fashioned *lobbying*. Of course we are. And just as moves have been made to facilitate voter turnout in recent years (albeit with limited success), so too reforms have been enacted that have the effect of facilitating lobbying. Probably as a consequence of,

[12] *Congressional Quarterly Weekly Report*, March 31, 1979, p. 574.

[13] Richard A. Brody, "The Puzzle of Political Participation in America," in Anthony King, ed., *The New American Political System* (Washington, D.C.: American Enterprise Institute, 1978), p. 324.

or in response to, the legitimacy of "demonstration democracy,"[14] Congress opened up many of its decision-making processes and thereby changed the patterns of access and advantage. Though I lack systematically derived data on what exactly has happened, impressionistic evidence suggests that some groups have maintained, perhaps even increased, their advantage; others have lost theirs; still others have gained access and advantage they did not have. In the short run, the new participants may be accommodated by enlarging the pie. The regulars keep what they have, and the budget is expanded to meet other demands. In the somewhat longer run, however, one may expect budgetary limits to be imposed, at which point real conflict emerges between the new and the old lobbyists (possibly with greater partisanship, as noted above).

The facilitation of lobbying is not necessarily enfeebling of political party. It is certainly possible to envisage a strong party system, buoyed by an active electorate, performing significant functions in the legislative process—that is, in representing interests, promoting policy, building coalitions, and getting support. To increase and promote access, however, without at the same time adding to the weight of the party system (or developing some means of cross-issue analysis) tends to result in the kind of "picket-fence politics" that is said to characterize the federal system.[15] To repeat, under these conditions the political party fails to perform its "expressive function."

It is worth noting as well that the increase in "politics group-on-group" has tended to emphasize two types of issues that are debilitating of political parties (though these issues may get to Washington in part because of the weakness of the parties). First, it has brought highly emotional and intensive issues into the legislature—for example, abortion, women's rights, environmental damage, nuclear power. If a relatively high degree of consensus is required for effective lawmaking, then we cannot expect much satisfaction with laws on these emotionally charged issues. The "politics of guilt" is difficult to deal with. Second, certain citizen groups, most notably Common Cause, concentrate on issues associated with the process rather than its output. That is not to say that other groups are not interested in process but rather that their interest is related to what comes out—namely, what they personally get from government. "Common Cause concentrates on issues having to do with government reform, such as regulation of campaign finance, regu-

[14] Amitai Etzioni's term in *Demonstration Democracy* (New York: Gordon and Breach, 1970).

[15] See Deil Wright, *Understanding Intergovernmental Relations* (North Scituate, Mass.: Duxbury, 1978), p. 62, where he illustrates "picket-fence federalism."

lation of lobbying, and requirements for open meetings in government."[16]

These emotional and process types of issues are likely to keep political parties off stride. No doubt party weakness permits these issues to get to government agendas in the first place. But having emotional issues and fundamental questions about political structure at the top of the congressional agenda clearly tests the capabilities of even the most resourceful party leaders.

Given the two-directional flow of recent reforms, I undertook this brief review to judge whether conditions favored the strengthening of party or of factions. I am forced to conclude that, on balance, factionalism prospers, party does not. There is even less incentive than usual for members of Congress to be loyal to their political party in these times.

How Others View This Matter

In connection with this assignment, I judged it useful to visit with other students of Congress.[17] I describe the meetings as visits and not interviews because my purpose was simply to get their general impressions on the role of party in the present Congress.

Certain general themes emerged as I reviewed my notes. Explicitly or implicitly, all agreed that the reforms go in two directions—more authority for the leadership, more resources for subcommittees and individual members. Also confirmed was the commonplace observation that party organization and functions differ between the Republicans and the Democrats and between the House and the Senate. Thus, I am reassured that generalizing about the role of party in Congress overall is as difficult for them as it is for me. They also stressed the importance of what goes on elsewhere—in elections, in the White House, in the economy—and thereby reiterated the dependency of political party on outside developments.

More specific comments can be organized into the following categories:[18]

16 Andrew S. McFarland, *Public Interest Lobbies: Decision Making on Energy* (Washington, D.C.: American Enterprise Institute, 1976), p. 57.

17 My sample included persons with various occupations and perspectives: Joel Aberbach and James Sundquist, Brookings Institution; David Cohen, Common Cause; Gerald Colbert, media adviser to Speaker O'Neill and executive director of a film on Congress; Al Hunt, *Wall Street Journal;* Thomas Mann and Austin Ranney, American Enterprise Institute; Walter Oleszek, Congressional Research Service, Library of Congress; Robert Peabody, Johns Hopkins University; and John Stewart, Senate Committee on Commerce, Science, and Transportation.

18 These excerpts are not necessarily accurate quotes. I did not tape the conversations. Rather, I took notes and later captured as much as possible on a tape recorder.

Presidential leadership

• The members think that what happens to the president does not happen to them as members of Congress. They are more or less independent of the president.

• There is nothing sustaining about the administration. The White House cannot bring us in. We in Congress are always willing to talk, but nothing is sustained. There is nothing to pull us in.

• House and Senate leaders really cannot pull together. What is really needed is an external force, such as the president, but that is not happening. It is hard to be a leader these days; there are few followers.

• Party leadership in the House is as strong as it has been in a long time; but there is no program to enact. Carter does not have a program. We have party but no program.

These comments essentially confirm the analysis offered earlier—namely, that presidential leadership is not forceful enough to drive the reforms in the direction of strengthened party function. The last comment poses the predicament—leadership potential in Congress that can be realized only with clearer direction from the White House.

Congressional party and leadership—the Democrats

• Changes in the committee assignment process have strengthened party leaders. For the most part, O'Neill gets his way.

• I think of the House Democrats when I think of party on the Hill. They are developing some party responsibility, and it is more than just Tip's doing. The vote on committee and subcommittee has injected party more into that level of operation; but the effects cannot always be controlled.[19] I misread Byrd. I thought he was the kind of guy who wanted trains to run on time, regardless of what was inside. But he has shown growth in politics. He is more substantive than I thought.

• Electing chairmen has strengthened the leadership. They are now in a good position to use the Steering Committee and the caucus to keep

[19] A recent example of uncontrolled effects would be the election of Henry A. Waxman (Democrat, California) as chairman of the Subcommittee on Health and the Environment, House Committee on Interstate and Foreign Commerce, over the senior member of the subcommittee, Richardson Preyer (Democrat, North Carolina). Though other senior subcommittee members were also defeated, the Waxman-Preyer upset was the most interesting because of Preyer's prestige in the House and because Waxman contributed to campaigns of several Commerce Committee members. Interestingly, given the themes of this paper, Waxman was quoted in *Science* as saying, "My commitment is not to Congress as an institution, but to the issues that this institution deals with"; 203 (March 30, 1979): 1321.

the membership somewhat in line. O'Neill has also professionalized his staff. Both O'Neill and Byrd make clear where they are and follow through—which is different from their predecessors. Byrd's personality is so different from O'Neill's. He tries to reach out, but he holds cards close to his chest. We find him to be a straight shooter, but people are wary of him.

Congressional party and leadership—the Republicans

- The House Republicans have a natural cohesiveness, but I am not impressed with the strength of their leadership. In recent years they have more or less abdicated. In the Senate, Baker has molded cohesiveness. He has done an extraordinary job.
- The House Republicans are far more disciplined—but around ideology. The policy committee is powerful and savvy politically. They use the committee assignment system well.
- The Republicans are better organized than the Democrats. They can get their people to the floor. They have good staff organization. They have good contact among Republican staff on committees. They keep each other informed.

It is interesting, but not unexpected, that most commentators agree with the statement above that "I think of the House Democrats when I think of party on the Hill." However well organized and disciplined, the House Republicans are, after all, in the minority. And senators are, by definition, unorganizable. Practically everyone I spoke with detected movement toward a strengthening party role in the House Democratic party, perhaps slight movement as well among Senate Democrats. These developments suggest that "political parties in waiting" still exist on Capitol Hill, possibly more prepared than in recent years to emerge, pending events elsewhere.

Subcommittees and the workload

- It is hard to turn back from decentralization once it starts. Kennedy wanted to reorganize the Judiciary Committee when he took over as chairman. There was a hue and cry even though the moves were relatively modest.
- The proliferation and strengthening of subcommittees has now gone too far. The increase in subcommittee power in order to reduce the power of the committee was probably a good thing, but it has gone too far.
- Compounding the problems of the leadership is the independence of the subcommittees—the growth of staff and budget. They can go anywhere. Also important is the increase in ad hoc groups—the steel

caucus, the black caucus, the solar coalition. There are about thirty of these groups, and some are quite active.

The whole workload is greatly increased. The increase in votes is important because of a greater number of amendments, which also reflects a breakdown in the role and effectiveness of committees. Committees are not given the sanctity they once were. More members have staff now that get into areas outside the member's area of expertise. The amending process is very active. Members are looking for ways to make their mark quickly.

• [*Subcommittee staffer*]: Party never touches us. The policy committee comes in only when we have a bill on the calendar and we want it scheduled. In determining our agenda, we do not look up to party leaders; we look around the country and around the world for the problems.

The two-directional thrust of congressional reform is well illustrated by these comments. Dispersion of authority and staff among subcommittees and individual members has had important effects on the workload and how it is managed. "Everybody is his own boss on Capitol Hill. Everybody has his own independent operation—it is almost a type of personal party bossism." Or, as someone else put it: "It is medieval. Everyone has his own little kingdom." It is pertinent that, whereas this comment has been made for decades about committees, it is now appropriate for subcommittees and, in some cases, for individual offices of senators and representatives.

The constituency

• The members have learned something about the mechanics of recent elections—about constituency surveys, about the decreased role of party in elections. I went around the district with Tim Wirth (Democrat, Colorado) recently. His campaign style was more or less: "Here I am, a bright, sharp guy, not one of those old Democrats coming home." He emphasized contacting him for any problems. Party was not mentioned.

• There is a qualitative difference in the members over the past. The notion of followership is not part of it anymore, making it difficult for the leaders to manage. In the past the members came out of party organizations and were familiar with that structure. Many are in Congress now as a result of challenging the establishment so they do not have any necessary allegiance to party.

That most members of Congress are primarily dependent on themselves for reelection is not a recent discovery. What is new is their uniformly greater resources back in the state and district. The word may be pronounced "ombudsman" but it is spelled "reelection." In a sense the member never has to leave the state or district now that professional staff can be allocated there. And, by the way, this staff performs functions formerly performed by local and state political parties.

I was not trying for, nor did I get, a systematic and comprehensive analysis of the role of political parties in Congress. I judge, however, that these conversations touched on many, if not all, the critical factors associated with the present and future status of party. One particularly acute student of Congress provided the perfect summary for these diverse analyses. "You tend to look for party in three places—ideology, elections, and institutions. What we find when we look today is a breakdown in all three." We both agreed that only the institutional change in the Speaker's power and the House Democratic party organization seemed to run counter to this generalization.

Can Our Parties Survive Our Politics?

The answer is, of course, yes. What we persist in calling "political parties" will survive. They are too strong to die, too weak to commit suicide. In a sense, our parties are our politics. The American political party is the ultimate dependent variable. Whether the congressional reforms of the past decade strengthen the role of party depends on other developments. Party itself is not sufficiently strong to capitalize on these reforms, to throw "its own weight into the demands it feels compelled to respond to." Our parties do not fulfill the *expressive function,* as described by Sartori.

> As Key put it, "political parties are basic institutions for the translation of mass preferences into public policy." In a similar vein a very dissimilar author, Schattschneider, declared that "the only kind of organization that can translate into fact the idea of majority rule is the political party." Both had in mind, it seems to me, the expressive function.[20]

But what if there are no mass preferences? Or no majority? Can American political parties create them? Sartori argues that "parties do not only *express;* they also *channel.*"

> *More* than expressing and reflecting public opinion parties shape, and indeed, manipulate, opinion. This can equally be conceded, excepting for the "more." I would only concede

[20] Sartori, *Parties and Party Systems,* p. 28.

> that parties *also* form and manipulate opinion. For the two sides of the coin—expression and manipulation—can hardly be treated as equivalent. Granted that parties are a two-way communication channel, the conclusion does not follow that parties are a transmission belt upward. There is manipulation and manipulation; and as long as parties are parts (in the plural), a party system lends itself to expression from below far more than to manipulation above.[21]

Thus Sartori concedes that even a party performing the expressive function well may not be in a position to shape mass preferences. Even by the most generous measures, it seems unlikely that congressional Democrats and Republicans are meeting the performance criteria for the expressive and manipulative functions.

What on earth are they doing? They are performing certain traditional functions (for example, committee assignments, scheduling, committee organization). They continue to serve as "upgoing transmission belts of claims and grievances"—that is, they facilitate factional interests. And, perhaps most important of all, they are surviving, hanging on until the effects of the 1960s, Vietnam, Watergate, and the political artlessness of the present administration have lessened or disappeared.

What are the parties likely to be doing in the 1980s? No one can say with certainty. What is apparent, however, is that reforms have been enacted that offer the potential for a more articulated and integrated party structure, particularly in the House of Representatives. Whether that potential is realized depends on the conditions cited earlier. At least the structure is now in place. Party caucuses (or conferences) are real entities in both parties and in both houses. Committee caucuses function in the House. Party leaders are alive, and those in the House majority party have greater formal powers than at any time since 1910. Should we emerge from this stranger-than-usual period of antipolitics, antiheroes, and proguilt with this structure still intact, it is at least conceivable that we will make one of our relatively infrequent moves from superfactionalism to moderate partyism.[22]

[21] Ibid., pp. 28–29.

[22] Lord Bryce argued that three methods have been used to get large assemblies to work: leave them with little to do, organize them into well-defined parties, and divide them into smaller bodies (that is, committees). We have opted for the latter throughout most of our history. With the reduction in the power of committee chairmen, it is possible that we will move toward the second solution. See James Bryce, *The American Commonwealth* 1 (New York: Macmillan, 1915): 156.

Parliamentary Change in Britain

Geoffrey Smith

Whatever the international reputation of Westminster may be, whatever historical or sentimental respect may still attach to it, there can be no doubt of the growing dissatisfaction at home with the British Parliament in recent years. There are three principal reasons for this. The first is that Parliament is seen as the symbol of government, and at a time when Britain's affairs have been conducted with evident lack of success it would be strange if the symbol were rising in popularity. As the casual visitor walks around the Palace of Westminster, he is aware of the sense of history, that great decisions were made in this place. He is not so easily persuaded that even competent ones are being made there today.

But this grievance has little to do directly with the operation of Parliament. It may indeed be maintained that if Parliament worked more effectively as an institution then the quality of governmental decisions would be improved and the prospects for national success thereby enhanced. This connection is not made, however, by most members of the general public who hold Parliament in less esteem because it is associated with the failures of government. They are judging not Parliament as an institution, whether legislative or scrutinizing, but the executive that operates in and through Parliament. If the effects of government were more to the public taste, if Britain were once again to become more prosperous than its neighbors, this particular source of criticism would melt away—even if there were no change whatsoever in the way that Parliament conducted its business.

The two other causes of dissatisfaction do, however, relate directly to the operations of Parliament. One is that Parliament is thought to be merely a rubber stamp for the decisions of government. Policy is worked out by ministers and their civil servants in the departments of state. Legislation is then passed through Parliament with only such minor amendments as are acceptable to ministers, and public expenditure is approved without even a serious attempt at scrutiny, let alone amendment. This domination by the executive is achieved by the tight discipline normally imposed on members of Parliament (MPs) by the party whips, so that ministers know that if their party has a majority of members in the House they can be virtually certain of getting their measures through Parliament without too much difficulty. The effect of this is to strengthen the inevitably considerable power of the bureaucracy because decisions reached within the government machine are not then subjected to serious parliamentary checks.

There is nothing new in this complaint. Indeed, as will be mentioned later, it has been less true recently than for many years. The more that legislation multiplies, however, the more that decisions of government affect the lives of individuals in great detail, and the louder the demand that MPs should do something about these details. The more that governments are seen to make mistakes, the more are MPs asked why they did not stop them. A plea of innocence through impotence may be convincing, but it hardly raises the standing of the person or the institution.

The other cause of discontent comes from within Parliament itself. A high proportion of MPs these days are professional in the sense that politics is their principal career. There are few Knights of the Shires left on the Tory benches, those members of comfortable means from attractive rural constituencies for whom it was sufficient just to be in the House of Commons without any aspirations to office. On the Labour side, the trade unions still sponsor members; but increasingly their support is given not to experienced workers from the pit or the shop floor but to young professional people—teachers, research workers, and the like. Many backbenchers of all parties continue to have outside jobs, but for most of them such occupations are nowadays an adjunct to their political careers, not the other way around. There are few MPs who have done better in their nonpolitical careers because they have entered Parliament.

Constituencies tend to favor younger candidates from whom much is demanded in terms of time and local service once they enter the House. The days are long past when the member with a safe seat might hope to get away with the annual visit to the constituency. Local surgeries for helping with the individual problems of constituents have become obligatory. The volume of correspondence from constituents has multiplied. Service in the House has also become more time-consuming, with an increasing quantity of legislation and a greater number of committees than in the past. It is time-consuming, but it is not satisfying. The young, aspiring MP has not largely sacrificed any other career, and possibly the comfort of his family as well, in order to be lobby fodder for his party in the Commons and a glorified welfare officer for his constituents at home. He wants to determine policies, to influence events.

He finds, however, that his opportunities for doing either are severely circumscribed on the backbenches and that his prospects of being called to the frontbench are limited by the laws of arithmetic. In a House where more and more members hope for office the army of the disappointed is bound to grow. This explains why there is mounting frustration among MPs and why it is the younger ones who are in general the most ardent supporters of parliamentary reform. The most powerful argument for reforming the procedures of Parliament is to create conditions in which government proposals may be scrutinized more carefully and the quality of decisions improved. There is also a strong case for procedural change in order to raise the prestige and authority of Parliament. These are the considerations of constitutional principle, and there are many distinguished champions of reform on both these grounds, among both MPs and others. What has given the demand an extra cutting edge, and made it more politically effective than for very many years, is that it accords with the personal ambitions of an increasing number of members who want to have work of political consequence on the backbenches, so that they have an alternative route to satisfaction even if they never tread the path to the frontbench.

For a good many years the cause of parliamentary reform in Britain has been associated above all with the creation of a strong committee system. This is partly because the experience of Congress suggests that powerful committees are necessary to a strong legislature; partly because British experience shows that it is on select committees that parliamentarians are most likely to rise above the customary dogfight of the party battle; and partly because common sense indicates that it is impossible for a legislature of 635 members to grapple with the intricacies of modern government in plenary session. Only committees can build up the necessary expertise in particular areas and examine policies in sufficient detail.

This has for long enough been common ground among reformers, but at last there is the prospect of action. In February 1976 a special Select Committee on Procedure was appointed by the House of Commons to consider how the House could carry out its functions more effectively. This committee, with its members drawn from four parties, proposed unanimously in August 1978 that a new structure of twelve select committees should be created, each to cover one or more government departments, so as to extend over the whole range of government activity. Shortly afterward, in a speech at Cambridge prior to the Conservative party conference in October—and again at the conference itself—Francis Pym, then shadow leader of the House, promised that in the first session after a general election a Conservative government would present to Parliament positive proposals based on this and other reports favoring stronger select committees. This commitment was subsequently confirmed by Norman St. John-Stevas, Pym's successor as shadow leader of the House, and now leader of the House in the new Conservative government.

Conservative policy makers had earlier been attracted by the idea of an economic affairs committee as a means of enforcing more rigorous control over public expenditure—a somewhat novel concept of a select committee as the potential ally of a harassed chancellor in his perpetual battle against a free-spending bureaucracy, or possibly even against his more profligate cabinet colleagues. Pym's commitment, however, went well beyond this limited concept to envisage a new structure of select committees along the lines of the report from the Select Committee on Procedure. He did not promise that a Conservative government would implement the report. The decision would quite properly be left to a free vote of the House. But his analysis was sympathetic, and the promise was definite that the House would be given the choice.

When the report was debated in the Commons in February 1979, Michael Foot, as leader of the House, gave a similar commitment, though from a very different personal position. Although he made no secret of his opposition to the proposal, he was forced by pressure from all sides to give an undertaking that the House would have an opportunity to take a decision on the report within the lifetime of that Parliament. Even though that did not prove to be possible, the effect is that both main parties are now committed to giving the House of Commons the chance to decide whether it wants a new structure of select committees—and, given the views that were expressed in that debate, there can be little doubt that the answer will be positive.

How much will this change in practice? It is not as if committees are unknown to the British parliamentary system. For nearly a century there have been standing committees to consider the details of legislation. There are also a wide range of select committees: a number of domestic committees concerned with the arrangements of the House of Commons, of which the Select Committee on Procedure is itself an example; three technical committees, the Statutory Instruments Committee, the Joint Consolidation Committee, and the European Legislation Committee; the Public Accounts Committee (PAC), which is concerned essentially with the audit of government expenditure; the committee overseeing the parliamentary commissioner for administration (the ombudsman); and five committees examining different aspects of government policy, the Expenditure Committee, which operates through six subcommittees, the Nationalised Industries Committee, the Science and Technology Committee, the Overseas Development Committee, and the Race Relations Committee.

The report recommends that the domestic and technical select committees should continue. So too with the PAC, though its powers should be strengthened. The proposed new structure of select committees is destined principally to sort out the remainder into a more coherent pattern. That is certainly necessary. The six subcommittees of the Expenditure Committee are the general subcommittee (in effect covering the Treasury), defense and external affairs, trade and industry, education and the arts, environment and the Home Office, employment and social services.

These, together with the Nationalised Industries Committee, the Science and Technology Committee, the Overseas Development Committee, the Race Relations Committee, and the Parliamentary Commissioner for Administration Committee will be replaced, if the Select Committee for Procedure's report is implemented, by twelve new departmental committees—for agriculture; defense; education, science, and the arts; energy; environment; foreign affairs; home affairs' industry and employment; social services; trade and consumer affairs; transport and the Treasury. (The report deliberately does not propose committees for Scotland, Wales, or Northern Ireland, but that does not mean that the principle of comprehensive coverage of government activities has been jettisoned.)

This would be a tidier arrangement than the present. It would mean that agriculture, for example, would be covered, as it is not now. It would cut out nearly all overlapping. It would mean that each committee's work was related directly to one or more government departments, instead of some committees covering a department and some dealing with a subject—such as science and technology—that ranges over a number of departments, some of them covered by separate committees.

This would not be enough in itself, however, to achieve the new balance of advantage between Parliament and government in the day-to-day working of the Constitution, to which the Select Committee aspires in the introduction to its report. It calculates that about 120 members would be required to man the proposed new committees, which would be only 15 more than the number now serving on the committees that would be replaced. This figure alone is enough to show that the structural recommendations do not involve a radical extension of the role of select committees. If that is to be the effect of the reforms, it must be because the new committees will be enabled to have a greater impact. Will that be so?

At the moment only two of the select committees scrutinizing the operations of government command widespread respect: the Public Accounts Committee and the general subcommittee of the Expenditure Committee. Many of the others do useful work. They publish reports that from time to time attract a good deal of public attention. But the product of their activities is uneven. The specialized subcommittees of the Expenditure Committee do not monitor the spending plans of the departments they are shadowing but prefer to choose particular topics for investigation. Even when a critical report attracts considerable notice, it does not necessarily influence action. It is embarrassing for the department concerned, but that department can delay its reply for a few months and the report may not even be debated in the House. Even when it is, the debate is unlikely to be related directly to any decision of substance by Parliament—and if it were, the party whips would be on so that the government would usually be in little danger of having its policy reversed. Select committees therefore have the power under present arrangements to cause embarrassment and to offer helpful ideas but not to force decisions against the wishes of the government. They flicker on the periphery of power.

How far would that be changed by the Select Committee's report? It has a number of recommendations for increasing the effectiveness of committees. It would strengthen their power to send for persons, papers, and records. A minister can now be compelled to attend a committee meeting only by the whole House, not by the committee itself. Nor is this a purely theoretical distinction. There was the instance in 1976 when Harold Lever, the chancellor of the duchy of Lancaster, was prevented by Sir Harold Wilson as prime minister from giving evidence to the trade and industry subcommittee of the Expenditure Committee on the question of whether the Chrysler Corporation in Britain should be helped by a large infusion of public funds. The ostensible grounds were that Lever was not the responsible minister, though he was known to be playing a particularly active role in the cabinet deliberations on the issue. The committee could have forced him to appear only if the whole House had been prepared in effect to reverse the prime minister's decision, assuming that the committee had been given an opportunity to raise the matter on the floor of the House. In a Parliament with a majority government this was no more than a theoretical possibility. The Select Committee on Procedure now recommends that committees should have the right to compel the attendance of ministers.

Select committees can now require the production of papers from departments that are not headed by a secretary of state but not from those that are—which effectively excludes all the major departments. The report would do away with this archaic distinction so as to give select committees the right to call for papers from all departments. It should also be made easier for select committees to enforce these powers, though it would be left to the House as a whole to decide whether a department was seeking to withhold papers on genuine grounds of national interest.

All departmental estimates for public expenditure should, it is suggested, be referred to the appropriate departmental committee, which would then examine them and report to the House. Select committees would also be given more staff, though here the fear of following too closely the example of Congress shines through the report. At present some twenty committees and subcommittees are serviced by twenty-six clerks of the House, fourteen secretaries, and thirteen executive or clerical staff. Most select committees have one or two part-time special advisers to assist them on specific inquiries; the Expenditure Committee has a full-time special adviser, who was formerly with the Department of Trade; and its defense and external affairs subcommittee has two full-time staff seconded to it. The only select committee that is serviced on anything approaching a reasonable scale is the Public Accounts Committee, which is supported by the comptroller and auditor general and his Exchequer and Audit Department.

The report recommends that each of the new committees should have at least one clerk, one executive or clerical officer, and one secretary. They should also be authorized to appoint part-time advisers on a more lasting basis, not just for specific inquiries, and to have permanent specialist assistants. It is clearly not envisaged, however, that select committees would take advantage of this right to make numerous appointments. What is striking about these staffing proposals is their breathtaking modesty. It is hard to believe that any American observer would suppose that this report will lead Parliament very far down the congressional road in this respect; but at least select committees should be a bit better equipped to challenge ministers and senior civil servants, supported by all the resources of the bureaucracy. In addition, the report suggests that the chairman of select committees should be paid a modest additional salary and that members of these committees, instead of being in effect nominated by the party whips, should be chosen by the Committee of Selection, a committee representing the whole House, which is already responsible for selecting the members of standing committees for processing legislation. Both these proposals are intended to increase the prestige and independence of select committees The payment of chairmen would, it is thought, encourage some members to see such appointments as an alternative to office as a career—a trend that may be beginning already. Further, if the whips are distanced from the process of selection they will have less chance of imposing their discipline on members of inconveniently independent mind, though it will not in practice be so easy to prevent the whips from exercising their influence on selection.

The report also proposes that government departments should reply to select committee reports within two months and that eight days a session should be made available for debating these reports on the floor of the House. This would go far to correct the present absurdity of many a select committee report left undebated and in effect ignored by the House on whose behalf the work has been done.

If all these recommendations were put into effect, select committees would be more fully informed and better serviced, command more respect, and be able to draw the attention of the House more readily to their reports. It would be reasonable to suppose that ministers and civil servants would pay rather more heed to such committees simply because they ought to have more intellectual weight and would be expected to deal more with the central policy issues. But would ministers and their advisers be forced to take greater account of them? It will be noted that the cumulative effect of the Select Committee on Procedure's proposals for select committees would be to ensure that the House would be better informed. No doubt that is desirable as an end in itself; but whether it would increase the power of the House in relation to the government—which is supposed to be the purpose of the exercise—would depend upon the uses to which this supply of information was put. That in turn would depend partly on the spirit of MPs and partly on procedure.

It is always dangerous to pontificate on the spirit of MPs, which is one of the less constant factors in political life. It is particularly hazardous at this time because the way in which MPs conduct themselves has been affected by the fact that, from April 1976 until the end of the last Parliament, no single party had an overall majority in the House of Commons. The assumptions made in this paper, and elsewhere in most political comment, about the ease with which the executive can get its measures through Parliament did not apply during this period of minority government.

This period has been characterized by two special factors, apart from the presence in office of a minority administration, the government wanted to avoid an election if at all possible, and for most of the time—from March 1977 until Parliament rose for the summer recess of 1978—the government was sustained by the Lib-Lab pact. The essence of this was that it was not a coalition but a parliamentary arrangement under which the Liberals promised to maintain the government in office by supporting it in any vote of confidence but did not undertake to give their backing to all policy measures. The combined effect of these two factors was that the government could be defeated on matters of policy without any fear of precipitating a general election—which was in practice, though certainly not in intent, to simulate the conditions of a fixed Parliament. There was no danger of the prime minister calling an election of his own volition and no danger of one being forced upon him because Labour and the Liberals had a majority of votes in the House when they combined, as they were pledged to do when the government's life was at stake. They were under no obligation to do so on other occasions, however, even though there was a complicated system of consultation between ministers and Liberal spokesmen.

Members took advantage of these changed circumstances to inflict numerous defeats upon the government. Some of these defeats occurred simply because the other parties joined forces against the Labour minority. On a number of other occasions—including some of the most important defeats that the government suffered—the administration lost only because of a rebellion in the Labour ranks. That was true of the emasculation of the dock work regulation bill in November 1976, when the late John Mackintosh and Brian Walden were what might be termed the decisive abstainers. Jeffrey Rooder and Audrey Wise led the move to have personal tax allowances raised against the wishes of the government. Labour defections determined that the Crown agents' inquiry should be held in public and that there should not be proportional representation in the elections for the European Parliament. But the most notable example of all was provided by the devolution. It was on the initiative of George Cunningham, supported by other Labour rebels, that the 40 percent requirement was stipulated for the Scottish and Welsh referendums—the provision that wrecked the government's plan for Scotland—and it was because there were so many rebels on its backbenches that the Labour government did not dare to go ahead with the devolution orders for Scotland after the referendum.

During this period of minority rule the balance has swung back somewhat toward Parliament in its relationship with the executive. Not entirely, by any means: otherwise the government would not have managed to get the devolution acts on the statute book in the first place when there was never a majority of MPs who positively favored them. The government still managed to get most of its legislation through—though little of it was of great consequence during this time—and its public expenditure proposals were as usual unchanged and unscrutinized. There was nonetheless a significant change in the parliamentary power game. This was partly because of the laws of parliamentary arithmetic; partly because a number of Labour MPs had the will to rebel and were able to do so without damaging repercussions from their constituency parties; and partly because the old myth was destroyed that a government has to be able to get every detail of its legislation through the House of Commons if it is to remain in office.

Will all this prove to have been only a temporary aberration? Will the new spirit of greater independence within Parliament fade away now that the laws of parliamentary arithmetic are once again on the side of the executive, with a majority government firmly installed in office? The mood of greater assertiveness among the younger MPs is likely to remain—this is simply another facet of the trend that makes them demand more select committees—but they are likely to be rebellious in actions as well as in spirit only if they do not thereby commit political suicide, which means that it would have to become generally acceptable for even a majority government to be defeated on substantive issues from time to time without resigning. Only then would the party rebel not be open to the charge of treason. It is the habit of making even the details of legislation an issue of confidence in the government that so cripples the exercise of proper parliamentary initiative.

It is by no means certain, however, that the British public is yet ready to regard it as proper for a government to remain in office after one or two important defeats in the House. This question has unfortunately become entwined with another which, although similar, is separate: Is there a point beyond which it is improper for a government to cling to office simply in order to postpone an election? Rightly or wrongly, it was widely alleged that James Callaghan declined to call an election in October 1978 not because there was some task that his government needed to complete, not because this was in the national interest, but just because he feared to face the electorate—remaining in office for no other purpose than to be there.

One does not have to accept the allegation in order to appreciate that there is a serious point here. The question arises because under the British system, whereby a prime minister can call a general election at virtually any time within the life of a five-year Parliament, there is public unease if he goes to the polls before the country is ready. What nameless horrors, it is asked, must be just around the corner? If, on the other hand, he delays when an election is generally expected, he is asked why he insists on clinging to office. There is, in other words, the concept of the fitting moment, and any prime minister ignores it at his peril.

It is quite possible to accept this concept and still to believe that it is proper for a government to remain in power after a few defeats. The defeats do not necessarily signal that the moment has come. The public, however, imbued with the tradition of strong governments, may not be prepared to make this distinction. It would be premature, therefore, to conclude that the last two and a half years of minority government were a turning point in British political history. If some of the attitudes displayed then are to persist and to be strengthened they will need to be nurtured by constitutional or procedural change.

The constitutional change that is most frequently mentioned in this context is proportional representation. This would make it much less likely that any single party would have a majority of seats and would therefore tilt the laws of parliamentary arithmetic in favor of the legislature rather than the executive. Under a system where no party was expected to have an overall majority, however, it would be much more probable that coalitions would be formed—in contrast to the Lib-Lab pact—and the leaders of the coalition parties might threaten their backbenchers with a dissolution if they did not support the government's policies. That would be the bad old system all over again. In this context, as has been suggested earlier, it would be more relevant to look toward fixed-term Parliaments.

That is to peer well into the future, however. If the balance of power is to be changed in the short term to the advantage of Parliament as against the executive it will be necessary to strengthen the authority of Parliament by changing its procedures. It is here that the Select Committee on Procedure's report is so weak. To make Parliament better informed may be admirable, but that alone will not make it more likely that Parliament will deny the government what it wants in terms of legislation or money—which is the essence of a legislature's power against an executive.

To be fair to the committee, it intends that there should be a further inquiry into the financial procedures of the House; and it is indeed of critical importance that Parliament should recapture control over public expenditure. At the moment, detailed estimates are approved on supply days—which are used, however, not to examine these estimates but to debate whatever topic the official opposition chooses. These estimates are then collected into a consolidated fund bill, which passes through the normal legislative procedures of the House; but there is so much in these bills that members have not digested that it is customary to use debates on them as occasions not for scrutinizing public expenditure but for raising constituency points or such other matters as an MP may choose. If the House is to recapture control over expenditure it must have a proper opportunity both to examine and to amend the government's proposals. The Select Committee on Procedure recommends that the new select committees should examine and comment on departmental estimates within their field but not that they should have the power to amend the estimates. Unless adequate opportunity is provided for that, they will be commenting into the void.

So far as legislation is concerned, it is recommended that standing committees should be authorized to have up to three sittings to take evidence on a bill before proceeding to examine it clause by clause. They should therefore be known as public bill committees, and they should include some members from the select committee covering the subject matter of the bill in question. This is obviously a compromise. Select committees will be able indirectly to influence the committees dealing with the legislation without themselves being those committees. This means that one set of committees will be acquiring the expertise, and another set of committees—each one of which is established simply for processing a particular bill—will be making the decisions. This is in substance the present arrangement, and it is one that makes it less likely that the executive will be embarrassed by committees, assured in their knowledge of the subject, refusing to give way before the pressure or persuasion of ministers.

There is, it is true, difficulty here. Unless select committees are able to make decisions—even if those decisions are subject to subsequent approval by the whole House, as are the decisions on legislation by standing committees—they will not be able to exercise power themselves and thereby directly affect the balance of advantage within Parliament. All they can then hope to do is to influence others who do have this power. The prospect held out in the report is that the new select committees, organized on more rational lines, might be able to do this rather better. It is not as radical a prospect as might be supposed from the comments of either its support or its critics.

If, however, select committees were to be given real power, there is the danger that they might then lose the very qualities that make them attractive: the greater readiness to examine evidence objectively and to consider issues on their merits without conducting every dialogue in terms of the party battle. Would select committees not resort to the adversarial style that characterizes British politics if they were taking decisions that mattered? The risk is a real one, but to be deterred by it is to confess that select committees have the limited appeal of the parliamentary eunuch, acceptable only as long as they are incapable.

Ultimately, if Parliament is to have more power, the parties must have less. There is no way around that dilemma. The strengthening of select committees should be seen not as a means of avoiding it but rather as a method of relaxing the grip of the parties in the cause of responsible government. Those with experience of what has happened to the American parties may object that the democratic system suffers even more when parties are too weak; but there is no danger in the very different circumstances of British politics that parties in the United Kingdom might be weakened to anything like that extent. The British

Parliament is certainly embarking on a period of reform, but it is all too likely that this will change the appearance rather than the substance of power.

It may be objected that to do more than that would do more harm than good, that the blessings of strong government would be sacrificed, and that the conventions of Britain's system of orderly rule would be upset. There is indeed much evidence that the public is attached to the belief, or one might say the myth, that strong government confers many blessings. But British governments are strong only in terms of what they are permitted to do within the provisions of the Constitution. A bare majority of seats in the House will enable them to get their policies through Parliament, in which case those policies will not then be challenged by the courts. That does not mean, however, that they have received the necessary degree of public approval for them to be implemented successfully. If governments had to fight harder to get their policies through the constitutional process there might then be a greater sense that these measures had received the imprimatur of political approval, as distinct from simply being the brainchildren of the executive.

One convention of British rule that might be upset by stronger select committees is that of ministerial responsibility. Powerful select committees would not be content for long with civil servants confining their evidence to factual information and eschewing their own ideas on policy. Such committees would want to know more about policy options. This would mean that particular civil servants might become associated with particular courses of action, and if this trend went far ministers might even come to feel that individual civil servants were maneuvering on their own account in their dealings with committees. That would damage relations between ministers and civil servants within their departments and might bring closer the day of political appointments to senior posts in the civil service. That would be unfortunate, but the trend is not likely to go that far. Already there has been a tendency for some very senior civil servants to be more outspoken before select committees and for the doctrine of ministerial responsibility to be weakened by the common knowledge that ministers cannot be personally responsible for everything that happens within their departments. These tendencies will go some way further if there are strong committees. But it would be impossible for Parliament to be strengthened without there being some other consequential adjustments. All Britain's history suggests that it is not a country where constitutional change is in danger of being too drastic or too rapid.

The Bundestag at the Intersection of Four Systems

Winfried Steffani

In one respect parliaments of Western democracies remained much the same during the past century: the equal rights of their members. Apart from that, however, the conditions of their existence changed a great deal, in some cases radically. Today, the legislatures of all Western democracies have to cope with the demands of a welfare state in highly developed industrial societies with their wide-ranging international involvements and dependencies.

Given the fundamental similarities of modern parliaments, each has its own set of particulars. A significant peculiarity of the German Bundestag is its position and operation within a complicated four-system network: First, there is the constitutional *system of separation of powers,* in which the Bundestag holds its own position as a state organ, like the government. On the other hand, the Constitution establishes, second, a *parliamentary system,* in which the state organs of Parliament and government are overlapped by the political separation of powers between the two institutions of government majority and opposition. Third, there is the *federal system*, which is important not only with regard to the Bundestag's authority vis-à-vis Länder Parliaments but also in relation to the Bundesrat, the other legislative assembly on the national level. Finally, and in the fourth place, there is the *constitutional system*; it provides for the institution of an independent Federal Supreme Court, whose purpose is to safeguard the Constitution against infringements by any state organ, including Parliament, on another.

Within this four-system network the Bundestag can appear at any given time as a government opponent, as a place for disputes between the government majority and the opposition, as a partner or rival of the Bundesrat, or as a state organ that has to submit to the verdict of the Federal Supreme Court.

All four systems do have an impact on the work of the Bundestag, which cannot evade any one of them. A meaningful investigation of the changes of the Bundestag within the political system of the Federal

Republic can be undertaken only when these four system levels and their connection are taken into account.

Because, in the course of time, each of these four systems was subject to more or less important alterations that by no means followed the same basic direction, the Bundestag—at different times—has been drawn into quite different system combinations. If we look back on the first thirty years of the German Bundestag, three significant system combinations can be distinguished, each marked by a series of specific characteristics: (1) the period of the Christian Democratic Union/ Christian Social Union (CDU/CSU) government with Social Democratic party (SPD) opposition from 1949 to 1966; (2) the period of the Great Coalition from 1966 to 1969; and (3) the period of the Social–Liberal Coalition from 1969 up to the present.

Before expanding on these system combinations, it is appropriate to give a description of the above-mentioned four-system network and a brief historical overview.

German Parliamentary History

The Bundestag is at the same time a new institution and the continuation of German parliamentary history.[1] Continuity and change in the national Parliament—apart from the Paulskirchen Assembly in 1848/ 1849 and parliamentary development on the state level—are marked by three dates: the years 1867, 1919, and 1949. In 1867 the first German national Parliament assembled under the name "Deutscher Reichstag" in what was later (after the foundation of the Deutsches Kaiserreich in 1871) to be the imperial capital, Berlin. In 1919 the Deutscher Reichstag became the Parliament of the first parliamentary republic in Germany. In September 1949—after the total breakdown of the German Reich in May 1945—the history of the national Parliament was taken up again under the name "Deutscher Bundestag" in the temporary capital, Bonn.

During the first fifty years of parliamentary history, the German Reichstag was the Parliament of a constitutional monarchy. That is, the Reichstag operated in legislation on an equal level with the Bundesrat as a chamber of Parliament, but the Reichstag was unable to institute the government (or the chancellor/prime minister) or to recall it for political reasons. Because democracy and monarchy can be reconciled only within the framework of a parliamentary system, the democratic suffrage to the Reichstag was only the first step toward introducing democratic means to the political system.

[1] See Gerhard Loewenberg, *Parliament in the German Political System* (Ithaca, N.Y.: Cornell University Press, 1967), pp. 4-39.

In a monarchy, only after the establishment of full parliamentarism can a democracy be said to have been achieved. When—shortly before the end of World War I on October 28, 1918—true parliamentarism *was* introduced, the German empire was already in a state of agony.

The proclamation of the Republic in Berlin on November 9, 1918, provided the first opportunity to choose a parliamentary or a presidential democracy. The National Assembly voted in favor of the parliamentary system. The Bundesrat was replaced by a weak successor (the Reichsrat), and the Weimar Constitution placed the Reichstag together with the Reichspräsident in the institutional center of the constitutional system.

The result was a challenge for political parties unknown until that time. In the imperial Parliament it had *not* been the primary task of political parties to keep the government in office. When party discipline was exercised, it was for reasons of ideology or creed. The introduction of the parliamentary system changed conditions fundamentally in this respect.

It was now up to the political parties in Parliament to accomplish the political task of supporting the government in office as long as possible. Party discipline became a necessity. Parties now had to prove their ability to form coalitions and majorities if the Reichstag was to secure its influence on the formation and duration of cabinets. A party discipline essentially motivated by ideology was bound to have negative effects upon a discipline called for by the system in order to stabilize a coalition. Consequently, in the transition from a constitutional monarchy to a parliamentary republic the Reichstag itself found it had to play a different role, a change with which parties were functionally unable to comply.

Ten years after the beginning of the parliamentary republic the democratic parties were in fundamental trouble. There was no democratic alternative to the parties of the Weimar Coalition—only an opposition hostile to the system, headed by National Socialists and Communists. On March 24, 1933, shortly after Hitler had seized power, a majority in Parliament passed a law—the so-called enabling act—that altered the Constitution to allow the power of legislation to pass from Parliament to the government, thus depriving the Reichstag of its power. During the next twelve years, until the end of the Hitler era, the Reichstag continued to exist formally only as an audience for Hitler's public addresses.

During the interregnum from the breakdown of the Third Reich until 1949, there was no national Parliament at all. The history of the German Bundestag begins with its first assembly on September 7, 1949.

Separation of Powers between Parliament (Bundestag) and Government

In reference to supreme power in West Germany, article 20(2).2 of the Constitution states: "It is to be executed by the people by way of elections and referendums and by special organs or legislation, executive power, and jurisdiction."[2] The phrase "by special organs" refers to the "classical" concept of separation of powers such as the division of Parliament from government and the relative independence of each. Incompatibility, the strict separation of parliamentary mandate and government office adhered to during the constitutional monarchy, was suspended but still practiced during the Weimar Republic and has now been replaced altogether by close ties between Parliament and government in the Federal Republic. Since the Federal Republic was established, nearly all members of the cabinet have also been members of Parliament (MPs). This is a significant political fact that overlies the judicially important fact that Parliament and government are independent state organs. Which principle ought to find visible expression, the political or the judicial one?

The British House of Commons—with well-known consequences—has preferred the political principle: seating arrangement and committee work emphasize the separation of government majority and opposition, not that of Parliament and cabinet. The Bundestag has chosen the opposite course, following the Reichstag tradition: the government bench is situated in visible contrast to the rest of Parliament; the division of majority and opposition is hardly noticeable. Initially, the government bench was almost suspended above the seats of the representatives. It was considered to be an act of reform and of shaking off the past when during President Gerstenmaier's term of office the seats of the ministers were lowered by inches, thereby making the distance between Parliament and the cabinet look a little less awesome.

The separation is not simply superficial. It has far-reaching consequences for parliamentary work. Members who take over a ministry on principle are not taken into account when seats are assigned at committee meetings. The same applies to members who take over the office of parliamentary secretary of state; they must be and must remain MPs in order to take office. It was regarded as a considerable breech of custom, however, when—in the early days of the Social-Liberal Coalition—a few parliamentary secretaries of state became deputy members of committees on the grounds of narrow majorities. An MP who has

[2] *Grundgesetz der Bundesrepublik Deutschland*, May 23, 1949, art. 20, para. 2, sentence 2.

risen to minister customarily forfeits his status as a regular committee member, but he gains at the same time significant privileges in the process of parliamentary proceedings. According to article 43(2) of the Constitution members of the cabinet and their deputies are allowed to speak at any time in the assembly and at committee meetings. They are not subjected to a majority vote.

Initially, the time government members used for their speeches was not counted as time allotted to parliamentary parties for this purpose or to parties that formed the government coalition or those to which the ministers belonged. This was greatly to the disadvantage of the opposition.

It was pretended that the government faced an independent Parliament where parliamentary parties commented independently on government attitudes. At the expense of equality it was disregarded in the debates that government and parliamentary majority were, in fact, a political unity facing the opposition. During the past decade, however, things have changed in favor of the opposition, although even now complete equality of government and opposition has not been effected. Standing orders show that according to current legal views Parliament and government are facing each other, not government majority and opposition. The original, basically still valid standing order drafted by the Reichstag in imperial days was, with few alterations, adapted for the Reichstag of the Weimar Republic and, finally, taken over by the Bundestag in 1951.

These standing orders account for minority rights but give no rights to the opposition. Minority rights can be made use of even by a minority within the government coalition. Specific rights of the opposition, expression for its fundamental significance as a constitutional institution, have not been realized in the German Constitutional and Standing Orders Law. In fact, the Federal Constitutional Court stated in its interpretation of the constitutional term "free democratic fundamental order" (art. 21) that "equal chances for all political parties including the right to constitutionally form and practice opposition" belong to the basic principles of this order. In spite of this, Hans Trossmann, former director at the German Bundestag during the 1960s, wrote a commentary on standing orders in which the key word "opposition" was not even mentioned.[3] German parliamentary law still puts the opposition in the general category of "minority."

[3] Cf. Hans Trossmann, *Parlamentsrecht und Praxis des Deutschen Bundestages—Kommentar in alphabetischer Ordnung . . .* (Bonn, 1967). The same applies to Trossmann's books, *Der Deutsche Bundestag: Vorgeschichte und Leistungen, Organisation und Arbeitsweise* (Darmstadt, 1971), and *Parlamentsrecht des Deutschen Bundestages: Kommentar zur Geschäftsordnung des Deutschen Bundestages unter Berücksichtigung des Verfassungsrechts* (Munich, 1977).

Separation of Powers between Government Majority and Opposition

The Constitution not only created Parliament (Bundestag) and government (Bundesregierung) as "specific organs" but also determined in detail their legal relationships. Accordingly, and contrary to the Weimar Constitution, Parliament has to elect the head of government (Bundeskanzler). Indeed, although the federal chancellor himself determines political guidelines, his future depends on the trust placed in him by Parliament, which can recall him at any time. This provides the basis for a parliamentary system.[4]

In the Weimar Republic every government member could be recalled by Parliament. The Bundestag can only issue a no-confidence vote against the federal chancellor; this is accomplished when a majority of its members votes to elect a new chancellor. This so-called constructive vote of no confidence requires that the negative vote of recall coincide with the positive step of a new election.

The Bundestag, in its legal relation to the government, is the most powerful Parliament in German history. The Bundestag is the first German Parliament that has the power to elect the chancellor and that can be dissolved only under extremely difficult conditions. What was meant to be Parliament's legal power over the government, however, has had the opposite effect politically: the strong position of the chancellor and his government. The main reason for this was the development of a new party system and especially the foundation of the CDU/CSU as a mass-movement, democratic, catchall party—in German party history, a development of extraordinary importance.

Initially, the multiparty system of the Weimar Republic seemed likely to continue. The first Bundestag had eight parliamentary parties, with nine members belonging to no party. Soon, however, the number of parties began to decrease. The second Bundestag (1953–1957) had six parliamentary parties; the third (1957–1961) had four; and, from the fourth Bundestag, in 1961, until today, there have been only three (see table 1). The initial multiparty system led to a three-party system in the Bundestag, and thus the separation of powers between government majority (as the unity of government and parliamentary majority) and opposition became a matter of fundamental importance.

For the first time Parliament had an opposition as a democratic alternative to the government. For the first time in German history all the parties in Parliament declared themselves to be ready for coalition.

[4] About the distinction of parliamentary and presidential government in reference to the political systems of the United Kingdom, the United States, and the Federal Republic of Germany, see Winfried Steffani, *Parlamentarische und präsidentielle Demokratie: Strukturelle Aspekte westlicher Demokratien* (Opladen: Westdeutscher Verlag, 1979).

TABLE 1

PARTY MEMBERSHIP IN THE GERMAN BUNDESTAG, 1949–1980

Term of Parliament	Parliamentary Parties (Fraktionen)									No Party in Parliament
	CDU/ CSU	SPD	FDP	DP	BP	KPD	WAV	Z	GB/ BHE	
1949–53	139	131	52	17	17	15	12	10	—	9
1953–57	250	162	53	15	—	—	—	3	27	—
1957–61	277	181	43	18	—	—	—	—	—	—
1961–65	251	203	67	—	—	—	—	—	—	—
1965–69	251	217	50	—	—	—	—	—	—	—
1969–72	250	237	31	—	—	—	—	—	—	—
1972–76	234	242	42	—	—	—	—	—	—	—
1976–80	254	224	40	—	—	—	—	—	—	—

NOTE: Party names are abbreviated as follows: Christian Democratic Union/ Christian Social Union (CDU/CSU), Social Democratic party (SPD), Free Democratic party (FDP), German party (DP), Bavarian (People's) party (BP), Communist party (KPD), Economic Reconstruction (WAV), Center party (Z), and All-German Block/Refugee party (GB/BHE).

SOURCE: Author.

During subsequent years, each of the three parties has, in fact, formed a government coalition with one of the other two.

In the election of 1969, the three parliamentary parties were given 94.4 percent of all votes; the percentage rose to 99.1 in 1972 and 1976. All federal governments have been coalition governments, even when—as in 1957, with the CDU/CSU—one party provided an absolute majority of all MPs. Consequently, from the fourth Bundestag on (with a brief interruption in November 1966), the opposition was formed by one party only. The party chief was *the* opposition leader.

On the government side, the election of the federal chancellor did not mean he had to submit entirely to the will of the parliamentary majority. Because the electoral prospects of a government majority depend on the political success and reputation of the government and its chief, it is in the interests of those legislators who appointed the chancellor to support him.[5] This, ironically, can create a situation in which Parliament sees its task as that of protecting the elected government unconditionally against criticism. Thus it is not that Parliament controls the government but vice versa. The chancellor becomes political leader of the parliamentary majority, faced by the critical eye of the opposition as a political alternative.

[5] See Uwe Thaysen, *Parlamentarisches Regierungssystem in der Bundesrepublik Deutschland,* 2nd ed. (Opladen: Leske Verlag, 1976), pp. 17-22.

A confident opposition will always underline the separation of powers between government majority and opposition and—for the sake of a free democratic development—strive for an equal opportunity to govern. On the other hand, a government majority will stress for its advantage as much as possible the separation of powers between Parliament and government. The tendency in the Federal Republic today is to bring more influence to bear on the *political* separation of powers—government versus opposition—than on the *legal* one—government versus Parliament. This tendency found its expression in the so-called Small Parliamentary Reform of 1969. The reform, affecting plenary work and parliamentary committees, strengthened the opposition in its minority role, with the result that the parliamentary system is increasingly though slowly gaining ground.

As committees have grown in importance in decision making, party and coalition discipline has been challenged. As a result of reforms, work and influence in the Bundestag have been shifted from the floor to the committees. To stop the trend to decentralization promoted by influential committees in the interest of a united party line, parliamentary parties procured a committee and working group system that turned out to function as an instrument of power, coordination, and control within the parties themselves. As a result, it is the parliamentary parties, forming a majority and an opposition, that today shape the parliamentary decision-making process. The Bundestag, in fact, is now a party parliament where the parties decide to a decisive extent the actions its members are going to take.

Bundestag and Bundesrat

Unlike the British Constitution, the German Constitution established not a pure parliamentary system but a federative one manifested by the existence of two legislative organs at the national level, the Bundestag and the Bundesrat. All bills have to be passed by the Bundestag. The Bundesrat, a construction to be found only in Germany, can in constitutional terms merely claim the right of participation. This means in fact, however, that amendments to the Constitution and bills requiring Bundesrat approval (*zustimmungspflichtige Gesetze,* today approximately 50 percent of all bills) have to be passed through both legislative organs. In these cases the Federal Republic is a two-chamber system. In the case of single laws (*einfache Gesetze*) the Bundesrat, which has only the right of veto, can be overridden by a majority vote in the Bundestag.

Elections for the Bundestag are the voters' chance to decide the government majority and the federal chancellorship, but this is not always enough to win a legislative majority. The parliamentary system of the Federal Republic allows a party or party coalition to carry through its legislative program only when it also succeeds in mobilizing a majority of the Bundesrat. The Federal Republic thus knows the problem of two majorities: one by direct (Bundestag) and one by indirect (Bundesrat) democratic authorization. Only the combined action of the two brings about a final and decisive legislative majority on the national level.

Like every other separation of power, this construction often is an issue of conflict, starting with the quality and structure of the two legislative organs. The Bundestag has been elected by all registered voters according to the "one man, one vote" principle. MPs win a free mandate belonging to them as individuals. They cannot be replaced by a deputy and are personally responsible for their political actions.

In the Bundesrat, on the other hand, the eleven Länder of the republic have, according to population, three to five votes at their disposal. This puts small Länder in a better position than large ones. Members of the Bundesrat have to be members, too, of their respective Land governments, which appoint and can recall them. They are obliged to follow the instructions of the Land government. The Land government, in its turn, has been authorized by a Land Parliament, which has been elected by the people. As can be seen, these two "democratic majorities" have quite different structures.

Conflict over the role of the Bundesrat centers on the question of whether a Bundesrat majority ought to follow a party line at all. Some regard the Bundesrat as an organ giving the states input into the federal lawmaking process. Others look upon the Bundesrat as a parliamentary organ subject, like the Bundestag, to the rules of democracy. According to the latter interpretation, parties become the means of influencing government decisions. In a parliamentary system democracy and parties are inextricably connected. The Bundesrat cannot be excluded from the principles obeyed in a democratic state controlled by political parties.

Parties forming the Bundestag—but not the Bundesrat—majority are bound to prefer the first interpretation. Reversed interests will argue the other way. Discussions throughout the past thirty years have demonstrated this course of argument about the role of the Bundesrat.

Although from 1949 until 1969 majorities of both Bundestag and Bundesrat were carried by the same party coalition, tension between the two organs existed from the very beginning. For the sake of cooperation, and for various internal reasons, the Bundestag gradually allowed the Bundesrat to carry more weight. By 1969, the Bundesrat had risen virtually to a point where its approval was necessary for a large amount of legislation.

The conflicts that had built up exploded in 1969, however, when—in the course of a new Social-Liberal Coalition—different majorities of Bundestag and Bundesrat made compromise necessary. On October 28, 1969, Chancellor Willy Brandt proclaimed in his government statement that "we shall venture more democracy" and announced a large-scale reform program. He did so in the face of a thin and, as it developed, rather vulnerable majority.

The CDU/CSU was now on the opposition bench, although in the election its party had received the largest number of votes. Used to exercising power and not happy with an opposition role, given the election results, CDU/CSU did not acquiesce without resorting to menace by hinting at the potential of its Bundesrat majority as a means of counteracting the government majority in the Bundestag.

The government's dilemma was clear: If it was to win over the Bundesrat majority, political reform proposals had to be modified considerably. On the other hand, the government could refuse to compromise and hold the Bundesrat responsible for the failure of reform proposals, although this meant admitting its own lack of power.

The Social-Liberal governing coalition relied on both strategies: adaptation and confrontation. The latter involved a reproach to CDU/CSU that it was abusing the Bundesrat for the ends of party politics. Adaptation, to the Social-Liberal government majority, meant getting approval from the CDU/CSU majority in the Bundesrat before passing its legislation. In fact, after the Great Coalition, from 1966–1969 to today, we have, to a great extent, a sort of "all-party cooperation."[6]

Parliament and the Constitutional Court

The Bundestag is not sovereign but subject to the Constitution. This applies to its outputs as well as to its procedures. Apart from appeals under constitutional law (*Verfassungsbeschwerde*) to which every citizen is entitled, legislation can cause conflicts or disputes at three possible stages:

- between the Bundestag and the Länder Parliaments
- between the Bundestag and the Bundesrat
- between the parliamentary majority and the opposition

If an agreement between state organs cannot be reached, opponents may put their case before the Constitutional Court. In the event of a

[6] Cf. Friedrich Karl Fromme, *Gesetzgebung im Widerstreit: Wer beherrscht den Bundesrat? Die Kontroverse 1969-1976* (Bonn, December 1976).

dispute over the interpretation of the constitutionality of a law (*abstrakte Normenkontrolle*), one-third of all MPs can also appeal to the Constitutional Court. Consequently, a strong opposition would be able to hinder the majority from interpreting the Constitution in its own way.

Proceedings initiated by the opposition against the government majority are mostly about the question of whether a factual decision is to be obtained by way of legislation or by constitutional amendments only. Because Bundesrat *and* Bundestag decide on constitutional questions with a two-thirds majority, the real question is whether a decision can be taken with or without the consent of the opposition. Thus having some control over the constitutionality of laws enlarges the opposition's ability to get the government majority into trouble. Conflicts of this kind put the Constitutional Court in the position of arbiter between government majority and opposition.

In the United States the verdict of the Supreme Court is almost the last resort because of the extraordinarily difficult amendment process of the Constitution. Not so in the Federal Republic. In Germany a vote of the Constitutional Court can be overridden or avoided by a timely change or amendment of the Constitution.

In thirty years the Constitution has been altered thirty-four times. Some of the important amendments (twelve) were initiated by the Great Coalition during its three years of administration, including the so-called Emergency Constitution of 1968, which affected twenty articles of the Constitution, and the Fiscal Reform Amendment of 1969. At this time the government majority had strong two-thirds majorities in both legislative organs.

In the Federal Republic the Constitutional Court has—as in other constitutional systems—the function of balance. At a time of more conservative politics the court tends to promote changes. If the government majority is all too keen on reforms the Constitutional Court may find it apt to point out constitutional limitations.

Three Significant System Combinations

On May 23, 1979, the Federal Republic had been in existence for thirty years, the age of a human generation. The history of and changes in the Bundestag in the parliamentary Federal Republic of Germany during these thirty years can be analyzed under two perspectives: first, with respect to general lines of development, taking the period as a whole and, second, by depicting certain periods or phases of development in relation to the then prevailing system combinations. Here we prefer the latter approach.

Chancellor Democracy (1949–1966). When Konrad Adenauer was elected the first chancellor in September 1949, he was then already seventy-three years of age. Nobody suspected the extent to which he was going to shape, during his time of office, not only politics and public policy but also the new Republic's style of government. As a description of Adenauer's era, the phrase "Chancellor Democracy" was soon in common use. Adenauer resigned in 1963 and was succeeded by Ludwig Erhard (CDU). Even though a newspaper in the mid-1960s compared Adenauer's and Erhard's style of government under the headline "Changeover from a Chancellor Democracy to an Interview Anarchy," this entire first phase is known as the Chancellor Democracy.

The specifics of this phase are as follows: the chancellor and his government could rely on relatively stable majorities in Parliament, disciplined by the challenge of a large parliamentary opposition that regarded itself as a government alternative. The repeated election success of rather poorly organized parties with a relatively small membership forming the government coalition and providing the chancellor was the result of the chancellor's popularity and his ability to make effective decisions. Thus, the chancellor elected by Parliament gained a strong leadership position within the government majority, which underlined the confrontation of majority and opposition.

In theory, this strong position should have been counterbalanced by an equal opportunity for the opposition in the debates that accompanied the parliamentary work. This was not the case, however. On the contrary, the judicial separation of powers between *Parliament* and *government* was employed; that is, after the government's address in Parliament the spokesman of the largest party—the chancellor's own party—was recognized. Although the opposition was an acknowledged and legitimate political power, its election defeat branded it a loser-minority, a group of permanent objectors.

The chancellor's dominant position within the parliamentary system was little affected by the federative system. The coalition parties of the Bundestag furnished the Bundesrat majority as well. Hence it followed that the same party coalition forming the majority in either legislative organ also prevailed on the national level, not only for single laws but also for those requiring explicit approval of both organs. Controversies between the majorities of Bundestag and Bundesrat, therefore, originated in diverse Länder interests rather than in programmatic or political issues.

Hence the phase of Chancellor Democracy meant a specific system combination, according to which

- the chancellor determined the policy guidelines within the government majority
- the government was backed by a strong parliamentary majority challenged by a relatively strong opposition
- in the process of parliamentary work and discussions the government turned the judicial separation of powers to its advantage
- the political program of the Bundesrat majority was in accordance with the parties of the government coalition
- the government majority gave the opposition little chance to call upon the Constitutional Court

The Great Coalition (1966–1969). The Great Coalition did not come into being immediately after a federal election; it emerged after the failure of Erhard's (CDU) second cabinet, when the Free Democratic party (FDP) left the coalition (October 28, 1966). Parliament chose the prime minister of Baden-Württemberg, Kurt Georg Kiesinger (CDU), to succeed Erhard in the chancellorship. The chairman of the Social Democratic party, Willy Brandt, became vice-chancellor and foreign minister. The government coalition formed by CDU/CSU and SPD counted 468 deputies. In opposition was the FDP with only 50 deputies.

Thus the political separation of powers between government majority and opposition, in fact, had ceased to exist; an overwhelming majority faced a tiny opposition, which was unable to act as a strong political counterpart. The rules of the parliamentary system were withdrawn, and more emphasis was put on the judicial separation of powers between Parliament and the federal government.

The formation of the Great Coalition turned out to be a severe challenge to the parliamentary system. Critical problems that could not be solved otherwise were said to be the coalition's basic raison d'être. Only joint action by the large parties (CDU/CSU and SPD) could bring about such constitutional changes as an emergency constitution and fiscal reform. Necessary compromises were worked out within the two parliamentary parties under the chairmanship of Rainer Barzel (CDU/CSU) and Helmut Schmidt (SPD), rather than by the government or the chancellor. An overwhelming parliamentary majority permitted a generous approach to party discipline.

In view of the fact that the party system made the Great Coalition acceptable only as a temporary arrangement, precautions had to be taken for the future. Because it was uncertain which party would be the opposition after the next general election everybody favored a comprehensive reform of standing orders, which would have the effect of strengthening the opposition.

A result was the "Small Parliamentary Reform" of 1969, which brought various important changes. Apart from a variety of procedural improvements, the reform took four directions:[7]

- streamlining and inspiring of plenary debates to promote a dialogue between government majority and opposition
- expansion and reorganization of committees to enlarge their powers of control (from this time on, the Bundestag could appoint commissions of inquiry set up by MPs and additional experts to help find solutions in cases of "important and comprehensive subject matters")
- general expansion of parliamentary publicity, starting with the right to open committee meetings to the public and to have more public hearings, not to mention the creation of a financially well-equipped Press and Information Center of the German Bundestag
- considerable improvements in administrative, secretarial, and research assistance to aid the Bundestag, the parliamentary committees, the parliamentary parties, and each individual MP

All of these parliamentary reforms contributed to an expansion of minority rights. They are the result of a Great Coalition open to new procedural reforms, which were carried to their full effect during the next parliamentary term.

The broad government coalition in the Bundestag corresponded to the political constellation of the Bundesrat. Necessary compromises could be achieved only within the framework of the government coalition: it could rather easily amend the Constitution; the opposition was too small in number to put in an appeal at the Constitutional Court.

The phase of the Great Coalition, therefore, is marked by a significant system combination, in which

- the chancellor and his cabinet cooperated with a relatively independent Parliament where the chairmen of either coalition partner earmarked the limits beyond which not even the chancellor could go in order to reach a compromise
- a government majority strong enough even to change the Constitution faced an extremely small opposition
- a similarly broad majority in the Bundesrat basically agreed with the politics of the government majority in the Bundestag
- the opposition could not produce a quorum to appeal to the Constitutional Court

[7] See Uwe Thaysen, *Parlamentsreform in Theorie und Praxis: Eine empirische Analyse der Parlamentsreform im 5. Deutschen Bundestag* (Opladen: Westdeutscher Verlag, 1972).

- oppositional forces, having no voice in either Bundestag or Bundesrat, or via the Constitutional Court, chose the way of extra-parliamentary opposition

Social-Liberal Coalition (1969–). Although the CDU/CSU remained the largest parliamentary party after the elections of 1969, the SPD and FDP formed a governing coalition under the chancellorship of Willy Brandt.

The parliamentary majority of the first government coalition, headed by a Social Democratic federal chancellor, was extremely thin and was labeled the Social-Liberal Coalition. Politically this was the first fundamental change of government in federal history. Because of the very close election result, the Christian Democrats were at first unwilling to adopt the role of opposition. They presumed that the new coalition would soon get into such difficulties that another change of government was in the offing; accordingly, their chosen course was strong confrontation.

After some MPs changed over from the parliamentary majority to the opposition, the Social-Liberal Coalition appeared damaged to such an extent that the chairman of CDU/CSU and its designated candidate for the office of chancellor, Rainer Barzel, decided to risk attempting the overthrow of the government by a vote of no confidence. The attempt failed, and the resulting voting stalemate paralyzed the Bundestag entirely.

On September 20, 1972, the chancellor asked for a vote of confidence to facilitate—by abstention of the government members—the self-dissolution of Parliament. This had the expected result. Chancellor Willy Brandt anticipated a clear majority for the Social-Liberal Coalition during the forthcoming election, an expectation fulfilled by the new elections of November 1972. For the first time the SPD was the largest parliamentary party—a position, however, it was fated to lose in the elections of 1976.

The parties of the Social-Liberal Coalition had won a majority in the Bundestag but not in the Bundesrat. The CDU and CSU managed to secure a majority in the Bundesrat during subsequent Länder elections, but this was the first German experience with different political majorities in the Bundestag and the Bundesrat. The government had to work under the condition of contrary majorities. This phase could therefore be labeled "Contrary Majorities."

The opposition parties of the Bundestag made it clear that they were going to cooperate in the Bundesrat only if their own views on subject matters were duly respected. Nor would they abstain from appealing to the Constitutional Court if the occasion arose. This narrowed the government majority's room for maneuvering. While the government majority—like its predecessors—tried to use the advantages of the judicial separation of powers, the opposition enjoyed the improvements of the Small Parliamentary Reform. The political separation of powers between government majority and opposition was more obvious than ever before. The Social-Liberal Coalition had a sufficient majority only for single legislation and not for laws requiring joint approval, let alone for constitutional amendments. The new government majority was forced frequently into compromise and often ended up before the Constitutional Court.

The government majority faced a dilemma: its coalition, which had promised far-reaching reforms to the electorate, was unable to realize them and was forced time and again to curb or compromise its proposals. As a consequence, people's initiatives (*Bürgerinitiativen*) sprang up throughout the country, mobilizing not only alternative strategies but also the resistance of intraparty groups fighting against government compromise in areas they regarded as essential.

The phase of Contrary Majorities—the period of the Social-Liberal Coalition—is marked by a significant system combination, the characteristics of which are

- a generally active government majority facing a strong opposition ready to steer a course of confrontation
- a chancellor who—within the framework of the political separation of powers—clearly leads the government majority in arguments with the opposition
- a government majority that, in a significant way, must come to terms with an opposition that controls the Bundesrat (Contrary Majorities)
- an opposition that, if necessary, will put its case before the Constitutional Court
- a Constitutional Court ready to protect the Constitution against the flood of far-reaching reforms instigated by the government majority
- an extraparliamentary opposition, in the form of people's initiatives, and an intraparty opposition on the government side in cases where compromises have been opposed for reasons of principle

In sum, we can say: The past thirty years of the German Bundestag show three phases of development marked, respectively, by three significant system combinations. The Bundestag's effectiveness, and that of the political groups operating in it, is to a large extent influenced by these fundamental system combinations. Similar constitutional or political combinations are feasible and are allowed for in the framework of the Constitution. The Bundestag has adapted its forms of organization and mode of work to these phases of development and has proved to be a flexible, large-scale organization (which still says little about its future ability to adapt).

In spite of the Bundestag's division into a complex committee system, which has created considerable problems of cooperation, the parliamentary parties have managed to maintain a guiding function to ensure their collective responsibility by way of an intraparty system of communications and control.

The Bundestag has developed into a complex party parliament. Its main continuing deficiency—in spite of remarkable improvements over the years—is its relationship and communications with the public.[8]

[8] See Leo Kissler, *Die Offentlichkeitsfunktion des Deutschen Bundestages: Theorie, Empirie, Reform* (Berlin: Duncker and Humblot, 1976).

The Working Conditions of Members of Parliament and Congress: Changing the Tools Changes the Job

Austin Ranney

However one may evaluate the ultimate impact of the events that took place in North America from 1776 to 1783, any fair-minded person must concede that the consequences were not unrelievedly bad. At the very least they spawned a new occupation for scholars, journalists, and politicians that has, profitably or unprofitably, engaged our forebears for centuries. This venerable occupation consists of Britons and Americans inspecting each other's political and governmental institutions—I do not speak of cuisine, music, or television programming—to see what models we might follow and what horrible examples we should avoid.

For many years, of course, the flow of both models and object lessons was mainly from east to west. In developing our new constitutional system, for example, we Americans borrowed the mother country's common law, its two-house legislature, and what a Frenchman told us—wrongly, it seems—was its dispersion of the legislative, executive, and judicial powers among different governmental agencies. We did not, of course, slavishly copy everything British: we rejected the hereditary monarchy, titles of nobility, concentration of power in the national government, and an unwritten constitution. In later years we copied British civil service reform, the British progressive income tax, and many British welfare-state social services and guarantees. In the twentieth century we have lagged well behind Britain in nationalizing business enterprises, although we think we have at least achieved parity in the close regulation of those enterprises to promote values such as safety in consumer products, safety in work conditions, and "affirmative action" in allocating places in universities.

More immediately relevant in the context of this volume is the fact that from the 1880s to the present day a succession of eminent American scholars and journalists—Woodrow Wilson and A. Lawrence Lowell at the turn of the century, E. E. Schattschneider in the 1940s, and David Broder and James MacGregor Burns in the 1970s—have urged our country to adopt what they call "responsible party government." They have argued that American government can never become truly effective *and* truly responsive until the Democratic and Republican parties become as centralized in control, as disciplined in legislative operation, and above all as cohesive in legislative voting as the Conservative and Labour parties are. In fact, of course, the American parties have developed in quite the opposite direction. They are now substantially *less* disciplined and cohesive than they were in the early 1900s. This is not the place to describe how and why this has come about, but it must be noted that the general adoption after 1903 of the direct primary system for making party nominations effectively eliminated any serious possibility that the Democratic and Republican parties would ever play a role in Washington very similar to that played in Westminster by the Conservative and Labour parties.

To be sure, for every commentator on either side of the Atlantic who has held up some institution on the other side as a model for his own country there has been another who has pointed out the foolishness of such an enterprise. After all, it is said, each nation's institutions have acquired their forms and operating modes from their country's unique historical experiences, contemporary social and economic conditions, and above all their citizens' special ways of viewing and taking part in public affairs. The institutions may flourish in their native soil, but they cannot be transplanted; any misguided effort to export them will result in their early demise or, worse, in their mutation into some kind of political monstrosities. Whatever may be the merits of this admonition, it has not in either country seriously inhibited the continung search for models and object lessons in the other, nor has it prevented the assembling of conferences comparing, say, the two national legislatures.

Warranted or not, the transatlantic search for models from the other side continues. In recent years, however, the flow of models to be admired and object lessons to be learned has shifted more to a west-to-east direction. This has been particularly evident in the growing number of articles by British scholars and journalists comparing various aspects of the House of Commons with their counterparts in the Congress, with most of the honors going to Congress. The matters most frequently mentioned are the low pay and primitive working conditions of back-bench members of Parliament (MPs), the haphazard organization and underutilization of parliamentary committees, and the powerless-ness and insignificance of the backbenchers resulting from the excessive power of the whips. The last of these complaints is especially bemusing for an American who, like me, has been concerned for so long with the doctrine of responsible party government and its condemnation of the excessive *weakness* of party leaders and party cohesion in Congress.

In this paper, however, I shall focus on the differences in the pay and other forms of support provided for backbench members of the

House of Commons and the House of Representatives. I propose to set forth in some detail the nature of those differences, offer some explanations for them, and speculate about the possible consequences of changing them.

Backbenchers' Salaries and Supplements in the House of Commons and the House of Representatives

Members' Salaries. A backbench MP is paid $12,916 per year (calculating the pound sterling at $2.06). He also receives an additional allowance of $793 per year for the cost of living in London. Total $13,709.

A member of Congress (MC) is paid $57,500 per year.[1]

Travel to Constituencies. An MP is given an allowance for travel between London and his constituency of up to $3,737 per year, depending upon the distances that must be traveled.

An MC is allowed thirty-three free round trips per year between Washington and his district. If he represents one of the Washington suburban districts in Maryland or Virginia, this amounts to only a few hundred dollars in taxi fares. The first-class round-trip air fare between Washington and Honolulu is now $865, and so each of Hawaii's two MCs can spend up to $28,545 per year on travel.

Salaries for Secretarial and Research Assistance. An MP is given an annual allotment of $7,595 for secretarial and research assistance. He can spend it all for help in Westminster or for help in his constituency, or he can divide it between the two. According to Godfrey Hodgson, however, not all MPs use their allotments. Hodgson reported in late 1978 that only 528 of the 635 MPs collected and spent their secretarial funds, and only 330 MPs employed secretarial help in Westminster. He also estimated that only about 200 MPs employed any kind of research assistant, and he added that at most times in recent years some 25 to 30 American undergraduates doing "junior year abroad" programs in London have worked as unpaid research assistants for MPs and have thereby constituted a significant portion of the research assistance enjoyed by MPs. Hodgson quotes Bruce George, Labour MP for Walsall South, on the appropriateness of such assistance: "It's not

[1] The data for members of Parliament are taken mainly from the new (5th) edition of David Butler and Anne Sloman, eds., *British Political Facts, 1900-1979* (London: Macmillan, 1979) as supplied to me by the senior editor. The data for congressmen are taken mainly from Richard E. Cohen, "Congressional Allowances are Really Perking Up," *National Journal,* February 4, 1978, pp. 180-83.

ideal that we have to take American college kids. Their parents are working in bars over there to subsidize their kids who are subsidising the British political system. But it's better than nothing."[2]

An MC is given $273,132 annually for "clerk hire"—that is, for employing secretaries, administrative assistants, legislative assistants, budget analysts, caseworkers, receptionists, news secretaries, and the like. He is allowed to hire as many as eighteen employees, but most congressmen prefer to hire fewer and pay them more. In 1978 the average congressman's staff numbered sixteen employees. Majorities of most MC staffs work in the MC's Washington office, but some are always assigned to the offices congressmen maintain in their districts, and a few congressmen use more employees in their districts than in Washington.

Office Space and Equipment. Not long ago very few backbench MPs were officially provided with private working space of any kind, but recently matters have improved: some kind of "writing place in an office" is now available for every MP who wants one. All but 40 or so ask for and receive such places, but the severe shortage of facilities means that only about 190 MPs are provided with whole rooms for their exclusive use, and the remaining 400 or so must share offices with other members. No public funds are provided for the rental or furnishing of space in which MPs conduct their periodic "surgeries" in their constituencies, and they must make those arrangements for themselves.

An MC is provided with office space both in Washington and in his district. The Washington offices are housed in five buildings near the Capitol—the Cannon, Longworth, and Rayburn House Office Buildings and two annexes created by remodeling other buildings. There is some variation in the size and quality of the offices, but the typical congressman has a suite of three rooms partitioned according to his preferences. The rooms are furnished and maintained at public expense, and the member is given an annual allowance of $5,200 for telephone equipment, $9,000 for the lease of electrical and mechanical equipment, and free long-distance telephone time of up to 15,000 minutes a year.

Each congressman is also given funds to rent and furnish one or more offices in his district. He is allowed to rent a total space of 2,500 square feet at a rate of from $5 to $18 per square foot, depending upon prevailing local rates, and he is given an additional $27,000 per year for furniture and equipment.

[2] Godfrey Hodgson, "America Comes to Aid British MPs," *New Statesman*, November 24, 1978, p. 686.

Other Support. The foregoing items substantially exhaust the publicly funded facilities provided for backbench MPs, but congressmen have a good deal more. They are also given annual allowances of $6,500 for office supplies, plus 480,000 envelopes. All official mail goes postage-free under the well-known "franking privilege" (note that if all of the 480,000 envelopes are sent out as first-class mail at fifteen cents per envelope, the total cash value of the free postage amounts to $72,000 per year). There are also annual allowances of $7,000 for "official expenses" (such as employment agency fees, purchase of radio and television time, flowers, and greeting cards) and $5,000 for the production and printing of "constituent communications" (mainly newsletters and questionnaires).

In addition to these readily quantifiable resources, MPs and MCs have some other support as well. The Library of the House of Commons has an excellent collection of materials and employs over a dozen researchers who, by all accounts, do a remarkably good job (considering their meager number) of digging up answers to several thousand questions submitted by MPs each year.

Members of Congress have first call on the resources of the Library of Congress, said by Sir Huw Wheldon, among others, to be the greatest research library in the world. Any congressman can at any time direct the Congressional Research Service (CRS) to do an in-depth analysis of any matter he specifies. The CRS employs over eight hundred researchers, some of whom are distinguished scholars in their fields (political scientists will recognize the names of Allen Schick, Louis Fisher, and Judith Parris). In addition, the General Accounting Office (GAO), which has a staff of over four thousand economists, political scientists, lawyers, engineers, and other professionals, not only conducts its own audits and investigations of the operation and impact of government programs but also conducts any special study requested by a member of Congress and provides advice and assistance to any member in drafting legislation.

Summing Up. Richard Cohen estimates—an exact figure is probably impossible—that the cash value of the support provided annually to each member of the House of Representatives is about $346,000, and this figure does not include his salary, his health and pension benefits, the services of the CRS or the GAO, or the many staff, service, and physical facilities furnished to each committee on which he serves. He adds that a senator can spend from $708,000 to more than $1.2 million per year, depending on the population of the state he represents.

It is very difficult for an American to estimate the cash value of the comparable annual support for a backbench MP, but surely the figure falls well below $20,000.

These figures, however rough and approximate, highlight what we all know to be the case: that by the standards of Congress backbench members of Parliament are paid very little and have extremely meager office facilities, secretarial and research assistance, and other forms of publicly funded support. If we were still living in the time when Westminster furnished the models for evaluating the institutions of Washington, we might now turn to the question of whether the pay and perquisites of congressmen should be drastically cut back so as to live down to the Westminster model. I sense, however, that this volume will more seriously consider questions of whether the working conditions of backbench MPs should be made more like those of congressmen, to what purpose, and with what likely costs and benefits. To those questions I now turn.

Who Decides? On What Grounds?

I take it that the levels of pay and other support for MPs and MCs alike depend on two main factors: who decides what the levels should be, and what tools the deciding authorities believe are necessary and proper for the job that legislators are supposed to do.

In both respects the differences between Congress and Parliament are vast. In the first instance, *Congress* is the authority that decides what Congress needs to do its job. Whatever may be their formal powers, the president, the Treasury, the Office of Management and Budget, and the other executive agencies of fiscal control play no part in fixing congressional pay or perquisites. The Supreme Court, of course, would not dream of intervening. The only external constraint on Congress's power to set its own pay and working conditions is the possibility that congressmen's constituents might become enraged at what they perceived to be an excessively greedy "pay grab" and express their rage at the polls. But at best even this constraint is a gun in the closet, rarely taken out and almost never fired.

In Westminster, on the other hand, the decisions about the pay and perquisites of backbench MPs are, like almost all other decisions, effectively made by the government. And the record shows that government estimates of the pay and support needed by backbenchers to do their jobs properly have consistently been much lower than the estimates made by most academic and journalistic Parliament watchers.

The great differences in the support for MPs and MCs have also resulted from very different perceptions of the legislators' proper jobs and the tools needed to accomplish them. At first glance the jobs of MPs and MCs seem quite similar. They attend their houses' plenary sessions; they introduce bills; they speak and vote; they serve on committees (though this is true for all MCs but for only some MPs); and they perform services for their constituents ranging from greeting them at the Capitol to intervening on their behalf in disputes with civil servants.

The differences between their jobs are much greater than their similarities, however. For one thing, the typical congressman has many more constituents to serve than the typical MP: the average population of a congressional district is 498,500, whereas the average population of a parliamentary constituency is 88,000. Far more important is the well-known fact that every congressman is, and is expected to be, an independent operator, whereas every backbench MP is, and is expected to be (by the government at least), a party man. That is, the congressman truly controls his vote and casts it in committees and in the House according to his own calculation of how best to serve the nation and his constituents. To be sure, on some matters he may seek guidance from and follow the lead of his party's chiefs and/or other especially respected colleagues on both sides of the aisle; but in law and in fact the final decision is his alone. Moreover, as any number of studies have shown, his constituents *want* him to behave independently. They invariably give the best marks to a congressman who is believed to "use his own judgment" rather than "do what the party bosses tell him." That being the case, the typical congressman understandably wants to cast the most intelligent and best-informed vote he can. To do so he needs the highest-quality and most independent information he can get. He needs to know how his constituents feel, and that requires reading (and answering) their letters, conducting polls, mailing questionnaires and analyzing the responses, reading local newspaper editorials, and the like. He needs all the information he can get about the issues, and he especially needs information that is not unduly slanted to advantage a particular executive agency or pressure group. To get such information he must make heavy use of his staff, the CRS, and the GAO. The more complex the nation's problems and the more multifarious the measures proposed to deal with them, the more resources he will feel—with some reason—that he needs to play his independent part in dealing with them. In recent years the congressman's job has grown more difficult in many ways, and it should not surprise us that congressmen have voted themselves more and better tools to do the job.

The backbench MP, on the other hand, is a party man, not an independent operator. On most public measures he votes as his party's whips direct, not according to how he independently evaluates the merits of the issues. I realize that this statement needs to be qualified, especially in the light of events since February 1974. I am aware of the significant recent increase in instances of defiance of the party whips by backbenchers.[3] I am quite persuaded by Anthony King's showing that the whips' disciplinary sanctions, commonly said to be the main factors that keep backbenchers trooping into the correct division lobbies, are in fact quite weak and that British party cohesion depends upon the beliefs of most backbenchers that the important struggle in Parliament is between Labour and the Conservatives, not between Parliament and the civil service or between the backbenchers and the government, and that a good MP supports his side in that struggle loyally and consistently.[4]

When all the appropriate qualifications have been made, however, the fact remains that, compared with the ordinary congessman, the backbench MP exercises very little control over his own vote and exercises very little independent judgment in joining one side or the other in votes on legislation. So long as that is the case, the backbencher really does not need very much office space, secretarial help, or research assistance to do the job that his paymaster, the government, expects him to do.

Thus the question becomes: Should the government give backbenchers a bit more support to help them do their present jobs a bit better; or should it give them a different job that might require substantially more support for them?

Should Backbenchers Receive More Support?

I know of no MP or commentator on Parliament who argues seriously that backbenchers should be provided with salaries, facilities, and staff that match or closely approach those lavished upon congressmen. For some, indeed, Congress provides an object lesson in the diffusion of responsibility and the confusion of policy that can result from giving too much power and support to backbenchers. Full parity in support for members of the two legislatures is not in question here.

Many students of Parliament have argued, however, that one need not regard Congress as the model to believe that Parliament should be given a more important and more dignified role than it now plays, that backbench MPs should be given more support than the cheeseparings

[3] John E. Schwarz, "The Quiet Revolution: The Awakening of the British House of Commons in the 1970s," manuscript.

[4] Anthony King, "The Chief Whip's Clothes," in Dick Leonard and Valentine Herman, eds., *The Backbencher and Parliament* (London: Macmillan, 1972), pp. 80-86.

now allowed them, and that one good device for making such improvements would be to enhance the number, activities, and support of select committees along the lines recommended by the 1978 report of the Select Committee on Procedure.

I find the case for such reforms quite persuasive. Their goals are evidently to improve the informational base and therefore the quality of the advice backbenchers give to the government (as distinct from giving them the wherewithal to make independent decisions and cast independent votes on legislation) and to improve the quality of backbench life by providing some goal other than ministerial office for those able and ambitious young backbenchers for whom the laws of arithmetic make attaining office impossible for many years. These seem to me to be worthy goals, the Select Committee's proposals seem likely to help attain them, and I gather that the Thatcher government is likely to allow the House a free vote to see if the members really want them.

Yet it seems appropriate to point out here, in the great tradition of transatlantic comparisons and admonitions, that the relationship between the size of the legislator's tool kit and the dimensions of his job works both ways. That is, Congress has certainly voted itself more staff support and better facilities because it feels it needs them to deal more effectively with its larger and more difficult post-Watergate job. It is also true, however, that the multitudes of newly added staff members have not been content merely to deal more efficiently with whatever chores have happened to come the way of their congressman. Rather, they have aggressively sought new initiatives for their employers, new legislative measures to press, new methods for controlling the bureaucracy, new ways of evaluating, disputing, and revising the president's recommendations, even new amendments to the federal Constitution. In short, the congressmen's new tools have not merely increased Congress's old job; they have significantly enlarged the job.

In my judgment the same logic applies to the tool kits of backbench MPs or any other legislators. If backbenchers are given *substantially* more and better tools (as distinct from the extremely modest improvements proposed by the Select Committee on Procedure), their jobs are bound to grow as well. The more secretarial and research assistance they have, the more they will acquire information about legislative issues that is independent of—and therefore somewhat different from—the information provided by the government and the civil service. The more the backbenchers' information differs from the government's, the more their understanding and evaluation of the issues are likely to differ as well. Even today many backbenchers in both of the leading parties have policy preferences that differ to some degree from those of their parties' leaders. If the backbenchers were to acquire substantially more independent information, those disagreements would surely deepen and multiply. And the more that happens, the more the government monopoly over policy making enforced by strong party discipline and cohesion that has constituted the core of the British system since the mid-nineteenth century is bound to weaken.

I do not anticipate any such changes in the near future; but I do believe that any government seeking to upgrade the importance, prestige, and support of backbench MPs would be well advised to think very carefully about just how much and in what ways it wants the backbenchers' role to expand, to recognize that any such expansion is likely to come more at the expense of the government than at the expense of the civil service, and to calculate very carefully what additional tools would change the backbenchers' job enough but not too much.

In making this calculation, perhaps such a government might find both useful models and instructive object lessons in the nature and impact of the expansion of congressmen's tools in the 1970s.

How to Strengthen Legislatures —Assuming That We Want To

Anthony King

Legislatures are in fashion at the moment. The affairs of the Western world have not been very well managed in recent years, and because they have been managed chiefly by executives—presidents, prime ministers, cabinets, and so forth—it is tempting to suppose that they might have been managed better had more influence been given to those other contenders for governmental power, the bodies we call legislatures. The grass always looks greener on the other side of the fence; there is always some possibility that it actually is greener.

In this essay, we intend to indicate some of the ways in which we might set about increasing the influence of legislative assemblies, assuming that that is what we want to do. Before we embark on this task, however, three preliminary points need to be made. All three suggest that we should be just a little cautious before assuming that significantly stronger legislatures would necessarily and always be conducive to the public good.

Three Notes of Caution

The first point is that there are no particular grounds in democratic theory for preferring the influence of legislatures to the influence of executives. The American president has as good a claim as any member of Congress to represent the American people; not only is he elected, in effect, by all of the people, but the claim of senators and representatives to be closer to the people than he is wears thin at a time when even the smallest congressional district numbers nearly a half-million inhabitants. What is true of the American president is also true of the French president. In the case of parliamentary systems, at least in Western Europe, the individual elector is no longer primarily choosing a local representative; he or she is choosing among the leaders and platforms of national political parties. Members of the Bundestag or the Italian Chamber of Deputies are not, and do not regard themselves as being, autonomous representatives of their localities. Rather, they are the local standard-bearers of national political organizations. The leaders of those organizations are at least as likely as their followers to be "in touch with the people."

The second point that needs to be made is that of course legislative influence by no means guarantees optimal outcomes. It is doubtful whether it even increases their likelihood. A Frenchman today may wish that there were more checks on executive power in his country; but almost no Frenchman wants to go back to the legislature-dominated politics of the Fourth Republic. Likewise, few Germans look back to Weimar with much nostalgia. In the United States, Congress may have deposed Nixon; but it also passed the Gulf of Tonkin Resolution by overwhelming majorities and in the late 1970s signally failed to respond to the challenge of reforming America's welfare system, or indeed to many of the other challenges facing the nation. Probably the most that can be said is that an influential legislature is desirable to the extent that it acts as a check on the abuse (as well as the use) of executive power and provides yet another forum (there are many others) for the debate, discussion, and investigation of governmental matters. At the very least, an active legislative assembly may offset the penchant that almost all executive institutions have for excessive rigidity and secrecy.

Finally, in considering the question of legislative influence we need to bear in mind that, in using terms like "the legislature" and "legislative," we are using a convenient, but crude, form of political shorthand. Legislatures are not monolithic entities any more than executives or interest groups are; they are made up of parties and factions, of ideological tendencies, of interest-group representatives, and of individuals with all kinds of axes to grind and career considerations to keep in mind. It is usually misleading to speak, without elaboration or qualification, of an increase or a decrease in a legislature's influence. What we are usually witnessing is an increase or a decrease in the influence of some specific section of the political community.

When for example, on the night of November 10, 1976, two right-wing Labour members of Parliament in Britain, John Mackintosh and Brian Walden, abstained on two crucial clauses of the dock labor bill, causing both to be defeated by 310 votes to 308, the power of Parliament vis-à-vis the executive in Britain was in some sense increased; but it is perhaps truer to say that the power of Mackintosh and Walden—or, more generally, of the moderate wing of the Labour party—was increased.[1] Those who advocate the giving of greater influence to legisla-

[1] On this specific episode, see Philip Norton, *Dissension in the House of Commons, 1974-1979* (Oxford: Clarendon Press, 1980), p. 436. More generally, the Labour government's loss of its overall majority in the same month greatly increased the power of every potential group of dissidents on the Labour benches

tures should be aware that in practice they are almost certainly giving greater power to certain (perhaps unforeseen and unforeseeable) individuals and groups within the political system. The groups may turn out to be benign, like the British Liberal party or the West German Free Democrats; but they may turn out to be less benign, like some of the extreme Protestants in Northern Ireland or the Communists in France or Italy. In short, Lenin's old question "Who, whom?" still needs to be asked—and answered—by those who would advocate increasing the influence of legislative institutions, whether in any one country or generally in the Western world.

All that said, let us proceed to consider how we might set about increasing the influence of a legislative assembly, if we had decided, for better or worse, that that was what we wanted to do. Our ideas can be offered in the form of practical observations. None of those offered below is strikingly novel, but all of them are based on the experience of a number of Western countries, and one or two of them may previously have escaped the reader's attention. They are set out in no particular order.

People

It stands to reasor that, other things being equal, the influence of any institution will vary directly with the quality of the people who compose it—with their intelligence, dedication, specialized skills, ability to work together, and so on. Quality in the case of members of legislatures probably also includes length of service, because certain relevant skills can be acquired only over a substantial period of time.

It follows that if we want to increase the influence of legislative assemblies, we should set about trying to improve the quality of their memberships. The trouble is that nobody quite knows how to do this. So much depends on the activities of a country's political parties, on its procedures for nominating parliamentary candidates, on the incidence and distribution of political ambition in the country, and on its structure of career opportunities generally. There is certainly no correlation, as there probably is in other occupations, between the quality of the parliamentary profession and the pay and working conditions of its members. British members of Parliament (MPs), for example, are paid a pittance compared with their opposite numbers in most other liberal democracies; and their working conditions would be regarded by members of most

and also of the parliamentary Liberal party; see David Butler and Dennis Kavanagh, *The British General Election of 1979* (London: Macmillan, 1980), chap. 2; and Howard R. Penniman, ed., *Britain at the Polls, 1979: The General Election* (Washington, D.C.: American Enterprise Institute, 1980), chap. 2.

other parliamentary assemblies as intolerable: they have little secretarial help, few of them have offices of their own, and they work hours that are long, unpredictable, and distinctly unsocial. Yet the quality of Britain's MPs seems to be as high as those in other countries, perhaps even higher. Even more puzzling, the quality of Britain's MPs appears, if anything, to have increased while the pay has worsened and the working conditions have deteriorated. The rewards of politics, it seems, are not quite like the rewards of other callings.

To complicate matters further, it is just conceivable that there may be, at least in parliamentary systems, an inverse relationship between the influence of a legislature and the quality of its members. Paradoxically, the weaker the legislature, the more impressive its members may be.

The explanation for such a phenomenon, if it exists, lies in the structure of political rewards in parliamentary systems. In a presidential system like that of the United States, a politically ambitious man or woman normally seeks either executive or legislative office—seeks to become either a state governor or attorney general, for example, or a member of the state legislature. Two separate career ladders exist. In addition, of course, service in the legislature may be seen as a means of increasing one's chances of pursuing a career in the executive; one may jump from one ladder to the other. In most parliamentary systems, however, only one political career ladder exists. The jobs at the top of the ladder are all in the cabinet (that is, in the executive branch); but the only way to reach the top of the ladder is by starting to climb it at the bottom (that is, in the legislative branch). In most parliamentary systems, in order to become prime minister or a leading member of the cabinet one has to become, and remain, a member of the legislature. In this way, all of a country's political talent is sucked into the country's parliamentary assembly, even though the assembly itself may not be very important. Indeed, the less important the assembly is, the more powerful, and therefore desirable, the cabinet and subcabinet posts are likely to be and the greater their attraction for able men and women.

Surely, however, if able men and women find themselves in the legislature, for whatever reason, will they exert themselves to increase its influence? No, not necessarily. In the first place, those who aspire to high office are unlikely to want to weaken the offices to which they aspire; the leaders of opposition parties in many parliaments have been notably reluctant to strengthen the legislature vis-à-vis the executive. In the second place, there is a tendency for two separate career ladders or tracks to develop inside legislative assemblies. One consists of those who have some reasonable expectation of one day holding ministerial office; such persons are unlikely to want to immerse themselves in purely legislative concerns. The other consists of those who, either because they are already ex-ministers or because their career ambitions have been frustrated, are forced to turn to the internal affairs of the legislature—chairing committees and so on—as a second-best alternative. In many parliamentary systems, people either ascend the ministerial ladder or they devote themselves to the affairs of the parliamentary institution; they do not do both. In practice, it is the most able (or at least the luckiest) who occupy rungs on the ministerial ladder; it is the less able (or at least the less lucky), the "professional backbenchers," who interest themselves in the affairs of the parliamentary assembly as such. Purely legislative work, in other words, comes to have the odor of failure about it.

It is not enough to recruit able members to a legislative assembly; it is desirable, as we have seen, to retain them. The legislature is unlikely to grow in influence if turnover among its membership is high; or, more precisely, its influence is unlikely to grow as fast as it would have done if its rate of turnover had been lower. Pay and working conditions may be of some importance here; but more important is likely to be the structure of power within the legislature. Able men and women will wish to remain in the legislature only if they have, and are seen to have, important work to do. One point to notice in this connection is that there is no necessary connection between the influence of a legislature, taken as a whole, and the power and influence of the individual members who compose it. Power within a relatively weak legislature may be concentrated; power within a more powerful one may be fragmented. The signs are that in recent years, although the importance of Congress within the American system has tended to increase, power within Congress has become more dispersed. Observers in the United States cite this dispersal—the weakening in the power of committee chairmen, for example, and the increase in the number of chairmanships—as a large part of the explanation for the increased incidence of voluntary retirements among both representatives and senators.[2] It is just possible that in parliamentary systems, too, moves to share power and influence more widely could have the unintended consequence of reducing the attractiveness, and therefore the retentive capacity, of political offices generally.

Still, one should not end this section of the paper on a gloomy note. There may be no surefire way of improving the quality of members of legislatures; but the recent experience of most Western democracies seems to suggest that, for a reason or reasons unknown, the quality of

[2] On congressional retirements in the 1970s, see *Congressional Quarterly Weekly Report,* January 12, 1980, pp. 79-82; and Tom Bethell, "Disadvantaged Congress," *Harper's,* April 1979, pp. 24-26.

legislators, like that of actors and orchestral musicians, has been gradually improving. It may be that, as in the theater and the concert hall, professionalism and the professional ethic in politics are driving out an older, more casual amateurism.

Knowledge and Staff

Knowledge, we are told, is power; and certainly, insofar as politics is a matter of reasoned debate, this is so. Of two politicians, one of whom knows more than the other, the more knowledgeable is also likely to be the more influential, other things being equal. Many legislators, conscious of their ignorance, especially as compared with executives, have sought in recent years to acquire more knowledge. In so doing, they have inevitably increased the sizes of their professional and semiprofessional staffs. The desire for more knowledge means, in practice, the desire for more bodies.

That knowledge, whether for politicians or anyone else, is a good thing that cannot be gainsaid. If members of the U.S. Congress had known more about what was really going on in Vietnam, they might not have passed the Gulf of Tonkin Resolution. Ignorance inhibited members of the British Parliament during the Suez crisis of 1956; it similarly reduced the effectiveness of the French National Assembly during the war in Algeria. Only when participants in political discussion are well informed can the validity of arguments be assessed and the truth of propositions tested. Legislatures are particularly important in this connection, because they are better placed than almost anybody outside of government to acquire knowledge and because they are almost unique in having the legal power to act on the basis of what they discover.

So much is commonplace. The difficulties arise when we raise the questions: How much knowledge? Knowledge of what? If a little knowledge is a dangerous thing, too much knowledge is equally dangerous; it becomes uninterpretable. And too much knowledge may easily be acquired if one does not know what one is looking for, or why.

One's response to these questions, in practical terms, is apt to depend on the country at which one is looking. Some legislatures have scarcely begun to equip themselves with the means of acquiring large amounts of knowledge; others have become quite formidable machines for information gathering and processing. The extreme cases are provided, as so often, by Britain and the United States. U.S. observers are amazed by the paucity of the resources of the British House of Commons. Backbench MPs in Britain have very little personal research support (one person working part time, at most); parliamentary committees have little or no specialist staff; and the House of Commons library is a very modest affair, though the people who work in it are competent enough. By contrast, in the United States both individual members of Congress and Congress's specialist committees possess professional staffs in abundance and ready access to the latest data-processing facilities. The Congressional Research Service has no real parallel in Britain. The Library of Congress is, of course, one of the world's largest data-storage and data-retrieval systems.

These differences between Britain and the United States largely reflect more profound differences in the political systems of the two countries. Congress is a genuine legislature, one of the few in the world; it actually makes laws. The British House of Commons is not really a legislative assembly in that sense; rather, like most such bodies in parliamentary systems, it is a sort of standing commission monitoring and criticizing the government of the day. The government governs (or tries to); the House of Commons keeps an eye on it. In order to be able to perform even this modest function, however, a quasi-legislature like that of the British needs knowledge and the means to acquire it, and undoubtedly backbench and opposition members of the House of Commons are weaker for lacking such knowledge and such means. To take only one example, the investigative select committees in Britain are considerably hampered, whether they know it or not, by their lack of full-time specialist staff. They cannot commission research except on a very small scale; perhaps more important, their questioning of expert witnesses, civil servants, and ministers is much less well informed and therefore frequently much less probing than it might be.

But if the British House of Commons lacks knowledge and staff, the U.S. Congress may just possibly have too much of both. No one should be dogmatic about saying what constitutes "too much" knowledge or "too many" staff, especially when the outputs of an enterprise like Congress are so difficult to quantify. All the same, one can suggest that representatives and senators, surrounded by staff aides of one kind and another, may possibly be neglecting tasks that they could perform well in favor of tasks that they cannot perform well, if indeed they can perform them at all.

It is often said of professors that most of them have never met a payroll. The same is less often said of legislators; but it is equally true of them. Most legislators have never managed a business or led a trade union; they have never conducted an international negotiation or negotiated a defense procurement contract; they have never managed a large government department or superintended the implementation of a complex government program. In short, unless they have served as ministers or reasonably high-level civil servants, they have never got their hands dirty in the conduct of public business. However well informed they may be, they are outsiders looking in. Professionals as legislators, they are usually amateurs at everything else.

The trouble is that large staffs and ready access to knowledge (of a kind) can tempt legislators into imagining that they know more than they really do, into supposing that the knowledge gained from reading reports and questioning witnesses is equivalent to the knowledge gained from practical experience, and, not least, into imagining that they are actually in a position to run a country's administration as distinct from merely helping to keep an eye on it. Large staffs and computers can, in other words, breed a sort of legislative hubris. Some observers think they have detected signs of just this hubris in the Ninety-fifth and Ninety-sixth Congresses in the United States.

The probability is that, with large staffs, legislators will become enmeshed in the intricacies of public policy; they will not remain detached from but, on the contrary, will become part of the pullulating "issue networks."[3] If they do, they are in danger of ceasing to perform their representative function of representing to those in power the hopes, fears, opinions, and aspirations of those who have elected them. They will become part of "them" instead of representatives of "us." Those who sat in the California legislature early in 1978 will know the feeling. If legislators lose touch with their constituents, they may still be reelected; they may benefit from being well known and from being assiduous in performing constituency services. But they may also, collectively, produce policies that are unacceptable to the mass electorate or to powerful interest groups, and their actions may lose the patina of democratic legitimacy. To put the same point differently, staff plus expertise may yield isolation.

A related point concerns responsibility, both in the sense that individuals may or may not feel responsible for their own actions and also in the sense that individuals may or may not be held accountable for their actions by others. It is a cliché that in the modern world individuals themselves feel less and less responsible and that responsibility becomes harder and harder for others to assign. The modern world is too interdependent; decision-making processes are too complex; lead times in the making of public policy are too long. This being so, it may be unfortunate if legislators engage themselves in the making of policy to the point where, because everyone is responsible for a policy, no one is. Large-scale staff support is similarly likely to lead to a certain dis-

[3] On issue networks, see Hugh Heclo, "Issue Networks and the Executive Establishment," in Anthony King, ed., *The New American Political System* (Washington, D.C.: American Enterprise Institute, 1978).

tancing, both psychological and political, of the legislator from his votes and other personal decisions.

Finally, if members of legislatures are neither administrators nor for the most part substantive experts, they are, or should be, experts in identifying the specifically political and moral components of large, complex issues that often contain substantial technical components as well. The question of the price at which oil can be extracted from shale is a technical question; the question of whether oil should be extracted at that price, of the associated costs and benefits for society at large, is a political question. Legislators who seek to turn themselves into technical experts are likely to fail at that task, and they are likely at the same time to cease to translate complex issues into terms that lay persons can understand—again, a certain distancing, a potential loss of democratic legitimacy, with legislators ceasing to function as politicians. From this point of view, staff is, at best, a mixed blessing.[4]

To sum up, British and American experience taken together suggests that members of legislatures need considerable staff support if they are to function effectively as monitors and critics of the executive, let alone as lawmakers in their own right; but American experience in the 1970s begins to make one wonder whether a great deal of knowledge and a great deal of staff support may not be bought at an overhigh price. Apart from anything else, staff is easy to acquire and hard to get rid of, as President Carter discovered.

Committees

It is scarcely too strong to say that any large body that does not do most of its work in committees is not a body that is doing serious work. Plenary sessions are not a suitable forum for detailed discussion, for close questioning, or for conducting negotiations; they tend to be great time wasters. Indeed, it is a useful rule of thumb that the more time a body like a legislature spends in plenary sessions, the less influential it is. By this measure, the legislatures of Britain and the old Commonwealth countries appear not to be very influential; they are merely debating chambers.

It would seem to follow that if a legislature lacking a well-developed committee system wishes to increase its influence it would do well to acquire one, whether for the purpose of conducting investigations or for the purpose of discussing and scrutinizing legislation—and, as we saw

[4] Since this essay was written, an excellent book on the political significance of the growth of congressional staffs has appeared: Michael J. Malbin, *Unelected Representatives: Congressional Staff and the Future of Representative Government* (New York: Basic Books, 1980).

earlier, committees, if they are to function effectively, need at least a modicum of staff. On the face of it, there seems no good reason why a legislature's investigative committees should not also, in general, be its legislative committees. The obvious principle around which a committee system can be organized is the substantive field of public policy or the government department; the two will usually overlap.

If British-type legislatures are interested, there is an appropriate model available for them to follow, or at least to adapt for their own purposes: that of West Germany. The relations between executive and legislature in West Germany are not dissimilar to those in countries like Britain, Australia, and New Zealand, yet the Federal Republic possesses a committee system that in its day-to-day operations resembles the American system fairly closely. Bills are referred to specialist committees on which sit those members of the Bundestag who have taken a particular interest in the general subject area into which the bills fall. The committees do not have their own specialist staffs, but they do have the next best thing: the ability, denied to their British opposite numbers, to have discussions with the civil servants who have been involved in preparing a bill. Much of the time of members of the Bundestag is taken up in such committee work; the committees operate to a considerable extent on a cross-party basis. It is presumably for a committee system along roughly these lines that would-be activists on the backbenches in the British House of Commons should be pressing. To say that it would not be feasible to introduce genuine American-style committees in Britain, though true, is beside the point; more appropriate models are close to hand, not just in West Germany but elsewhere on the Continent.[5]

By this stage of the argument, however, the skeptic will long since have grown impatient. "Higher quality members, more information, more staff, a proper system of committees—these are all very well," he has already said to himself, "but they will increase a legislature's

[5] On West Germany, see Gerhard Loewenberg, *Parliament in the German Political System* (Ithaca, N.Y.: Cornell University Press, 1967), esp. chaps. 4, 6; William Safran, *Veto-Group Politics: The Case of Health-Insurance Reform in West Germany* (San Francisco: Chandler, 1967); Gerard Braunthal, *The West German Legislative Process: A Case Study of Two Transportation Bills* (Ithaca, N.Y.: Cornell University Press, 1972); and Gerhard Loewenberg and Samuel C. Patterson, *Comparing Legislatures* (Boston: Little, Brown, 1979), pp. 135-38, 204-6. On France, see Philip M. Williams, *The French Parliament, 1958-1967* (London: George Allen and Unwin, 1968); and Jack Hayward, *The One and Indivisible French Republic* (London: Weidenfeld and Nicolson, 1973), chap. 3. Less has been written on Italy, but see Giuseppe Di Palma, "Institutional Rules and Legislative Outcomes in the Italian Parliament," *Legislative Studies Quarterly* 1 (May 1976): 147-79.

influence only very marginally so long as the members of the legislature allow party loyalty to determine how they will cast their votes. Why should a minister pay much attention to backbench suggestions and criticisms if he knows that he will always get his way once the bells ring and the vote is called?" The skeptic's point is well taken. And here, at last, we come to the crux of the matter.

Votes

The influence of members of a legislature depends ultimately on their votes. If they are prepared to cast their votes in defiance of the government or the administration, then they will have a good deal of influence; they will be a political force to be reckoned with. If they are not so prepared, then they will have relatively little influence; the government or the administration will feel it can ignore them. Representatives and senators in the United States are powerful not merely because of the separation of powers but also because they are so undisciplined. That a legislature can throw its weight around even in a parliamentary system is attested to by the experience of the Fourth Republic in France.

A puzzling feature of so many parliamentary democracies is that backbench MPs, knowing their power, nevertheless persist in refusing to use it. In Britain, with one minor wartime exception, no government enjoying a working majority in the House of Commons was defeated on a matter of any real importance in the more than three-quarters of a century between 1895 and 1972. This is not the place for a full discussion of the sources of party cohesion in the legislatures of countries with parliamentary systems, but some of the factors bearing on the point may be cited:

- the high level of spontaneous agreement that would probably exist among co-partisans anyway, even in the absence of other factors
- the willingness of governments to make concessions to dissidents in their own party in order to prevent revolts in Parliament
- the desire of backbench MPs for promotion to ministerial office and their fear that if they vote against the government they will not get it
- the fear of sanctions, such as being expelled from the parliamentary party or being denied renomination by one's party at the next election
- the fear that the electorate will not vote for a publicly disunited party

- strong feelings of party loyalty and party solidarity such that a backbencher voting against his own government feels himself guilty of an act of betrayal and is looked on as a traitor by his colleagues.

Above all, members of the governing party in parliamentary systems typically vote with the government because they fear that, if they do not, the government will fall and either the opposition will take power or an election will be called.

These are potentially very powerful constraints and sanctions, especially if, as is often the case, several of them operate in conjunction. An ambitious MP—and many MPs are ambitious—is going to think long and hard before risking his prospects of promotion and possibly even his parliamentary seat by voting against his government. No member of Parliament wants to be thought responsible for reducing his party's chances of winning the next election. Few are likely to want to incur the odium of "letting down the side." American readers, in particular, should not underestimate the moral and emotional strength of partisanship in many parliamentary democracies. Voting against one's party is like a Bostonian in the stands at Fenway Park rooting vociferously for the Yankees. One can do it, but it is dangerous.

If legislators are to increase their influence, however, those who normally support the governing party have to be prepared to vote against their own government from time to time, and to do so in sufficient numbers to defeat it or at least badly frighten it. In this connection, a series of recent events in Britain is of considerable significance. On the night of November 22, 1972, a set of draft immigration rules introduced into the House of Commons by the then Conservative government was defeated by a combination of the Labour opposition and a considerable number of dissident backbench Conservatives. The draft rules were important to the government; the government did not conceal its chagrin at their defeat. It did not resign, however—far from it. It simply withdrew the defeated rules and a few months later introduced a new set of rules designed to meet the bulk of the backbenchers' objections. Since November 1972, successive British governments have been defeated in the House of Commons on a considerable number of occasions as the result of defections by members of their own party; and several of the issues on which they have been defeated have been, by any standards, important. One of them was mentioned toward the beginning of this essay. Yet no government resigned or even hinted at resigning until the Callaghan government was defeated on a formal no-confidence motion in late March 1979.[6]

[6] On the growing incidence of backbench rebellion in the British House of Commons, see Norton, *Dissension, 1974-1979,* and also two other books by Norton:

The moral is clear. The belief that a government defeated in the House of Commons on a matter of substantial importance is bound to resign or to dissolve Parliament is, and probably always was, a myth. A government is bound to resign only if it has formally declared that the relevant motion is to be treated as one of confidence. Otherwise the government will not resign or dissolve Parliament. Why should it? It does not want to risk letting the opposition in or losing an election any more than backbenchers do. If anything, its stake is greater than theirs. This lesson—that the British Constitution no longer says quite what it used to say—has not been lost on at least some backbench MPs, and it will be surprising if the incidence of backbench dissent on the government side does not remain substantially higher in the future than it was in the first part of this century. In retrospect, it is mildly mysterious that party cohesion in Britain remained for so long at such a high level.

In short, legislators in many countries have the power to increase their influence. Their power lies in their votes. It is up to them to decide whether or not they want to use it. In Britain at least, MPs are discovering that they can vote against their party with far greater impunity than they had previously thought. Perhaps backbench MPs in other countries will make the same discovery.

Another Note of Caution

We end where we began, on a cautionary note. Legislators in many countries, like blacks, women, and nonsmokers, are feeling their strength at the moment and want to use it. One can sympathize. They have seen the power of their institutions decline over the past hundred years or so. They have seen both the misuse and the abuse of executive authority. They know that political executives are not all-wise and that they frequently make mistakes that could have been avoided if only the relevant proposals had been subjected to close scrutiny and in good time. All of this is true; yet we should not lose sight of the fact that legislatures are not governments and that their size, their composition, their internal organization, and their methods of operation make them ill suited for the conduct of a wide range of public business. In the twentieth century, legislature-dominated governments have not, with rare exceptions, been good governments. One thinks immediately of pre-1933 Germany, of France for most of this century, and of Italy for much of the period since 1945. So, two cheers for legislatures in Western democracies—but maybe not three.

Conservative Dissidents: Dissent within the Parliamentary Conservative Party, 1970-74 (London: Temple Smith, 1978) and *Dissension in the House of Commons: Intra-party Dissent in the House of Commons' Division Lobbies, 1945-1974* (London: Macmillan, 1975).

Discussion

Session I

The Role of the Legislature in a Presidential System

GEOFFREY SMITH, moderator: The most distinctive of the political systems that we shall be looking at is the presidential system.

The author of our first paper, "The Two Congresses and How They Are Changing," is Roger H. Davidson, professor of political science at the University of California, Santa Barbara. He has worked on both Senate and House reorganization committees and is the author of numerous books on Congress. The second paper, "Can Our Parties Survive Our Politics?" is by Charles O. Jones, professor of political science at the University of Pittsburgh. He is also editor of the *American Political Science Review* and the author of many books on the American political system.

The discussants are two distinguished congressmen: Bob Eckhardt, Democratic representative from Texas, who might be described as a living example of change in Congress in the sense that he has recently bucked the seniority system by being elected, in preference to a more senior member, chairman of the Oversight and Investigation Subcommittee of the Commerce Committee of the House; and Charles Rose, Democratic representative from North Carolina, who is chairman of three subcommittees and an experienced member of the House.

ROGER H. DAVIDSON: My paper proceeds from the general proposition that the American Congress should be understood as two institutions combined into one. To use Edmund Burke's phrases, our legislature is both a deliberative assembly of the whole nation and a Congress of ambassadors from different areas and constituencies. This dual character of Congress is mandated by the Constitution. It seems to be reflected in the job descriptions or role perceptions of members of Congress. And it is also, interestingly enough, reflected in the perceptions that the public has of Congress. The public seems to view individual members in a somewhat different light from the institution as a whole, as a deliberative body.

The Congress has been vastly altered over the past decade or decade and a half and perhaps is as radically changed as any of our major institutions. My paper addresses the substance of these changes, their consequences—some of the reforms have produced a new generation of problems—and the possible future agenda for the politics of change in the next generation. The bulk of my paper is devoted to cataloging the forces for change in two aspects of congressional activity: first, the Congress as a policy-making body, as an institution, as a collective or collegial body; and second, the Congress as a body of "political entrepreneurs," the individual members, their careers, and their constituency activities.

Dealing with Congress as an institution, I discuss the heavy demands and work loads, the declining resources in relation to those demands, the unfamiliar shape of some of the problems, and the fact that they do not accord strictly with the jurisdictions or congressional time tables or schedules. I also discuss briefly the shifts in party and factional structures. The major changes in Congress as an institution include adjustments in the handling of work loads, the proliferation of committees and subcommittees, the democratization or spreading around of initiatives and influence, and the impressive growth of a staff bureaucracy, or, I should say, staff bureaucracies—plural—on Capitol Hill.

The unresolved problems for Congress as an institution revolve around the question of leadership and of committee alignment. The leadership problem presents a paradox in that, on paper, congressional leaders are probably more powerful today than at any time since 1910. The leaders themselves in the House and Senate are perhaps as able and skillful as any one could imagine in those jobs. Yet, it is my feeling that their power is tenuous and rests on a tenuous base. There is a problem not only with the partisan leadership but also with the policy leadership in the committees and subcommittees because it has been fragmented in the past ten years. Another problem is that of committee jurisdictions and realignments, which perhaps I emphasize particularly because of my own experience with the Select Committee on Committees.

Turning to the individual members of Congress, their careers, and their constituency work, I discuss the decline of political party organizations in the constituencies; the changing nature of the congressional career, both inside and outside the institution; rising and insistent demands from the constituency for errand-running and service; and the pervasive cynicism of the public toward politics and politicians. The major changes in the congressional member's life include an increase in the scale of service to his constituency. Errand-running has always been a feature of our political system, but the emphasis is greater today than it has been in a long time. This leads to conflicts in the member's role and schedule; it makes the job of being a legislator in the United States physically and perhaps mentally wearing—the result being a slight downturn in the length of the average congressional career. For the future, we will have to devote more attention than we have in the past to looking sympathetically and carefully at the working conditions of our national legislators, at the rewards and the incentives of public service, as well as at the monetary and psychological costs.

In short, today's Congress, like the political system itself—the political parties and interest groups—is fragmented. It is fractionalized. It is decentralized. The channels for participation are relatively more open than they were a generation ago. Congress usually reflects American political life, and we are now going through a period of atomization. I do not know where that will end, but I suspect there will have to be a galvanizing issue or problem to provide some organizing principle for the legislative branch in the years to come.

CHARLES O. JONES: An important theme throughout these deliberations is: Can a free legislature be both powerful and well integrated into the decision-making system? My paper addresses a part of this potent question by discussing the role of political parties in Congress, following an active period of reform—probably the greatest period of reform in congressional history.

I have sworn off the study of political parties many times. It is too frustrating to study them in the United States. I tell my students that the American political party is like the fog. We know it is there, but we do not know where it came from. We do not know where it is going, and we are not altogether sure about its purpose while it is there. Why study fog? But I keep coming back to parties in my research and writing because they are, in a sense, the ultimate dependent variable. Their status tells much about what else is going on.

My paper takes another crack at the whole subject, but this time I have tried to ease my own burden and perplexity by simply accepting that we in the United States have political parties in the making. Sometimes we come fairly close to having a political party; sometimes we are very far away, but we are never quite there.

Have we come closer or gone further away with the reforms of the past decade? In proper political science fashion, I have listed and classified many of the reforms. Not surprisingly, I find multi-directional pulls in the nature of these reforms and their apparent purposes: a pull in the direction of the subcommittees and the individual members; a pull toward substance and power within this substance; and another pull, as a consequence of these reforms, in the direction of leadership and party units that is toward an effective and well-integrated process.

What of the future? If a party in the United States is the ultimate dependent variable, on what does its future depend? I try to identify some of those important forces, and most seemed to fall in the general political context: first, conditions facilitating presidential leadership—the president and his support; second, congressional leaders and their support; the issues that we face at any one time; and—something we would not have added several years ago—the demands for participation on the part of many public interest groups, various specialist groups, and citizen groups that have developed recently. These interest groups were not even mentioned in the literature twenty years ago. This is a new category, a new force.

I make some coarse judgments about these conditions, and aside from the House leadership, I see little that facilitates an expansive role of the party. The developments in the House party leadership are important, but, as one of the people I interviewed in Washington said, "We've got party but no program," which he found a bit ironic.

My central question is, Can our parties survive our politics? The answer is, of course, yes. Political parties will survive because they are too strong to die, too weak to commit suicide. In a sense, our parties are our politics. No one can say with certainty what the parties are likely to do in the 1980s. It is apparent, however, that the reforms enacted offer the potential for a more articulated and integrated party structure, particularly in the House. Whether that potential is realized depends on certain conditions. At least the structure is now in place, and if it emerges intact from this strange period of antipolitics, antiheroes, and guilt, it is conceivable that we will make one of our relatively infrequent moves from superfactionalism to modern partyism.

BOB ECKHARDT: Professor Davidson talks about the two Congresses, which is a good way of putting it, but I would describe it in terms of three functions—the function of lawmaker, of ombudsman, and of educator—which every congressman performs. I think Professor Davidson would associate the first two functions with his first Congress and the second and third functions with his second Congress. All three are important functions, which are both motivated salubriously and tainted regrettably by that dichotomy between institutional and individual activities, which Professor Davidson talks about.

The individual as opposed to the institutional activities lead the congressman toward faction, as Professor Jones mentioned, rather than toward party. I think it is appropriate to define those terms here. As I understand it, both Burke and Sartori particularly, with the refinement of Professor Jones, would define "party" as a group or an association of persons who have the general welfare of the public in mind, but from a particular direction or position; whereas "faction" would be used in the sense that Publius used it—that is, the three writers of the *Federalist Papers:* a group whose special interests direct their activities toward their own ends. I agree that the direction should be toward party and against faction.

I would like to expound a bit on the third function, which has been treated somewhat lightly in both papers. The function of educator makes of Congress a sounding board, a lectern, and a stump and is extremely important. It is one that most of the members elected from New York tend to use extensively. I have sometimes said, maybe a little harshly, that they have been elected to the *New York Times* rather than the U.S. Congress, and they have used the Congress merely as a place from which to express views that may change the course of the country.

I do not mean to say this in any pejorative sense. For instance, Al Lowenstein used Congress in that way, and I think he used it rather well, with respect to the Vietnam war. Bella Abzug has been frequently the subject of disparagement, but she was a very capable congresswoman and brought many matters forcefully to the attention of the American people by utilizing Congress in this way. On the other side of the aisle, the same is true of Robert Bauman and John Rousselot, perhaps not as constructively. Nevertheless, the use of Congress as an educational medium is extremely important.

In all these functions—that of lawmaker, ombudsman, and educator—there is always a good and a bad influence. The twin evils are faction and money. The influence of money and the manner in which money and organized, professional public relations are used today in politics very much affect the operation of the U.S. Congress.

A few years ago I went to a Ditchley Foundation meeting with a misconception of how the British political system is financed. I was in favor of some kind of public financing for American political campaigns, and I was under the impression at that time that this might follow a British pattern. I was entirely wrong. But the important point is that the British did not understand our problem because it dces not exist in their country. As I understand it, the money that goes to political campaigns in Britain is more or less fungible with funds that go to the party. I think this has a strong influence on the manner in which the party functions in Britain.

In the United States, contributions go directly to candidates. The tendency, of course, is strongly in the direction of faction and against party because of the method of financing. For instance, the railroads, which may be against a coal-slurry pipeline, would get friends on their side from both parties. They would form a faction to support railroad carriage of coal, which is an issue not at all related to either party. The opposition would also spring up from both sides of the aisle. Although the administration may favor the movement of coal by slurry pipeline, this becomes relatively meaningless as a party proposition, because the support of candidates is across party lines. It seems to me that this important aspect of the American system is a very dangerous development.

Both papers have addressed the issue of congressional reform. Although there have been many reforms, all of them have had some negative fallout. For instance, ever since a 1970 reform, it is possible to get a vote on almost every issue with the electronic voting device at the insistence of only twenty-five members of the House. It is good to be able to measure a developing position in Congress. This was absolutely impossible during the gradual development of opposition toward the Vietnam war. From about 1967 until the end of the war the majorities of both parties were in favor of the president's position, and it was very difficult, with no recorded votes, to get any indication of a growing sentiment against it.

Nevertheless, this reform has had some negative effects. I came to Congress from the Texas legislature, where everything was done not in the committee of the whole but in the body itself, and every demagogic issue could be brought up and voted on. I remember how relieved I was that Congress could chuck out the purely demagogic issues. Examples of such issues might be attaching to an appropriation for the National Institutes of Health a provision that none of the funds be used to experiment on human fetuses, which of course none of the funds were to be used for anyway; or providing in a general transportation bill that none of the funds be used for busing children to schools to achieve racial balance, which none of the funds were to be used for anyway. In my first years in the Congress, we could eliminate these issues by taking a vote, without a record, in the committee of the whole House, on what was called a teller vote. Members simply passed down the aisle and were counted by advocates of both sides, and no record was made of who voted or how they voted. I do not suggest that we go back to this system, but I do suggest that we find ways to prevent the waste of time on such issues.

There are several other serious questions about the negative fallout of the reforms, particularly with respect to the weakening of the floor of the House, which is becoming more like the New York Stock Exchange than an area in which serious debate is possible—a place where transactions are made, but opinions are not changed by discussion. But these questions can be taken up in later discussion.

CHARLES ROSE: I would first like to look at Roger Davidson's work on the two Congresses and how they are changing. Davidson notes that the government and the Congress are continually asked to resolve all manner of problems. I would like to talk a minute about that.

Any discussion of our various parliaments is not going to be complete until we understand the national or the world framework in which they are attempting to do their work. In the United States we in the Congress share the perception that we are continually asked to resolve all manner of problems. In fact, we have gone out of our way to be asked to resolve problems. We beat the bushes, as it were, to stir up things that we might be able to resolve. I would juxtapose that comment with Davidson's observation about role conflicts: Which came first, the congressional apparatus for servicing the constituency or the public's expectation that such service should be given?

I will plead guilty to being among those who have sought to increase our ability to service our constituencies. Although we have serviced them in ways that we could manage, we have basically been unwilling to admit to those areas that we are incapable of managing. We should go back and find a way to have a frank discussion with our constituencies as to what is our true and proper role in our respective countries. Unfortunately, we are not likely to move to such a frank discussion any time soon.

We have a serious problem in the United States because we have encouraged our people to think that their government and, in particular, their Congress can solve many of their problems, especially their social problems. By this system we have encouraged people to do less and less for themselves and almost nothing for each other. They have learned to look to the government to feed the hungry and heal the sick. The postindustrial age of modern technology and science has given rise to crisis after crisis that the American people have dumped on the doorstep of Congress and that we are totally unable to handle.

Some of us have formed a group in the Congress to forestall crisis. We call it "The Futures Clearing House." We were impressed with Alvin Toffler's urging that democracy, by definition "participatory," must learn in this postindustrial age to anticipate crisis. As we go down the road toward anticipating crisis, we suddenly face the expectations that we have raised in the minds of our constituencies. In America those expectations are perhaps a great deal higher than in

Europe. And when they are combined with a moderate crisis such as a few million barrels of oil a day cut off from Iran, Americans walk around helplessly, wondering where to look for guidance.

I hope that by dissecting Congress and the political processes that make it up we can find a better source of the guidance that is sought within the U.S. Congress. But most congressmen know instinctively that we have made a bit too grand a place for ourselves in American society. We have overadvertised our capability, and the system that we are now running discourages people from helping each other and from helping themselves.

Knowing that our ultimate abilities are fairly limited, we congressmen have created veritable cottage industries, mailing things back and forth to our constituents. We send out a great many baby books and agricultural handbooks. As an Indian constituent once told me: "Congressman, we have heard a great deal of thunder; we have seen a lot of lightning; but we have not felt the first drop of rain."

I would close with an observation that a local lady made on television recently as to why she did not vote—a problem which seems to be plaguing Great Britain as well as the United States. When asked, "Did you vote?" she said, "Of course not." And when asked, "Why not?" she said, "It just encourages them." [Laughter.]

MICHAEL MALBIN, American Enterprise Institute: My question is addressed to Mr. Eckhardt and then to anyone else who would like to answer it.

There is a running debate in the United States about the effect of the reforms of the 1970s. Mr. Eckhardt began to speak about it. Part of that debate can be summarized in one question: Has the former dominance of about 15 important committee chairmen in each chamber been replaced by a system in which about 200 or so subcommittee chairmen are now the dominant forces in Congress, each in his own field? As I see it, one would have to look at different stages of the process to begin to answer that.

At the beginning of the legislative process, issues get on the agenda of Congress in a different way from that of other parliaments. What Hugh Heclo has labeled "issue networks"—subcommittee chairmen, staff, interest groups on all sides of an issue, and people in the agencies—seem to control a great deal of what gets on our political agenda: what intiatives will be proposed and whether they are proposed as congressional or administrative initiatives.

At the next stage of the process are the congressional committees, where negotiation takes place, or legislation is marked up, or perhaps a bill is killed. Here, there is a different nexus of power; subcommittees and full committees are important, and party leaders start to exert influence. When the issue gets to the floor, the situation seems to change again. Mr. Eckhardt has spoken most eloquently on the thesis that subcommittees are not very powerful on the floor. I would like to ask him to address this question.

REPRESENTATIVE ECKHARDT: Again, there is good news and bad news about the reforms. On the whole, it was a good thing to get away from the dominance of old chairmen, who were frequently at odds with the majority party. Of course, that was more or less a regional phenomenon related to the fact that southerners stayed in office for a long time, regardless of their connection with the actual movement of government.

The old system was not good; the new system also has its flaws, but I think they can be corrected. The trouble with the new system is that it gives authority to many more subcommittee chairmen. These subcommittee chairmen are backed by good and competent staffs, and this part is good. But we have put members on so many subcommittees and given them so much responsibility that there are not enough people who are experts on matters that come to the floor.

In the last session of Congress, I headed a small subcommittee that had heavy responsibility for dealing with very complex and controversial measures of, for example, the Federal Trade Commission. When I, as subcommittee chairman, presented a bill for the committee, the chances were that my committee chairman would not be on the floor. There would be maybe three members of the subcommittee present, only one of whom had heard much of the evidence in the case. A "Dear Colleague" letter handed out at the door could influence those coming on the floor to a greater extent, perhaps, than the long, tedious, and hard work of a subcommittee chairman, his minority ranking member, and the whole staff of the subcommittee. That is what I mean when I say the floor has been weakened by otherwise desirable reforms.

I think the situation can be corrected. One improvement would be to call for a caucus of the full committee before important bills come on the floor, so that knowledgeable persons would be present. Another would be to consider important bills on a special day when about five minutes would be allowed for the vote—not for the debate—so that anyone not on the floor would not get to vote.

In the old teller system, only one bell was rung to summon members to vote, and by the time everybody got through the lines, the vote was over. This system eliminated all the paddle-ball players and those who were out of town, but it did get on the floor those who wanted to influence legislation. It was a selective means of getting those who were the most knowledgeable about the subjects and the most sincere in their legislative functions. We could restore that. In short, the reforms tend to bring more talent and more attention to various elements of legislation, but they fail to create party activity in the best sense—the drive that is necessary to put through desirable legislation.

TUNJI OLAGUNJU, deputy secretary, Cabinet Office, Nigeria: I wonder whether the kinds of reforms mentioned were necessitated because the American government in the 1970s faced issues with which the two-party system was not able to cope. The expertise of the new subcommittees and committees was needed to resolve these issues.

If these issues do raise the question of wider participation in the party system, does the two-party system really guarantee this? Or will Americans start thinking about a system with five national parties to allow individual expression and participation? Are there other alternatives in some new, national parties?

AUSTIN RANNEY, American Enterprise Institute: The alternative to the collapse of the American party system is not necessarily the development of a multiple party system of the European model. It may very well be some kind of no-party system. I think Professor Roger Davidson is in a good position to comment on what such politics would be like, because in that regard, as in all others, California provides the model of the future. There has been no party politics there for some time. It produces leaders such as the present governor. The development of the European Parliament may well provide a model of politics along similar lines, as British Conservatives try to align themselves with Christian Democrats from Italy or Germany, and the like. I would only say that if, after his unsuccessful try for the presidency, Governor Brown seeks to become a British subject, or a citizen of the Federal Republic or some other country, we may well see what the future leadership of the European Parliament is going to be like. It is something Europeans might want to think about and alert their immigration officers to. [Laughter.]

PROFESSOR DAVIDSON: This is a very live issue in the United States, particularly among political scientists, many of whom have a traditionally high investment in political parties as institutions. There is a difference of opinion on the utility of political parties, as we normally understand them, and their future. It is just as well to get that issue out on the table. I would not want to give the impression that American political observers are all of one mind. Many political scientists, journalists, and close observers of the American political system lament the fact that the parties have been weakened, and they would like to see the political party system strengthened and refurbished.

I gather that this is Professor Jones's view. My own feeling—and it is a hunch—is that the traditional party system in the United States is dead and beyond reviving. It seems to me that the real party system in the United States is a fluid and changing system of factionalism in which candidates and interest groups try to position themselves to attract the voting market. The parties have been fatally weakened, if not by the reforms earlier in the century, certainly by the reforms of the last decade or decade and a half. The modern campaign finance legislation, the changes in the process of candidate selection, and new technology that enables groups to get at voters in different ways have made it possible for any group with a minimum of financing and support to perform some of the functions traditionally associated with the political party. The result is a floating system of factionalism.

The true party system in the Congress consists not so much of Democrats and Republicans but of the forty-five or so voting blocs—forty-five is the most recent count I have read; they are organized, many have staff, and some have whip systems of their own. These voting blocs include a black caucus, an Irish caucus, an Italian caucus, an iron and steel caucus, a rural caucus, the balanced-budget group, and so on. It seems to be an emerging party system and may be indicative of things to come. It does not seem to me that the Democrats and the Republicans have successfully encompassed the kinds of issues which are agitating individuals and voting blocs in our country.

TOM MCNALLY, member, British Parliament: With regard to political parties in America, it is still true that it is almost impossible to run except as a Republican or a Democrat. It is a paradox that, despite the weakening of the party system, people are not running as independents and being successful. I believe that 18 percent of Americans register as Republicans these days, and yet the percentage of Republicans in the House is much larger than that, and most people want to run as a Republican or a Democrat.

The British always find the American system strange because of the enormous strength of the popular vote and the number of incumbents that are returned. Chuck Whalen, I believe, held his seat year after year as a Republican, but since his departure, the vote has gone dramatically Democratic. The ability of the individual to retain the seat seems to rest, in British terms, on much more than the 500 votes that Dr. David Butler ascribes to the personality of the candidate.

I would like to present two views of what the Congress has been doing. The last time I was in the United States, a senior congressman told me that in his view an era had come to an end. It had probably begun with Roosevelt and reached its zenith with Kennedy, Johnson, and Nixon, with the presidency taking to itself powers that it had no right to take. He said that the Congress is now reasserting the proper balance within the Constitution.

I put this view to a member of the present administration, however, and he saw the Congress as weakening and crippling good government by trying to handle more than it could properly manage. From the outside, there is an occasional worry that the Congress is doing just that, particularly in matters of foreign affairs. As a result of guilt about the Gulf of Tonkin Resolution and Vietnam, and the suspicion following Watergate, it is not simply that there is a particularly artless administration in the White House, but that there is a grim determination in Congress not to let history repeat itself. This makes it almost impossible for any president to carry out his role as the chief executive.

REPRESENTATIVE ECKHARDT: That is a very perceptive view of what is happening. The question is whether, with the weakening of government as a total institution, we can meet the extremely complex and difficult developments in the world today.

Congress envisages itself as virtually independent with respect to policy making and also with respect to administration. This is reflected in, for instance, the Anti-Impoundment Bill, which I thought was good, and the War Powers Act, which I thought was bad because it gave away more congressional authority than it preserved in an area in which Congress should have the final say. It is also reflected more positively in what is called the legislative veto; that is, the authority of Congress to deal with the details of administration, after an act is passed, by requiring the administrators to bring back the final action—for instance, a rule—for Congress to overturn.

We are very rapidly approaching a situation in which Congress is asserting that it has the power to act as an independent agency, but it cannot possibly have it. It is almost impossible, for instance, to generate a national energy policy out of Congress alone. Congress can do much in this direction and did actually work miracles under Tip O'Neill in establishing an energy program in the Ad Hoc Energy Committee. That was a salutary and extremely innovative process, but the president was essentially for the program, and so is the leadership.

Right now, with respect to oil policy, the majority of the Democrats in Congress are opposed to the position of the president, and a majority of the minority party are in favor of it. It is almost what we had toward the end of the Vietnam war. The result was exactly the opposite of what would have happened in Britain. Instead of going out of power in Congress, the majority party brought down the president, and then it ended the Vietnam war under an administration of the other party. Something like that could possibly happen with respect to the energy program.

ANTHONY KING, University of Essex: I am not a comparative analyst of statute books, but if I were, I think I would find that the United Kingdom does not have many statutes, and those that exist are, by and large, set up very much as a framework. The extreme case that I have encountered is the Education Act of 1944, which, as I recall, says merely that the secretary of state for education shall see to it that local authorities provide a good educational service. It has a few more detailed provisions, but those are its aims. I suspect, however, that the U.S. federal statute book contains far more statutes than Great Britain has, and that they go into enormous detail setting out exactly how the policy aim is to be pursued. In addition, as Representative Eckhardt has just said, there are procedures whereby the little that is left to the executive branch often has to be brought back to Congress for another look and may be thrown out. In France, of course, that curious document, the Constitution of the Fifth Republic, makes an effort to distinguish between the domain of the law and the statute, on the one hand, and the rule-making domain, the legislature, on the other.

For the performance of its educational role, wouldn't it be desirable if Congress were to concern itself much less with the details of policy and of administration and concentrated on a more limited number of larger questions? I haven't the foggiest idea how this objective—if it is desirable—could be achieved, but I am very conscious that all the current pressures for more subcommittees and more staff, and the suspicion that Congressmen have of the executive branch, are pushing in the other direction. My question is whether this objective is desirable and whether there is any conceivable way in which Congress might go some distance toward achieving it.

NORMAN J. ORNSTEIN, American Enterprise Institute: Tony King is absolutely right about the difference in the number of pages in the statute books of the United Kingdom and the United States, but there are some interesting trends in Congress that I think ought to be brought out here.

Over the past decades, the number of public laws that have been passed by Congress has been cut in half, while the number of roll-call votes taken on the floor of the House and Senate has more than quadrupled, and the number of meetings of committees and subcommittees has also quadrupled. The average length of a statute has more than doubled while the number of statutes has been cut in half. There are fewer laws passed, more and more activity, and longer and longer bills coming up on the floor. Of course, all these things are interrelated.

One result is omnibus bills that cover a variety of areas and try to be both comprehensive and detailed. With more votes on the floor and more amendments added to bills, legislation becomes jerry-built, often going in contradictory directions. In many instances, the result is bad law, and Congress then needs to go back to the issues in a later omnibus bill, which may not deal with the same subjects, to try and correct things that have happened.

REPRESENTATIVE ECKHARDT: To respond to Anthony King's point, it is true that we have gone into great detail in federal legislation and written a lot of words, but we have also delegated a tremendous amount of authority to both the executive department and to the independent regulatory agencies. It is a bit deceptive to consider the detail of the legislation as confining. In many respects, it is exactly the opposite. It delegates authority within so-called guidelines, but these guidelines are frequently extremely lenient. For instance, under the Federal Trade Commission Act, the FTC, which is an independent regulatory agency, can make rules to prevent unfair or deceptive practices. The terms are very broad.

As another example, various laws have been passed with respect to the control of the price of oil. The Energy Policy and Conservation Act, if passed, would delegate authority to the Department of Energy to establish oil prices at various rates for new and old oil and other categories, as long as the average price is $7.66 plus 10 percent per year for inflation. In addition, the department would have authority to allocate oil to various regions of the country and to refineries, and to put into effect an entitlement program, which would exchange money from one refinery to another to equalize the opportunity of receiving oil.

Although legislation is more complex and the delegation of authority is more refined, the executive is by no means more greatly restrained than in the past. I think Congress has actually moved in the other direction. There are both institutional and political reasons why legislation is often more detailed. In many areas, such as air pollution control, it is extremely detailed because Congress has sought to set the standard.

It makes a difference who is president. Here the separation of powers and the separation of elections are significant. It is one thing for a Congress to enact legislation to be administered by a president with whom they have friendly relations and a great deal of confidence. It is another matter for a Democratic majority in Congress to enact legislation over a long period of time for a Republican president.

MANFRED SCHULTE, member, German Bundestag: Professor Davidson spoke about the growing influence in Congress of the staff and of the staff bureaucracy. Any discussion of parliamentary problems must consider the vital role of the staff. The American Congress has big staffs, and we in Germany still have small staffs. What is the real role of the staff in the Congress? Is the staff very close to decision making? Is the staff member the decision maker to some extent?

PROFESSOR DAVIDSON: There has been a trend in the last twenty years toward more direct involvement of the staff in the business of negotiating legislative agreements and actually writing legislation. When I first started frequenting the halls of Congress on Capitol Hill, members of the House of Representatives did most of their own legislative research and in many cases even wrote legislative provisions. In the Senate, this was less true. Because the senators represent larger constituencies, they earlier went to more staff control. Today, it seems that almost all of the hard legislative work on the Senate side is done through staff negotiations.

It is sometimes hard to know whether one is dealing with the senator himself or with the staff individual, and sometimes perhaps there is poor communication between the two. My own impression is that this is becoming more and more the case in the House of Representatives. Over the past five years—perhaps since the "subcommittee bill of rights" and the development of staff in the subcommittee—staff seem to play a more active role in the legislative process in the House of Representatives, but it is not yet as extreme a situation as in the U.S. Senate.

SHIRLEY WILLIAMS, former British secretary of state for education and science: I wonder whether we are beginning to see a trade-off between the decline of party discipline and authority, on the one side, and, on the other, the tendency for the legislature to come together against the executive in the absence of such party discipline or loyalty. In other words, is a pattern emerging in which the choice lies between these two tendencies?

That leads me to two questions. First, why do Americans still run—to pick up Tom McNally's point—as Republicans and Democrats? What does it mean when they say that about themselves?

A second rather different question has to do with the frustration of the expectations of the electorate. Many problems such as those of energy policy are going to emerge in the next decade. How can a system of factions deal with them? When legislators engage in an enjoyable system of repealing one another's legislation—which is the British answer to the problem—how can they come to grips with these long-term problems? It would be useful to compare the effectiveness of different types of legislatures, those with a strong party system and those without.

CHARLES WHALEN, former member, U.S. Congress: Candidates run as Republicans and Democrats because that is the way the election system is set up. Many independents are now running as Republicans or Democrats against the Republican and Democratic parties collectively, which I think is a bad trend.

MR. RANNEY: Both Professors Davidson and Jones alluded to one angle of what is going on in Congress that seems to me important enough to add to the agenda. Very briefly, it is that from the standpoint of the outside observer, things have not looked so rosy, particularly in the House of Representatives, in a long time. The grip of seniority has been substantially broken. Not only are there eighteen or nineteen really juicy leadership positions now, but there are many subcommittee chairmanships. Staff has been greatly increased, as I tried to show in my paper, with something on the order of $350,000 to $400,000 a year of support, in addition to salaries and other perks. It looks really marvelous.

As has been alluded to here several times, for an incumbent member of Congress, whether a Republican or a Democrat, the chances of being reelected are overwhelmingly strong. And yet there is now a higher turnover in Congress than in a very long time. As a matter of fact, the great proportion of the members of both Houses of Congress have been elected since 1972. In some ways, Congress is the least experienced now under circumstances which should have produced the most seniority.

I would like Professor Davidson or Representatives Eckhardt or Rose to comment on the increase in the turnover, its causes, and what its consequences will be for the nature of the legislative process.

MR. SMITH: Most of those points will be taken up in later sessions.

HENRY HUBBARD, *Newsweek:* In talking about the weakening of the party, somebody mentioned caucuses and extraparliamentary groups within the legislature. Although there are many of them, such as the steel caucus and the rural caucus, it is important not to exaggerate their influence. Most of them exist for a single issue and are often merely publicity devices to send press releases to a congressman's home district to explain his interest in steel, if he belongs to a steel caucus, or to announce that he visited the president, who was influenced by what he had to say.

The institutions with more important influence on the Congress, however, are the outside interest groups. Their power depends on the velocity of communication in the United States, a system which has been highly refined by some of these groups. The Chamber of Commerce and other institutions, for example, used to visit congressmen to explain why they should vote a certain way, but these groups no longer operate that way. When a piece of legislation is coming up for a subcommittee vote, they activate an elaborate telephone communication system. Within an hour or two, they can have, on the tables of every one of their regional offices in the United States, advice on what is to be voted, and instructions on the kind of lobbying they want done.

The regional offices, in turn, communicate to friendly businessmen in the community, who communicate to Washington by mailgram or telegram. On the desk of a congressman, the morning of the vote in his subcommittee, there will be a highly intimidating stack of mail or telegrams or telephone messages.

The effectiveness of this barrage, I suppose, depends on how timid the Congress is—and the Congress has been very timid in the past few years. This trend can be combated, but in recent years the fight has not been effective. The speed and the sophistication of communication are corrupting the legislative process to a great extent.

REPRESENTATIVE ROSE: I agree with Henry Hubbard's observation. The speed of communication has affected the Congress greatly. Specifically, special interest groups have begun to use computerized mailing lists to target the Congress. Most congressmen who receive large targeted mailings no longer quiver and shake as much as they initially did. If they are clever, they take those targeted lists and computerize them themselves, so that they have a spear to throw back in the other direction.

I have always said that if a special interest group has a better mailing list of my constituents than I do, they will own me. If I cannot reach my people as quickly as or quicker than they can, then I will worry about what they might say or imply about my intentions when I voted a particular way. I got into quite a heated argument with Reed Larson of the Right-To-Work Committee on that issue. He thinks it is horrible that I use the taxpayers' money to mail computerized postcards, although he sent me postcards by the bushel, urging me to do certain things or not to do certain things, for fear that the union bosses were taking over the electoral process. I wrote to him and told him what a great fellow I thought Reed Larson was, but that his point was hogwash, and gave him the reasons.

I want to speed up communication even more. I would like Congress to have its own telecommunication satellite, so that I could sit in my office in Washington and have video conferences with my constituents back home.

MR. SMITH: Thank you very much. On that note I am afraid we will have to end the first session.

Session II

The Role of the Legislature in a Parliamentary System

NELSON POLSBY, moderator: The panel for this session consists of three specialists on the German parliamentary system and two on the British parliamentary system. In the American format, that is roughly proportional representation, according to population. We have decided jointly that we will move conversation on to the floor as rapidly as possible and reserve at least some of the time for extended comment.

The first paper, "Parliamentary Change in Britain," is by Geoffrey Smith of the *London Times,* who has made me and possibly others extremely nostalgic for *Times* leaders.[1] He begins his paper with the word "whatever," just as in every good fourth leader of the *Times.* There will be a comment from Kenneth Baker, member of the British Parliament and chairman of the Hansard Society in succession to the late John Mackintosh, in whose honor we are having a moment of noise.

The German participants will be Professor Michael Hereth, of the Armed Forces Academy of Hamburg, and two representatives of the significant legislature-watching group of political scientists at the University of Hamburg, Professor Uwe Thaysen and Professor Winfried Steffani. Professor Steffani is author of the paper entitled "The Bundestag at the Intersection of Four Systems."

GEOFFREY SMITH: I must say I thought that all the best leaders began, not with the word "whatever," but with the word "moreover." [Laughter.]

To continue what I said in my paper, I suggest that there is a growing mood for parliamentary reform in Britain to strengthen the position of Parliament in its relation to the executive and to the government of the day. The demand for Parliament to be stronger in its dealings with government comes for a variety of reasons and from different sources. It is politically significant at the moment because it is coming increasingly from the younger members of Parliament, who are dissatisfied with the role that they find accorded to them under the existing procedures.

[1] *London Times* editorials. At the time of the conference, the *Times* was on strike.

Specifically, the demand for reform seeks to create a stronger system of select committees. In Britain we have two kinds of parliamentary committees. To oversimplify considerably, one kind of committee deals with legislation. After a bill has received its second reading, which means that it has been approved in principle by the whole House, it is sent to a standing committee, which examines the details of that legislation, clause by clause, and reports the bill back to the whole House, which then can deal with the changes as it thinks fit. That standing committee is always created for the purpose of examining the particular bill in question. Despite its name, it is, in practice, an ad hoc committee, and when it has accomplished its task it is then dissolved.

Then there are select committees, whose broad task is to examine government policy and activities. Roughly, the select committees have the task of oversight. They are a hodge-podge. Some examine the work of individual government departments; some examine particular fields of activity such as the Select Committee on Race Relations and Immigration. One, the Public Accounts Committee, examines the whole field of government activity and performs an auditing function.

The demand has been to create a more effective structure of select committees, and a special select committee on procedure has been set up. Several people at this conference are members of that committee. In August 1978 it recommended a new structure of twelve select committees to take the place of most, though not all, of the select committees that we have at the moment; these twelve new committees would be shadowing government departments. The effect would be a more coherent structure. It would be a tidier arrangement that would get rid of overlapping. And all areas of government would, in fact, be covered by a select committee, which is not the case at the moment.

The select committee's report has been once debated in the House,[2] the general measure of approval, and there is an understanding that it will be debated again shortly. There is a strong demand for the House to have the opportunity of coming to a decision on this. If the report is approved, there would be a new structure of committees, which would have more power in certain areas. They would have greater power to call for people and papers—more evidence, therefore—to be presented to them. They would have more staff. There would be greater oppor-

[2] Late in 1979, the House of Commons approved the committee report creating fourteen departmental select committees. They were: Agriculture; Defence; Education, Science, Arts; Employment; Energy; Environment; Foreign Affairs; Home Affairs; Industry and Trade; Scottish Affairs; Social Services; Transport; Treasury and Civil Service; and Welsh Affairs. Eight were chaired initially by Conservative MPs; six by Labourites.

tunity to debate their reports on the floor of the House of Commons, and so on. But the influence of the select committees would still depend on the power of publicity. It is the standing committees that deal with legislation. The select committees have only the power of publicity.

In my paper, I suggest that although there is a very strong case for improving the strength of Parliament and for having stronger select committees, this particular select committee report goes only part of the way. I am in a minority of one. I must emphasize for Americans, Germans, and others at this conference that this is no accident. The debate, as it has proceeded in Britain, is essentially between those who favor strong select committees, who like the select committee report and want to see it implemented, and those who do not want to see stronger select committees and want to bury the select committee report.

I want to see stronger select committees. I believe that the select committee report does not go far enough because it does not give any effective power to the new select committees that are postulated. In British politics, as in politics elsewhere, influence follows power, and it is no use creating a new structure of tidier committees with more influence without actually giving them power. Therefore, while I approve the general thrust and purpose, I end on a skeptical note.

KENNETH BAKER: Geoffrey Smith has outlined the mood for parliamentary change in the United Kingdom. It is very strong because British politics is developing in a way that is in complete contradistinction to that of American politics.

Over the past few years, the powers of the American president have withered away as a result of the building up of the powers of Congress and, of course, the crisis of authority following Watergate. Even if the president had an energy policy and people understood it, it is likely to be weakened or, indeed, reversed in a matter of days by pressures in Congress. There is a lack of authority at the center.

In the British system, however, the trend has gone very much the other way. The power of the executive has become greater, and to those who study British politics, let me enter just one caveat: Do not generalize from the past two years of minority government under Mr. Callaghan, which are unique in our parliamentary history. It is necessary to go back more than a hundred years, to the 1867 Reform Act, to find the degree of flexibility and instability that the government has shown in getting through its policies in the past two years.

With the recent general election in the United Kingdom, "normal service" has been resumed. [Laughter.] Not only do we have the return of the Conservative government—that, we know, is normal—but also a party with a clear overall majority that can withstand, short of major economic calamities, probably a four- or five-year term. I think that many of my colleagues on the backbenches in the Conservative party were persuaded to do something about the growing power of the executive.

The power of our prime minister is infinitely greater than the power of the president in the American system. That power derives principally from considerable patronage both within the House of Commons and outside it. We, as legislators, do not have any influence upon this patronage and cannot check or question it. Indeed, the amount of patronage that is in the hands of the prime minister would make even Sir Robert Walpole blush. When he was prime minister he appointed so many of his family to lucrative posts in government that his rule was known as the "Robertaucracy." [Laughter.]

In addition, the power of the prime minister stems from the power of the executive within the legislature. The government exercises virtually complete control of the agenda of the House of Commons. The order paper is in the hands, not of the House of Commons, but of the leader of the House, who is a member of the British Cabinet.

To illustrate the problem, one of the minor proposals in our select committee was for the House of Commons, which normally sits on Friday from 10:00 o'clock until 4:00 o'clock, to adjourn at 2:30 on Fridays so that members could go home early. We cannot actually debate that without the approval of a member of the Cabinet, because the executive has to find time for each debate. It was recently explained to me that the U.S. House of Representatives had decided a couple of years ago to change its hours of sitting. The difference between the American and the British system is that we, as backbenchers, cannot effectively do that. We could possibly use certain procedures of the House to change the hours, but not without the actual support of the executive.

Geoffrey Smith has mentioned the growing restlessness of backbenchers about their role. I have been in the House for ten years, and certainly, the nature of members of Parliament has changed over those years. They tend to be younger and from more professional and expert backgrounds, and they really do not want to spend much of their time in the House of Commons as underpaid social welfare workers, nor do they want to be treated largely as lobby fodder for their parties. They want a more interesting and more creative role, and my colleagues on both sides of the House are pressing for a more effective committee system.

The role of the backbencher in our system is very strange indeed. Now that normal service has been resumed, the spectacular successes of one or two backbenchers—such as George Cunningham—in the last Parliament simply cannot be repeated.

Geoffrey Smith has mentioned the details of the changes—the twelve departmental committees that will examine the estimates. He would like it to go further and asked why we did not recommend select committees that would have the power to propose legislation. The answer is that we have to make changes slowly. If our committee had come out with such a proposal, the possibility of getting it through the House of Commons would have been almost nil. We have to take one step at a time.

How will it change our system? To some extent, it depends upon how effective the committees are once they are established. It will depend upon the personality and drive of the chairmen of the committees and the caliber of the members who are on the committees. They will be given a very free hand to examine any area of expenditure of the twelve major departments. And they will be able to produce reports, which will have the right of being debated on the floor of the House, because another of our proposals was to set aside eight Mondays a year when the reports come back on substantive motions. We also recommended an improvement in staffing, though nothing on the scale that Congress has.

I would also like to see the chairmen of these select committees receive a salary over and above their salaries as members of Parliament. This was carried by a majority vote in our select committee on procedure, but I suspect the House will not approve it, which is a pity. If the chairmen of the select committees were paid, it would enhance their role as chairmen and open up another career pattern for backbenchers that does not fit into the general career ladder that Anthony King refers to.[3]

In the longer term, two implications of these changes give rise to anxiety in Britain. The first is that the chamber of the House of Commons will cease to be the center of debate. Michael Foot uses this argument, and Enoch Powell has used it in the past, although he was on our committee and agrees with our proposals. I do not see this danger. The chamber of the House of Commons will continue to be the center of national debate. But the House of Commons itself, sitting in plenary session, is not an effective instrument to call government departments and ministers to account. It is impossible to call people to the bar of the House to examine them in detail. In my view, it can be done only by detailed examination and cross-examination in committee. I do not believe that the nature of the chamber of the House is going to change.

The second anxiety is that procedural changes in the House of Commons are going to break down the party political system—the

[3] See, Anthony King, "How to Strengthen Legislatures—Assuming that We Want To," in this volume.

adversary nature of British politics. Of course, that is not going to happen.

A select committee tends to weaken the party bonds to some extent. These bonds are very strong in the adversary nature of the chamber itself and in standing committees, but I do not believe that the party system will be destroyed or even undermined, as some critics say.

The essence of the British political system is the party system. One cannot envisage British politics without it. Many people may be very dissatisfied with the system, but if there are changes in it they will be much more fundamental than changes of procedure in the House of Commons; they will affect our electoral system and things of that sort.

We are merely trying to redress the imbalance between the executive and the legislative arms. It has tipped far too much in favor of the executive.

WINFRIED STEFFANI: About fourteen years ago, when I was in the United States to study the House of Representatives, I was informed that Mr. Polsby was a brilliant expert on its organization. I asked him about a particular proposal to reform the House, and his answer was that he had been studying the House of Representatives for only five years and was still trying to understand how it works. So he was not prepared yet to discuss issues such as reform.

Today we are speaking not only about the organization of the U.S. House of Representatives, the British House of Commons, and the German Bundestag, but also about the broader setting for these institutions. A long debate has been going on for about 200 years on the difference between the American and the British systems, and the main issues have been rather similar throughout the 200 years. The American Constitution does not mention parties, but the parties have a special function in the system. In Great Britain, the party formally makes the rules of the whole government. The Parliament cannot be understood without understanding the action and behavior of the parties.

In Germany we watch the British system, where the parties are in the center. The British say they cannot use the instruments of the American system, such as powerful committees, and still keep the parties in the center of the system. In the United States, they say that if their parties become stronger, their special governmental system would not work in the familiar way. The American parties have a different function from the British parties, and so they cannot learn much from each other.

In Germany, we have tried to make a mixture of both governmental systems. I point out in my paper how the framework for this special system combines some parts taken over from the United States and some from the British system.

I have titled my paper "The Bundestag at the Intersection of Four Systems." These four systems are: First, the classical separation of powers. I call it the judicial separation of powers. The Parliament and the government are separate state organs in their own right.

Second is the parliamentary system, which has a political separation of powers between the "governmental majority," a unit of the government and the parliamentary majority, on the one side, and the parliamentary opposition, on the other.

Third is the federal system, in which we have two legislative chambers. The Bundestag does not always represent a majority on legislative issues, because in 50 percent of our legislation, it is necessary to have the consent of the other legislative organ, the Bundesrat, and therefore majorities are needed in both legislative organs. In all these cases, the national majority is not identical with the majority of the Bundestag. Two majorities have to consent. Problems develop if one party has a majority only in the Bundestag and not also in the Bundesrat.

On the fourth level is the constitutional system, in which a federal court can set strong limits for the legislative process. Sometimes there is trouble between the separate interests in this field, as in the United States.

During the thirty years of our Constitution, we have had three combinations of these four systems. The first phase, from 1949 to 1966, was the so-called Chancellor Democracy. The chancellor had a very strong position and a disciplined party in parliament, which brought him into office, so that he could give guidelines for policy against a rather strong opposition. The Bundesrat had the same political majority as the Bundestag. A constitutional court, the Supreme Court, was not often called upon to decide political issues, because the majority was rather conservative compared with the opposition and therefore behaved in a reformist way only in the strict framework of the Constitution.

In the second phase, from 1966 to 1969, a rather different system developed in which the separation between the government and the Parliament was much stronger than earlier, because we had the Great Coalition. The majority in the House was more than 460 members, and the opposition, with only 50 members, was very weak; there was the same majority in the other chamber. Because this large majority could change the Constitution, the Supreme Court was no longer very important. If the Great Coalition wanted to act on political issues, it could change the Constitution. The majority parties were the masters of the system. In comparison with the first phase, there were different relations among the four systems—the judicial separation of powers, the political separation of powers, the federal system, and the constitutional system with the Supreme Court.

Since 1969 we have the third phase. The majority in the Bundestag now tries to force reform policy and sees itself as rather progressive, but for the first time both legislative chambers have different party majorities. Since 1969 the party forming the opposition in the Bundestag has the majority in the Bundesrat. On many issues it has therefore been necessary for the parties to work in an all-party coalition. This is very difficult for the governing majority in the Bundestag.

In this discussion of the role of the Parliament in the whole system, and the role of the parties and of committees within Parliament, it is sometimes implied that if the committees are very strong, then the parties have to be weak. It is also implied that if we want to have strong parties, as in Great Britain, the special committees cannot have too much power because it would be difficult to bring both together under one system.

We in Germany are trying to go a third route. We have a party parliament, with strong guidelines made by the parties, and at the same time we have a rather strong committee system. One can have a weak party system if the constitution allows a government a long period in office, as in the United States. The main function of the parties in parliamentary systems is to stabilize the government, but this is not the case in the United States. Under the U.S. Constitution the parties can behave almost as they wish.

In France the civil service and the administration have long ruled the system, but under a parliamentary system the parties have to solve the problem of having a stabilized government to ensure a long period in office. They have to function through discipline to enable an administration or a government to stay in office. If we are to have a stabilized system in Germany, our parties have to bring about a majority in Parliament, so that the government can manage a longer time in office. It is, I think, a major change in our history that we have for the first time developed a party system which is able to resolve this problem.

In the first session of the Bundestag, from 1949 through 1953, there were nine parties in Parliament, along with nine independent members. In the second Bundestag, there were six parties in Parliament and no independent members. Then, in the third Bundestag, four parties, and since 1961 until today, there have been three parties in the Bundestag. This phenomenon is more important than many sentences written in the Constitution. Furthermore, all these parties in Parliament can—for the first time in German history—form coalitions with one another. In the past two elections (1972 and 1976) about 90 percent of the voters turned out, and 99.1 percent of the voters voted for one of these three parties in Parliament.

This looks like a very stabilized system. All the parties are in principle for coalitions, so that there is always in the Bundestag an opposition, which can take over the government without the problem of a fundamental change in the political system.

As a parliamentary system we need disciplined parties to have a government in office. In order to have both strong committees and still strong party discipline, we have developed a very complicated system of committees. They have the power the British speak about, because there is no distinction between standing committees and select committees. Our standing committees have the function of the British select committees and sometimes the functions of an American investigating committee.

In addition, the parties have developed a substructure to coordinate the broad party system, the party on the floor of Parliament, and the party groups in the parliamentary committees. How this works in detail, and whether it can serve as a model for other governments, is a topic for later discussion.

UWE THAYSEN: I would like to add a brief comment on a specific policy area in the German political system. The energy issue, especially the case of nuclear plants, has, in contrast to what the textbooks say, strengthened the parties at the local and the Länder levels.[4] This is because the Länder have special rights to decide certain questions, for instance, where nuclear power plants should be built. Since this decision is up to the Länder, the Länder level has gained importance during the past few years.

The growing importance of the Länder and local levels of the parties can be clearly demonstrated by the example of a debate going on in Lower Saxony on a crucial element of energy policy. The government of Lower Saxony—again, it was the party of the opposition—decided not to concede to the federal government its authority to set policy on energy and power plants. The federal government is therefore not able to implement its concepts of energy security and energy provision. I think the local and the Länder levels of the parties are strengthened by these questions at stake at the moment, although this is quite contrary to many predictions that modern problems are going to strengthen the federal government.

MICHAEL HERETH: When I began to study political science, we were taught that the English Parliament was the model for all parliaments. Recently I read Neville Johnson's book on the English political system,

[4] The Länder are the German equivalent of American states.

and I was very interested that an Englishman recommended transforming all English politics into what we may call the German illnesses. [Laughter.] Today it is quite funny to read of an approach to the House of Commons which seems to imply learning from Germany. But I do not think that the English really learn from Germany; they are learning from their own problems.

In any case, the federal Parliament in Germany can indeed give some information about what would happen if England were to introduce procedures comparable to those we have in the Federal Republic. But there are some problems, which I think should be introduced into the debate of this reform.

First, there would be an important change in the nature of careers of parliamentarians. In the Federal Republic, a parliamentarian who hopes to become a senior minister one day would normally rise from deputy chairman, to chairman, and so on, and finally to minister. If at each of these stages he receives more money in return for his services, this will be regarded as a professional career. I do not oppose it, but the type of political career English parliamentarians now have would be changed to the type we have in Germany. Our parliamentarians are able to handle a bill and manage it through all the committees, but they are not able to speak in a way that voters understand, which is a typical German problem. I do not think that the committee system entirely is responsible for that; the whole political culture of Germany is not much inclined toward good rhetoric. But I think it has something to do with our committee system, and that system would probably produce a problem in England, too.

Second, I cannot agree with Mr. Smith that giving the committees power will result in a decline of party power. The *distribution* of power will change, but there will be neither more nor less power within the party. A parliament organized in committees will produce the distribution of power we have in Germany. The man who leads the administration will no longer be the only one who has the say *within* the parliamentary party. The chairmen of the committees and the chairman of the parliamentary group of the governing majority are also influential. They and their deputies are the ones who bargain with the minister and the junior ministers. The problem is not one of diminishing the power of parties, but rather of changing the distribution of power within the parties, which also produces a different pattern of political careers.

This leads to my third point: this kind of political career within parliament is tolerable because it is not the only one in a federal order. England, however, does not have the type of powerful and widely known politician who is not a member of the House and who has an essentially local base of power, having been or being mayor of an important city or prime minister of a state of the Federal Republic. When careers within parliament are made attractive by the existence of committees, a type of influential politician is created who is not very attractive to the public. In Germany, however, there is an alternative: the leader of the opposition in Parliament will not be a candidate for the chancellorship; the candidate will be a state prime minister of the Christian Democratic Union or of the Christian Social Union.

This is the result of the nonrhetorical and more committee-oriented parliamentary government we have in Germany. I think it works because there is a second line of political power outside Parliament. This does not, I think, exist in England in the same way because of the sovereignty of Parliament, which until today is really a sovereignty of government.

SYDNEY IRVING, former member, British Parliament: The causes and consequences of reform are many and varied. At the beginning of this last session of Parliament, we had quite a fierce debate—both inside and outside Parliament—about the need for change. I, like Kenneth Baker, want to see a strong Parliament ensuring a curb on the executive, but I have some reservations about the select committee recommendations.

I do not think it is self-evident that the new departmental committees are going to have the power that the members of the select committee on procedure wanted them to have—and they formed a very effective lobby in support of their own recommendations. Geoffrey Smith said quite clearly that they ought to have more power. But the select committee itself ruled out the one way of giving them greater power, as Kenneth Baker pointed out. In the United States the committees have some control over legislation, and the seniority system gives them the power to make the executive listen. In England, however, there will be no reason for the executive to listen to the departmental committees any more than to the existing select committees.

The members of the select committee made one or two fundamental mistakes, which I hope will be corrected in the course of the debate. They are going to set up twelve new committees with ten members each. I believe that spreads our resources far too thinly. Ten members will not allow proper representation of even the parties in the House. Instead of a strong body of members, with the best-known, most articulate, and most determined members concentrated on a limited number of committees and challenging the executive in specific ways, the resources of members, of staff, of accommodations, and of expertise will be spread right across the board. One or two of these committees may be effective, but it would be very easy for the department to control some of the less popular ones. The permanent secretary can, in fact, feed them with so much paper that they cannot keep up with it. And it then becomes a situation in which bureaucracy is talking to bureaucracy.

I would therefore hope that instead of having twelve select committees, they would establish four select committees, say, foreign affairs; treasury; trade and industry; and home affairs. If these committees were firmly established and given all the support they need, with the backing of the strongest members in the House, they would become effective and would be a better stepping stone to curb the executive than the present recommendations are likely to be.

GEORGE CUNNINGHAM, member, British Parliament: We should not get into too much detail on the recommendations of the procedure committee on the British Parliament. If we were to do so, I would want to argue that last point, because I am sure it is impossible to take a very untidy system of committees and half-tidy it up. It can be left a mess, as it is at the moment, or it can be tidied up, but if it is only half-tidied it will be a worse mess than at the moment.

A point of general significance to all countries represented here is whether it is good to have committees responsible for the three principal functions of the legislature: that is, considering legislation, considering money, and doing general studies of policy options for, say, transport. In the American system the committees do have all those functions. In the present Canadian system, if I remember correctly, the standing committees—which in our terms means select committees—are responsible for both legislation and money, but not for any general studies. My understanding is that the money job does not get properly done by the new Canadian committees, because there is not time to do both the money side of things and the legislation.

There might be a general lesson to be learned, you can get the advantages of a good committee system and a tidy committee system without the disadvantages I have just mentioned for Canada in having politicians who are too much engaged in a committee career. It would be advantageous to have committees which are not assigned so many responsibilities. In other words, the general functions, the legislative functions, and the expenditure functions would be separated; the committees would do the general work and the expenditure work, but would not handle the detailed consideration of bills. It would be interesting to hear the thoughts of people from other countries, where these functions are concentrated in one committee, as to the advantage of splitting them up.

PROFESSOR POLSBY: I am hoping, as this conference goes along, that some mention will be made of the word "competence" for legislative committees and the words "civil service" will pass someone's lips. Then perhaps we may enter into the heart of the discussion.

GERHARD KUNZ, member, German Bundestag: One has to consider the question of what parliament means today. This question has different answers for the American, the English, and the German parliaments. In the case of the German Parliament, I think it has a meaning for the whole institution. Parliament in the material sense usually means the opposition. Coalition is, roughly, something like the notary's office of the government—an institution that helps the government to enforce its views and the role of the delegates. As a delegate for seven years in the opposition, I found the role of an opposition delegate to be much more rewarding than the role of the delegates in the majority party, which of course is understandable. Parliament as we have it now in Germany is concentrated on the opposition. It therefore becomes more and more difficult to exercise control over proposed laws. One does not concentrate on unnecessary details; one has to control the premises, the main supports of the law. That becomes more difficult because it requires a great deal of knowledge and a great deal of groundwork. The respective government expert works at least two years on a proposal, and the parliamentary correspondent has at most six weeks before he knows the subject well enough to feel comfortable with it.

In Germany I see a growing influence of the so-called public interest movement. I believe this also exists in other countries, though perhaps in a somewhat different form. The politics of the energy issue, as conducted in Germany, do not lie in the hands of the Parliament or in the hands of the state government, but to a great extent in the hands of the public interest movement, no matter how it is qualified. This is not a judgment but a fact. More important, in my view, than the question of how a committee works are the broader questions regarding the challenges that face the Parliament.

BOB ECKHARDT, U.S. representative (Democrat, Texas): I would like to try to clarify some of the comparisons and differences that Mr. Smith has indicated between the proposed British select committee system and the existing U.S. system. As I understand it, the select committee would be roughly comparable to the American standing committees. They would provide a kind of bank of continuing expertise originating from the parliamentary body itself. And I gather that the bank of expertise, which emanates in the American system from the administration, would come in the British system from the government.

We have recently devised, in connection with the energy bill, an ad hoc committee, which is roughly equivalent to what the British call a standing committee, organized around a specific act. But there is a distinct difference between the American standing committee and the proposed British select committee. Our standing committee "marks up" a bill. That sounds rather pejorative. It puts ugly marks on the president's proposals, so to speak, to amend and ultimately fashion a piece of legislation. I understand that this is not envisaged in the present select committee proposal, but Mr. Smith hopes that it would be. I gather there is little possibility that Mr. Smith's proposal will be accepted, but in either event these twelve select committees obviously would not replace the standing committees, because they could not, in effect, mark up a bill.

MR. BAKER: In the British Parliament the so-called marking up is done in our standing committees, which are special ad hoc committees. The one important change would be that the committees *might* be allowed to take evidence from outside interests. Some people are opposed to this, but it is the only change we are recommending on the standing committees. At the first four sessions, that ad hoc mark-up committee would also be allowed to hear evidence from various interests.

REPRESENTATIVE ECKHARDT: As I see it, the British are moving modestly toward the American system of establishing a bank of expertise, and we are moving modestly toward your system and setting up a committee with more administrative or executive clout. Our ad hoc committee would usually be more closely related to a bill emanating from the administration.

TOM MCNALLY, member, British Parliament: I have had five weeks' experience as a parliamentarian, but I did have five years as a kind of civil servant, as a special adviser to Jim Callaghan. The first motion that I signed when I went into the House of Commons was to implement the select committee report. I did so because the five years as a civil servant convinced me of the massive imbalance between the resources available to ministers and civil servants and those available to the legislators who were trying to check that power. The resources that a minister has at his disposal are almost beyond belief.

It may rather shock the legislators that I have discovered ministers are not much interested in having legislation scrutinized by the House of Commons. They want to get it through as quickly and as quietly as possible. Therefore, when discussing giving powers to select committees, it is important to realize that a large body of members of Parliament have no interest whatsoever in increasing the power of the backbenchers. When I told my erstwhile boss that I had signed that motion, he simply said, "You will regret it one day." [Laughter.]

We have already heard from Kenneth Baker about the last Parliament. Despite the numerical weakness of the government in the House of Commons, it did get most of its legislation through. Again, it showed the power of the legislative branch, even when it was parliamentarily weak.

It did have side effects, mostly on the government backbenchers. The government backbencher who conducts independent inquiry is not popular with his own government and not popular with his own whips. The balance of interest is to the opposition, and the task of the clever opposition is to ensnare, in a committee report, enough government backbenchers to embarrass the government. For example, when our own select committee looked into the steel industry and exposed mismanagement and misjudgment on the part of ministers and administrators, that immediately became a political issue. The government backbenchers who had signed that report were quickly whipped into line to vote for the minister and vote down the report that they had already signed. Similarly, the committee on immigration produced a report that was marginally more favorable to the current Conservative policy on immigration than was the standing of the government at the time. Immediately, the Labour party rushed around to the people who had signed the report asking, "What are you up to, playing into the Tories' hands?"

It is unreal to imagine that there are no truths and consequences, particularly for government backbenchers. In the end, the government will want its legislation, and the power of party discipline will come to bear down heavily, even on those members who want to play a totally dispassionate role in the select committees on which they serve.

David Marquand, University of Salford: At last we are beginning to get some of the sordid truths of the British system out into the open. I would like, if I might, to bring out another sordid truth.

Why not ask all the members of Parliament who are present here to testify on oath which they would prefer to be—parliamentary secretary at a ministry or the chairman of a select committee? Because until backbench members of Parliament would rather be a chairman of a select committee than part of the executive, the reforms we are discussing are not going to make much real difference.

This procedure committee report has given me, I am afraid, a terrible feeling of déjà vu. I was a member of a select committee on procedure which sat in the 1960s. We went through the whole question of how to strengthen committees against the executive. After much thought, we decided to set up an expenditure committee, which would be divided along functional lines. This meant that each subcommittee of the expenditure committee would have a lever of power, since it would control blocks of government expenditure. In this way, Parliament's control over the executive would be enormously increased.

Now, a new procedure committee report is proposing to abolish the expenditure committee. It is perfectly true that the expenditure committee proposal did not, in fact, make a great deal of difference to what happened. The question is, why not? The expenditure subcommittees did some useful academic work and published some interesting reports, some of which were never debated; others were debated in very thinly attended Houses. Not much notice was taken of them. The reason was that the expenditure committee made no difference to the career prospects of individual members of Parliament—above all their career prospects in terms of their membership of their political parties.

Among the members of Parliament who have actually stopped the government from doing what it wants, nearly all have had a very strong independent base. One of the papers that we are discussing today mentions the famous episode of Brian Walden and John Mackintosh, who defeated or emasculated the Callaghan government's dock labor bill. Both men were able to destroy that legislation on the floor of the House, not through a committee system, but because each had a very strong constituency base. They knew that the ties of party loyalty would not constrain them, that their constituents would not care if they defeated their own government on the floor of the House.

Most members of Parliament are not in that position. They know perfectly well that their party supporters in their constituencies expect them to support the government, except on the rare issues when the members of the party are themselves rebelling against the government position.

There will be a fundamental change in the balance of power between the executive and the legislature in our system if and when the electoral system is changed—either through proportional representation or perhaps through a primary system—to ensure each member of Parliament the strength that an American congressman has. Then he will know that he has been elected independently of his party and can, if necessary, rely on a power base that is independent of his party. These committee changes are not going to make much difference until that has happened.

MR. SMITH: I find myself half agreeing enormously with David Marquand and half disagreeing, because it seemed to me that part of his analysis does not quite relate to the other.

Two forms of discipline are imposed upon members of Parliament in Britain, and they do not always have precisely the same effect upon individuals. One is the influence of the constituency party upon the member, and the other is the influence of the whip upon the member. Clearly, in a confidence vote, when the future of the government itself is at stake, both forms of influence will be brought to bear in exactly the same way. But a great many votes of consequence in the House of Commons are not votes of confidence, and the future of the government therefore does not depend on them.

I believe that the scope for a member of Parliament to rebel on those questions without, in fact, bringing down the wrath of his constituency, is much greater than is often supposed. George Cunningham has rebelled on a number of particular questions; so have Jeffrey Wilk and Audrey Wise. The whole of the last Parliament offered examples of individual backbenchers rebelling and occasioning the defeat of the government on issues of policy that were not matters of confidence, largely because of the particular circumstances of that Parliament. And because the life of the government was not itself at stake, they rebelled, in most instances, with impunity so far as their own constituencies were concerned.

The other form of pressure, the pressure of the whips, is always strong upon those members who are looking for advancement in their personal careers, because the first step on the ministerial ladder will be taken largely, if not entirely, on the advice of the whips. The member who is out of step with the whips will find himself at a disadvantage in his personal career.

I believe that this is generally the case, and even if it is not what will happen, it is what most members of Parliament believe will happen. Here, I come to David Marquand's point about the need for individual members to feel that there is an alternative career structure, which they could either regard as a satisfactory alternative or might even, ideally, prefer. That point becomes important only if one believes that constituency pressure can be largely discounted when the life of the government is not at stake.

To come back to Professor Steffani's point, there has to be a certain relaxation of party discipline in Britain if these committees are going to be effective. Discipline can be relaxed in different ways. The individual members of a committee of the governing side may collectively decide to reject the advice of their leaders, in which case they will cause affront to the whips. Or, as quite often happened in recent years, an individual member of the governing party may actually support people of the opposition party.

SHIRLEY WILLIAMS, former British secretary of state for education and science: I think that Geoffrey Smith has left out two things of importance. One is that governments have recently been inclined to make far fewer votes of confidence than in the past. The strength of the discipline of the 1940s and 1950s was that every major issue was treated as a matter of possible resignation of the government. Under the last two or three governments, many issues have ceased to be so treated, and I think that members of Parliament can exploit that more than they have.

The second point is that under the Wilson government it was a positive advantage to be a rebel, because the rebels were, in effect, bought off by the whips and put in the government at a low level. No one should assume that obedience to the whip is necessarily the high road to office. It may be just the reverse: an obedient party member may be treated as a complaisant backbencher, who can be left in that happy position for years to come.

I do not wholly agree with Tom McNally, who described in forthright and somewhat cynical terms the reasons the executive is against reform. As one who is in favor of reform, I would say that members of Parliament will have to swallow some of their party differences if they are actually to bring about reform. They are going to have to revolt together against the executive.

There is, however, strong argument on the part of the executive for parliamentary reform, and I speak as someone who was for ten years a member of the executive. Frankly, a Cabinet minister does not worry much about appearing before select committees or about appearing for parliamentary question time—though sometimes one loses out or reveals something one did not want to reveal. The real worries of a member of the executive are about facing the great corporate power of outside interests, the trade unions, business, individual professional groups, and so forth.

I became more and more conscious, as a member of the executive, that even a select committee would be merely another straw added to the burden. At least in the European system the real burden lies in the fact that major interest groups will not cooperate in a particular program or on a particular piece of legislation. For example, in the 1966 to 1970 government, when I was in the ministry of education for a time, the Plaudin report recommended a major expansion of nursery school education. It depended upon schools' being able to employ, besides a fully qualified teacher, a number of assistants. If it had been possible to do that, there could have been universal nursery education in Britain within seven or eight years. The unions made it clear, however, that they would not accept assistants of this kind; every single class had to be taught by a fully qualified teacher, even for children as young as three.

That was never made public. The government felt that one of its responsibilities was not to reveal this kind of pressure, and the organizations got away with it. One could say exactly the same thing about the professional organization of doctors in regard to some of the reforms in the health service. One could say the same about industry in regard to traineeships for young people entering employment. The pressure is not for one issue only; it exists across the board.

If reform would force some of these major vested interests to be accountable for what they say, force them to give evidence for the positions that they take, force them to state before Parliament their reasons for undertaking actions which are counterproductive to what society needs and wants, then I would be passionately in favor of parliamentary reform. What worries me is not that parliamentary reform is directed at the executive—it ought to be—but that it is directed *solely* at the executive. The immense and growing strength of the special interest groups has been disregarded, and we really need to bring these groups to book if we are to have an effective and accountable democracy.

I would like to ask our American and German colleagues whether such special interests are brought effectively to book under their systems, because I think we have left out a whole chapter in this discussion.

DAVID BUTLER, Nuffield College, Oxford: I am interested in what Tom McNally and Shirley Williams say about the law of anticipated reactions: the extent to which ministers say to their civil servants, "I would not like to defend that in the House," and the extent to which the House of Commons represents a sounding board, which actually restrains ministers. Few amendments are made to bills by backbenchers or by the opposition, but a large number of amendments are made by ministers—at a later stage in the proceedings—in response to objections that have been ventilated by the opposition, by wicked outside interests, and the like.

I am all for expanding the sounding board, but I do not think one ought to be terribly worried about giving legislators a larger role in the nitty-gritty of amending Clause I, Subsection 33.

CLIVE LANDA, political director, Tory Reform Group: Could I support from outside the parliamentary system much of what Shirley Williams was saying? In the ten years she has been part of the executive, I have been part of various outside interest groups, trying to persuade ministers and parties to take different views. I would claim, among our various successes, killing a bill introduced by a backbench member of Parliament, which was supported by his own government. That must be pretty fundamental in trying to upset the role of the backbencher. One or two other escapades in which I have been involved led backbench members of Parliament to comment that we perhaps saw more of the ministers than they did themselves.

From my cooperation with the German Christian Democrats I believe that the same pattern of behavior has led to similar successes of extraparliamentary activity in the Federal Republic. In Scandinavia and elsewhere it is possible that in the last ten years other parliamentary institutions have seen a growth in that sort of activity.

How does one harness Parliament to that situation? It seems to me that the select committee is doing the equivalent to what the British call closing the stable door after the horse has bolted. The distribution of power has altered. It is no use now trying to alter the existing framework and roles to try and recapture the past. That is why Geoffrey Smith is certainly not in a minority of one. There is at least one other who believes that the report is irrelevant to this discussion.

We need to find a way of capturing those outside interest groups without going to the American system. It is frightening that in the American system, especially since the recent law on campaign contributions, the outside interest group can now literally buy what it wants. If the interest group can get together sufficient funds for a campaign—and some campaigns need in excess of a million dollars—they have a substantial chance of buying the influence they want in the Congress and certain committees. This is not to suggest that the people involved in the political system are, in any sense, corrupt, but they have to play the game by the rules of the system. If we in Great Britain are going to take that route, we have to dissipate the influence on the executive.

I do not have prescriptive solutions or answers, which is why I am outside the parliamentary system, seeking to influence events. That seems to be the place to get results.

THOMAS FOLEY, U.S. representative (Democrat, Washington): To suggest that the current campaign financing system permits the election of the finest Congress that money can buy is a bit of a misstatement, to say the least. Money follows position; position does not follow money. If one comes from an area where the railroad unions are strong, and they are organized against the coal-slurry pipeline bill, for example, one is naturally going to be drawn to support the railroad union position. As a consequence, the railroad union political action committees will probably offer a contribution. But I would like to make it clear to our colleagues from other countries, who may not be familiar with our system, that members of Congress do not go out on the stump and say, "What am I offered to take a position on this or that bill?" The constituency would quickly discover such an offer and would run the member right out of office. We have to report contributions, after all.

Mrs. Shirley Williams knows our system very well and knows that special interest groups have enormous power. It is my view, however, that their power is due less to their financial contributions than to their ability to organize and mobilize support in constituencies.

Americans do not tend to think in terms of being Republicans or Democrats, or supporting a party platform. They do not ask, "Are you going to vote Democratic or Republican in this congressional election?" The question is, "Are you going to vote for Whalen or some incompetent opponent of his?" It is a highly personalized situation. Consequently, a member of Congress has the constant job of trying to keep the support of a broad coalition of interest groups in his constituency.

This makes it easy to oppose the government. There is no party discipline. If the Speaker of the House was to go beyond the accepted benign, arm-on-shoulder type of persuasion and exert stronger pressure, such as a threat of retaliation, to get a member to vote a certain way, there would be a scandal in the House. We have gone much too far in this direction.

In addition to their enormous influence in the Congress, which comes primarily from their capacity to organize constituencies behind a particular position, special interest groups are not without influence in the executive branch. The British members are shocked to learn that in the United States the executive branch has no capacity of its own to introduce legislation in the Congress except through individual members, and on some occasions it has been unable to persuade even one of the 535 House and Senate members to sponsor a particular bill. At present, one of the major administration policies, cost containment in hospitals, is not able to get out of the subcommittee of the Ways and Means Committee. Three members are being constantly pressured by the executive branch to change their position, but the hospital associations of the members' own districts are strongly against it. The House would probably vote for the bill if it could reach the floor, but this probably will not happen.

I do not know if the British want to make their committees that powerful. The power over legislation held by a subcommittee chairman of the U.S. House or the Senate, much less a full committee chairman, cannot be compared with that of a junior minister of the Crown or an assistant secretary. The junior minister of the Crown is comparatively insignificant, mostly anonymous, and has a much lower rank in terms of power or protocol.

It is sometimes surprising to congressmen who go abroad to find an assistant secretary of a department accorded great attention as if he actually had much to do with policy. In point of fact, only in rare circumstances do assistant secretaries have much influence over legislation, and then it is only those of outstanding merit, who have assiduously courted their congressional relations.

MICHAEL RYLE, clerk, British House of Commons: There has been far too much talk about power in the House of Commons. The British Parliament has not exercised power directly for many, many years. It provides a forum where the public exercise of power by the government must be portrayed and displayed, and where interest groups are also required to display their influence publicly. In other words, it is *through* Parliament that the power is exercised, not *by* Parliament.

I would like to illustrate an oversimplistic way of looking at how select committees might fit into this structure. If we think of select committees not as power leaders, but as forums for public criticism and as providing an opportunity both for pressure groups to put their points of view publicly on record, and for parliaments to look critically at the pressure groups, then a possible role for the twelve new specialist committees becomes apparent. The committees would not be totally valueless, although they would not make a great change in the balance of power.

It is very difficult to speculate. The only thing that can safely be said is that they will not operate as might be expected. They will be less successful than the protagonists suggest and not as dangerous as the opponents believe. That has been the feature of all our procedural changes over the years.

To speculate a bit, however, it seems most significant that, for the first time, the committees are going to be genuinely specialized. Instead of a trade and industry subcommittee of the expenditure committee, which moves from an inquiry into the motor industry to an inquiry into the fishing industry, there will be select committees which will attract members who want a worthy place where they can devote their time and efforts to a particular field of interest.

I agree that if the committees had legislative powers, they would be automatically powerful. But even without legislative powers, it might be that the outside pressure groups would begin to feel that these bodies were worth lobbying. It is then a circular argument: if the bodies are worth lobbying, the members will find it worth being on them because they touch the levers of power and their actions receive the appropriate publicity and respect.

We do not know what use the committees will make of staff—I hope they do not cease to be political. Nor do we know the extent to which their reports will have real influence. But I do not think we should be dismayed at opening up new avenues for Parliament to exercise a critical function in an effective way. In other words, we want to see not more power, but more effective criticism.

HEINRICH OBERREUTER, Free University, Berlin: Mr. Steffani and Mr. Thaysen have spoken about the role of federalism in the current political situation of the Federal Republic, and since I live in Munich and teach in Berlin, I have to defend federalism. The role of the upper house has been somewhat exaggerated here, and the basic conditions have changed little in the Federal Republic in the historical context. The all-party coalition in the legislature has existed in the Federal Republic since 1949, and the unanimous approval of legislation in the German lower house has always hovered around 87 to 96 percent of all bills. Federalism has changed nothing in that. The forced compromise in legislation belongs to the parliamentary political culture.

More generally, I suspect that we are asking for a standard, a historical point from which to judge that a parliament today has gotten into a powerless position. This approach to the problem might be right for Great Britain, but if I remember the book by Butt, *The Power of Parliament,* this seems questionable. For Germany, this historical point of the decline of a powerful parliament to one with functional difficulties does not apply, because we never had a powerful parliament.

Many discussions do not consider the change in governmental tasks over the last hundred years. At least during the nineteenth century, there were few governmental tasks in the areas of foreign policy legislation, taxation, and domestic policies. At the moment, however, the dominant social welfare politics have led to an increase in the number of tasks and consequently also in the powers of the executive branch. One consequence of this power game is that parliament today more than ever is forced to specialize. The opposite side of this development, of course, is that the lack of representativeness of committees causes discontent and misunderstanding and has been criticized in German views on parliamentary decisions.

A second consequence—which seems to be common to all the political systems discussed here—is that the role of the delegate undergoes a change from that of lawmaker to that of ombudsman, or to what Kenneth Baker described as the underpaid social welfare worker. I do not see this entirely as a problem, but as a positive part of the delegates' work. The legitimacy of a political system depends greatly on the fact that delegates are able to facilitate communication between the parliament and the public. The social welfare work serves this legitimizing function.

Finally, I would not see the role of the interest groups as negative, as one or two previous speakers have done. I think that the role of parliament to develop sovereign legislative processes is not in harmony with the challenge to develop a democratic political system. Even if parliament is supposed to have a strong role, a democratic political system depends on the fact that organized and nonorganized interests can participate in the legislative decision process.

IAN WRIGGLESWORTH, member, British Parliament: One important question, which is asked by more and more young and new members in the House of Commons, is that of the resources available to members. There is enormous pressure within the British Parliament—and I hope it increases—to provide the means to do the job. Tom McNally will probably confirm that one of the great weaknesses of the British members is that the resources to do the job are very slim. He has been five weeks in the place, but I do not know whether he has a desk yet, or a secretary, or anything else. It is virtually impossible to run the constituency, to do the party job and the parliamentary job, and to be an effective member of the select committee, with enormous amounts of paper to handle, with no staff and inadequate office facilities. Most people know this situation in Westminster, but there is considerable pressure now for reform.

I should like to comment also on Shirley Williams's remarks about the corporatist pressure from outside. If it is true that pressure groups are stopping the government from doing what it wants, it is rather surprising that the executive does not enroll Parliament to come to its aid by exposing these pressures rather more than it has done in the past. The sort of powers being proposed by the procedure committee—enabling standing committees to take evidence from pressure groups and, indeed, making that a binding part of the process—would surely help to expose those pressures. I am not sure that the government actually does want to get these pressures from behind closed doors, out into the open; but if the government does, then the way to do so is to use the select committee and the standing committee procedures to expose the pressures. The last government said that it wanted to do that, but I do not see any evidence that it did. And I fear that members of the new executive are getting cold feet about some of the proposals they supported when they were in opposition.

PROFESSOR POLSBY: Thank you all very much. This is the end of our second session.

Session III
The Role of the Junior Legislator

PETER G. RICHARDS, moderator: The subject under discussion is the role of the backbencher, or the junior legislator. In the earlier discussion Kenneth Baker warned that normal service was now being resumed, because the government once again has a clear majority in the Commons. This means that the backbenchers such as George Cunningham will no longer be introducing major and successful challenges to government policy. Shirley Williams stressed that it has been established that not all votes in the House are to be regarded as votes of confidence, and this could mean a more relaxed attitude to parliamentary party discipline. We shall have to see what the future holds.

The panel consists of four members of four different legislatures: Representative Butler Derrick from South Carolina in the U.S. Congress; George Cunningham, a Labour member of Parliament for a London constituency; Klaus Daweke, a member of the German Bundestag; and Mark MacGuigan, a liberal member of the Canadian Parliament from Ontario. They will talk about their own experiences in their separate legislatures. They will probably be talking about the attitudes of some of the younger and more vigorous members of the legislatures, because, of course, they themselves are among the younger and more vigorous members. That is why they are here. Perhaps the one thing that worries me a bit is that this panel may not be entirely representative of the totality of legislators. I am sure that there are older and less active legislators, who might have rather different views.

I propose to call on the panel members in the order in which they appear in the program.

BUTLER DERRICK: I was elected in 1974 and began my service in 1975. Sam Rayburn, a prominent speaker of the House a decade or so ago, said, "To get along, you go along." Probably this has been disproved since 1974. I am allowed to vote on every vote in the Congress. I am paid $57,500 a year. I get more than $300,000 a year for staff, and other emoluments such as a haircut for $6 in the House barbershop.

Before I was elected to Congress, the kings of the House were the committee chairmen. They were elected by the Democratic caucus, but by one vote. Their names, along with the names of the committee members, were selected by the committee on committees, the Ways and Means Committtee. It was merely a formality that the Democratic caucus approved the committee chairmen, as well as the members of the committee. The committee chairmen were all-powerful, and their rule was not questioned until 1975, during the 94th Congress, of which I was a member.

When we came out of the throes of Watergate, the Democratic caucus was revived. As a result, three major committee chairmen were deposed. This would have been unthinkable even two or three years before then. The freshmen members of the 94th Congress had the audacity to ask the chairmen their views on the seniority system—a system I found repugnant at the time, but like more as time goes on. The chairmen were also asked how they felt about the Vietnam war and other issues, and as a result of those interviews, most of the seventy-six freshmen Democrats threw their weight against the election of three major chairmen and brought about their defeat. This almost immediately democratized the House of Representatives, and committee chairmen began seeking out their members and courting their pleasure in anticipation of the next election.

In addition, my class in 1975 asked the leadership to put a freshman member on the exclusive committees, the Ways and Means, Appropriations, and the Rules Committee, along with the Budget Committee, which is not an exclusive committee. It was the first time in the history of the Congress that a freshman member was put on an exclusive committee, at least in this manner. The committee chairmen, mindful of the next election, started recognizing freshmen members in committee. And because of that, the freshmen members began to participate more than in the past. For example, I was on the Budget Committee and was a subcommittee chairman at the beginning of my second term; I now serve on the Rules Committee, which would have been unheard of a decade or less ago.

In the last session, particularly, the leadership started to use specific task forces on legislation, instead of going through the regular whip system. As a second-term member, I was head of the budget task force, which was in charge of getting the budget resolution through the House. Several of my contemporaries, as well as one freshman member, held similar positions. The Democratic caucus recently went on record as being opposed to President Carter's plan to decontrol petroleum. This effort was led by a member from Connecticut, who was elected the same time I was. It is not unusual now for many members of my class to have subcommittee chairmanships at this stage, and to ascend to positions of leadership in all issue areas.

These changes were, I think, generally positive, but there have been some negative side effects. One is that there is not the party discipline in the House that there was a decade ago, and it is therefore more difficult for the majority party to get its legislation through. It takes quite a bit more courting.

In the parliamentary system members vote along a party line, but this is certainly not the case in the U.S. Congress. I would say that a member represents primarily his district and its needs. For instance, two-thirds of those employed in my district are employed in textiles. It would be absolute suicide for me to vote against legislation that would be helpful to the textile industry. If there were fairly equal pulls on both ends, I think most members would vote along party lines, and in some instances, when called upon by the leadership in a positive manner, members would perhaps vote against their usual position. But I think the first allegiance in the House is to the constituency and to one's own personal preference.

GEORGE CUNNINGHAM: The British and the Americans have little in common regarding the role of the backbencher. If there is a problem of the backbencher in British politics, it does not exist in the United States. It does in Canada, and I think it does in Germany. It exists only in a legislature in which the executive is present and in which there is therefore a contest between the backbencher—that is, the non-ministerial member—and the executive in the parliament. Although the British can share many experiences with America, the role of the backbencher is not one of them.

In the British House of Commons, it might well be said, there is no party discipline. When I receive the whip—that is, a piece of paper which indicates how someone wishes me to vote—it does not come from my party caucus. It has not been decided by all the Labour members in the House of Commons. When we were in government it was decided by the government, not the party. Now that we are in opposition, it is decided by the leadership of the party, not the party as a whole.

By contrast with, say, Germany, the party—it would be called the faction or caucus in the United States and Canada—does not meet to discuss how to vote on a bill the government is proposing. And the caucus does not then proceed to make a decision on that and recommend that all its members vote accordingly. Instead, the leadership of the party—or the government, if we are in power—takes a position on how it wants me to behave. Because I have not been involved in reaching that decision, I feel free to decide whether to comply with the advice tendered by the leadership.

For the past year, I have been in the British delegation to the European Parliament, which has the group system in the continental pattern. Because it is the groups—the parties or caucuses—which reach a decision as to what a member should do, each member of the caucus feels more morally obliged to toe the line than if he had not had an opportunity to help decide. That is not the case in the British Parliament. When a member votes against his own side there, he votes against a decision recommended by his leadership and not by the group to which he belongs.

Although there has been some discussion about procedure and the structure of legislatures, I do not think that the problem in the British House of Commons has much to do with procedure, or the structure, or the committee system. I want to see changes in all those things, and I think they will affect the attitudes and behavior of members. But it is not procedure and structure that is wrong; it is attitudes. The two are to a great extent, independent of each other.

Anthony King's paper points out the curious fact that in Britain the members still possess all the powers that they ever had. They have lost not a single power. Not one word goes onto the statute book but they say yea to it. Not one penny is spent but they say yea to it. And yet, having all this power, they do not exercise it. They abdicate it upward to their leaders, whether to the government in power or to the leaders of the party in opposition.

The first question is whether this is a good thing, and, second, if it should be changed, why did it happen? Why have elected people been given power, and yet they choose not to exercise it?

There are many reasons that might be advanced, such as the power of the party machine, which might, if annoyed with me, disenfranchise me, as it were, as a member of the Labour party. The caucus in the House of Commons also might disenfranchise me as a member of that caucus, although it could not stop me from being an MP for the time being. Another reason might be simply a feeling of party loyalty, which is very important.

More significant than any of those institutional reasons, however, is habit. It is merely habit to vote the way of the herd. Once such a habit is established, it is rather difficult to change. It upsets other people, and given the number of hours we spend with our colleagues in the House of Commons, we do not want to upset them too much. I do not think you need to look for institutional reasons as much as simply habit.

Another thing that we are up against is the attitude represented by Mr. Ryle, who says it is influence that the House of Commons should exercise, and not power.

MICHAEL RYLE, clerk, British House of Commons: I did not say "should." I said "does."

MR. CUNNINGHAM: Well, I think you implied it should, as well as it does.

It was said earlier that there is no influence without power. It is possible to lead a person to the police station if he knows that he will be handcuffed if necessary. If we do not sometimes exercise our power and show that we have the will to exercise it, then we will not exercise any influence at all. Only if have a big stick can we get away with using little sticks. There is no reason at all to stop British members of Parliament from exercising the power that they possess. There is no reason they should not do so except a lack of will.

My final point: the Cunningham thesis about British democracy is that what is wrong is the public. Once, when abortion was an active subject, there was a question whether to set up a committee, and the government decided that there would be what we call a "free" vote; that is, no recommendation would be tendered by the government. One of my constituents wrote to me and said, "It is disgraceful that Barbara Castle is allowing you a free vote on this matter." I would hope that people in the United States would not write to their congressmen with such sentiments. What can be done with a public that does not insist that its representatives exercise their judgment according to what they think the public truly wants?

There will be some good done if members simply exercise this power, but unless the public forces the member to exercise power, it will not necessarily be done. We cannot rely on those who have voted independently over the past few years to do so voluntarily; the public must demand that members do so. The question for the future is how to get the public to change its attitudes and insist upon that slight increase in independence of judgment. Without it we might as well have a referendum every five years to decide the government, and then not bother with the House of Commons except at election time.

KLAUS DAWEKE: After hearing critiques of the various parliaments, I do not think we have such a bad deal with the Bundestag, in view of the rights and the power of other delegates. This could be because we received hints from our French and English and American friends at the end of the Second World War on how to build up a parliamentary democracy, and perhaps we did not do some things that were at the time already considered negative. For instance, the Bundestag has a very well-developed scientific service at the disposal of any delegate, and there are almost 400 staffers. We have supplied the parties with very good resources compared with the English. For instance, my party has about 250 staff. Regarding the individual member, we found a compromise between the English and the American way; each member has a certain sum that allows him to hire two or three staff members.

Nevertheless, the frustrations of a young delegate who first enters our Parliament are no smaller than those our English colleagues have spoken of. There is frustration not only if one sits on the hard bench of opposition, but also if one rules in the majority—in fact, the frustrations may be even larger there. It starts with the entrance into Parliament. In any reputable firm, a newcomer gets introduced; that is, someone shows him around and explains how the firm works. The colleagues in the Bundestag do not do that. They are, after all, not colleagues, but prima donnas who were elected from their own constituencies; they never learned how to dance in a ballet, however, and therefore are very jealous of their rights and powers. They act in anything but a collegial manner. That begins with the fact that in his constituency the delegate has been number one, but when he reaches the Bundestag he becomes part of the mass of 253. In the whole Parliament there are 518 people who all want to do the same work. Furthermore, the parliamentary democracy, in its inner structure, is actually an oligarchy, with the power in the hands of either the government or the leadership of the opposition.

The question that has been posed remains: What is the role of the young delegate and of the backbencher? According to one of my colleagues, delegates are an anonymous, nameless, bunch of cattle used to secure majorities or to document the power of the opposition. How does a delegate react to this experience? There are some delegates who focus inwardly and retreat. An interesting phenomenon is that often those who were elected as contact-loving extroverts are the ones who are pushed back into the position of introverted schoolboys. Another possibility is that the delegate recognizes that he has been pushed into a hierarchy and accepts the fact that right now he is at the bottom of the pyramid. Then he specializes; that is, he looks for a marketable niche that offers a politically unoccupied field, where he can show some success, even if only moderate success.

A third way in which many delegates react is to realize that it is not possible for the average delegate to be successful in the legislature—and who wants to be without success?—and therefore they look for successful experiences in their constituencies. That is what Professor

Oberreuter previously described as a byproduct. The "underpaid social worker" is, in my view, a role gratefully taken because it allows even a backbencher to show considerable success. If he works intensively within the constituency it also has the advantage of helping to ensure his reelection. He becomes indispensable at home and his margin widens, so that he can free himself from work in election circles and become available for the hoped-for ascent within the hierarchy. As I see it, these are the normal reactions.

I believe that if the government or the party was to withhold all information from a young delegate, he would naturally rebel. Because neither the government nor the party leadership has any interest in handing on their knowledge of power, they do exactly the opposite. They produce so much paper that the young delegate cannot attempt to read it all or to follow up on it. He cannot complain about the lack of information—but, in fact, he does not have any. As a result, he often does not have the political overview of the really important issues.

MARK MACGUIGAN: The underlying question in all of these discussions is how to achieve a reasonable balance between the executive interest and the legislative interest. I would submit that such a balance is always found very much in the context of a particular system.

If I have any quarrel with Professor King's otherwise admirable paper, it is that perhaps he tries to generalize too much on this conflict and does not locate the problem sufficiently within the boundaries of particular systems. I think it differs in each system. The U.S. system, for example, suffers very much from an overgrowth of the legislative interest. Parliamentary systems, of course, have a preponderance of the executive interest, which we are all, in various ways, striving to overcome.

The preponderance of the executive interest in Canada is made slightly more tolerable than seems to be the case in England, according to Mr. Cunningham's comments, by the institution of the caucus, whether on the government side or the opposition side. The leaders of the party, whether they are the Cabinet or the opposition front bench, have weekly meetings with all the elected members of the caucus. Although the caucus is not a good instrument for the fine-tuning of legislation, there is no instance in my eleven years' experience in the House in which the government dared to ignore the negative feelings of members of the government caucus about any piece of legislation or policy. Any time a large number of members have strong negative feelings, that is the end of the particular government initiative, whatever it may be and however embarrassing it may be for the government to withdraw from it. We therefore do not usually find ourselves with a great gulf between the executive and the members of the same party who are not the executive. I think that avoids a bit of conflict that might otherwise occur.

In Canada during the past decade there has been a steady movement toward strengthening the legislative interest and helping the backbencher. I want to outline this movement briefly, and more suggestively than completely, and draw a few general conclusions for the future, which I hope may prove instructive. I want to talk about five areas in which there has been significant progress, some of the trade-offs that had to be made to achieve that progress, the incompleteness which still remains in those areas, and then about prospects for the future.

In the first area—salary and facilities—there has been a great deal of progress since I was elected in 1968. Our staff has grown from one to four, which is not a large number, but represents a significant increase in work capacity. We now have the ability to telephone anywhere in Canada from anywhere in the country, and we can use ten of our weekly air tickets to our constituency for travel anywhere within Canada. This makes us, as backbenchers, available, for instance, to speak to the party in various parts of the country at no expense. When your side is in government, this gives a political presence to backbenchers which they would not otherwise have.

As for salary, we get an annual automatic increase based on the composite industrial index, up to a maximum of 7 percent. In this case backbenchers did not have to endure any offsets. These were unmitigated gains—except to the public treasury, of course. The gains are incomplete, however, with respect to the amount of assistance that we are allowed.

The second area of progress is the introduction of radio and television broadcasting. The Americans, I know, have subsequently moved in this direction, too, but I am not sure if it is now fully instituted. The proceedings of the Canadian House are fully broadcast and recorded by radio and television. That does not mean that everything is carried immediately by all stations. There are, however, about fifty cable stations across Canada, which carry every moment, precious or otherwise, of parliamentary proceedings. I should think that anybody who was subjected to a steady diet of it would find it very boring. In Australia, by the way, a radio network does the same thing and has for many years. Of course, the highlights are captured by the National News, and in Ontario the educational network broadcasts the full hour of the day's question period late every night, and that has quite a large audience.

All these programs have had a larger audience than anyone would have anticipated, and they have given a great deal more presence to the backbencher in popular consciousness across the country. Especially those in the opposition—which is my lot since the recent change of government—are able to acquire a much higher profile than would otherwise be the case. Even government backbenchers get more currency this way than they otherwise would. Of course, the ministry is also shown, either to advantage or disadvantage, each day in the question period.

The chief incompleteness here is with respect to committees, which do not yet have any broadcast coverage, even by radio. Of course, it might be expensive for the public purse to introduce television coverage of committees, because we do not leave broadcasting to the private networks—we provide it as a service of the House. It is entirely in the control of the House itself, handled by officials of the House, and there are strict rules that must be followed. The tapes are then made available to the media. In the case of committees, this could easily be done for radio without substantial expense. Television, however, would of course require expensive equipment in all the committee rooms and would be understandably slower to achieve.

The third area is election financing. First, candidates for recognized political parties receive election subsidies from the public purse. In fact, both the national parties and the individual candidates receive subsidies. In my case in this past election the subsidy amounted to $12,000, and I was allowed to spend about $26,000. The governmental subsidy is therefore a considerable proportion of the allowable expenses.

There is also a tax credit for political contributions—not merely a deduction, but an actual credit to the amount of tax, which is 75 percent for the first hundred dollars, then 50 percent, and finally 33⅓ percent, to a maximum credit of $500. Complete disclosure of all contributions over $100 is required, which is, I suppose, one of the offsets here.

In theory, the election financing system could operate very much to the advantage of the party rather than the backbencher, because the tax credit in nonelection periods is given only for contributions to the national party. During the election period it is given for contributions to candidates, but only to candidates who are certified by a recognized national party. In the case of an independent candidate, for instance, no tax credit is allowed, and he receives no subsidy of any kind.

As a result, a number of new parties have sprung up. There is one called the Garden party. Another is the Rhinoceros party. Although it is a joke party operating mostly in the province of Quebec, it obtained more votes in several Quebec constituencies than the Conservative candidate of the present government.

Rather than favoring the parties, however, election financing has had just the opposite effect. It has put funds into the hands of the individual candidates, because they have not only found it easy to raise money, but have also been allowed to keep most of it. Although in nonelection periods the tax credit is given for contributions to the party, in my party the local constituency gets back 75 percent of the money contributed, the party retaining only 25 percent. In election periods, money which is contributed locally goes entirely to the candidate, and the official receipt is issued by his official agent.

An enormous pool of potential funds is thus available to individual candidates. As a result, although previously the parties had raised money nationally, which they gave the candidates during elections, in this election the candidates were asked to assign one-third of the government subsidy to the party to make the national campaign possible. This change has therefore been a strong plus for the backbencher.

The fourth area is the committee system. We introduced a new system of standing committees in 1969, with no distinction between standing and select committees. The same standing committees do the job of legislation, scrutinize the spending estimates, and when there is a general order of reference, as is now frequently the case, also conduct special studies. The incompleteness of this reform is that standing committees still have no control over their own agendas, and I believe that giving them this control is an important step still to be taken. The committees are not given staff as a right, but only by special order of the House, and this situation is very unsatisfactory when the members are already short of staff in their individual capacities.

The existing committees are too numerous and too large, and we need more precise control over expenditures. I have to disagree, however, with what George Cunningham said earlier about Canadian committees. His committee was right in saying that we are not carrying out all of the committee roles properly, but the remedy is not to have two kinds of committees, select and standing. It is rather to give us additional powers to do the job properly.

I am of a mind with Geoffrey Smith that the proposed changes in Britain do not go nearly far enough. The combination of expertise and power must be offered by a single committee structure, which will permit more adequate control of the executive. Unlike Mr. Ryle, I would not be satisfied merely to achieve influence—I want committees to have power as well. On that point, I think Mr. Cunningham and I agree, but we disagree on the implementation.

It is hard to say whether the changes which we have had, and may still have, will work without fundamental changes in the electoral system. But we have been greatly aided in Canada by an extraneous development—minority government. We have had minority government for nine of the last twenty-two years, and we have once again elected a minority government. This, of course, means that backbenchers, not only in the opposition party, but also in the government party, have a much greater opportunity to influence what goes on in the House, both in caucus—in fact, especially in caucus—and on the floor of the House. The frequency of minority government will help achieve more legislative power, even in the absence of more fundamental changes—although perhaps not if we soon return to an extended period of majority government.

Although we have come a long way in Canada since 1968, we still have some way to go to acquire adequate facilities, especially staff assistance, to enable us to take hold of the committee system and do the kind of legislative job that should be done. We lack control of committee agendas, and lack even willingness on the part of members to do what needs to be done.

As George Cunningham suggested, this is partly a question of habit, or perhaps of cowardice, but it is also largely a result of the fact that members do not have enough time because of the amount of social work they have to do. Our present staff is not adequate to do both that job and a legislative job, and we need at least twice the staff we now have to do a legislative job properly.

I differ with George Cunningham on the role of the public. There is a large question of the extent of public support for parliamentary reform, but I tend to think that the public will follow our leadership. We cannot expect the initiative to come from the public; it has to come from Parliament. I believe the public really wants to see us in a more active role, but it is easily led or easily misled, as the case may be. If the initiative for change comes from us, I am convinced that the public will respond and support the more democratic system we are all aiming for.

GERHARD KUNZ, member, German Bundestag: I cannot completely agree with my colleague Klaus Daweke, but I can, of course, understand his view. As parliamentary leader, I have given this question some thought. There is so much work in Parliament that the individual has a difficult time grasping it. The party management often tries very hard to find someone who will take on tasks because the scope of parliamentary work has grown immensely.

I see the problem of the backbencher in a different light. Every legislator needs publicity. Without it, he loses the opportunity to communicate his views to the rank-and-file voter. The legislator has to stand by while a privileged few are always put in the foreground by the media, but hardly any notice is taken of him. Recognizing the need for publicity, some of our young delegates came up with an idea that I want to share but not necessarily recommend here. They got together and voiced their own opinions on current issues. Their opinions were not very far from those of their parties, but, lo and behold, all the media were interested in them because the message was "man bites dog" and not "dog bites man." When something like that happens, I become worried about parliamentarism. We experience this fragmentation more and more, and it is dictated not by political necessity but by the miserable lack of opportunities for individuals to participate in the publicity of politics. It would be interesting to hear what American, English, and Canadian politicians have to say to the question of the delegate's publicity and to explore how one could improve the situation with the available means.

CLIFFORD HACKETT, U.S. Senate staff: My comment is in the nature of a historical footnote. I know Mr. Derrick did not want to leave the impression that the revolt against committee chairmen started only in 1974, or had its roots only in Watergate. In my recollection, it went back much further. I started working for a House member in 1967, and the original reforms in the House certainly had their roots in the Vietnam era and in a revolt against the leadership of Speaker McCormack in 1968. The revolt failed with the challenger getting less than a hundred votes, but nonetheless it caused the creation of the Hansen committee, which produced the first reforms in 1971. Among other things, these reforms gave every subcommittee chairman the right to name one staff person to his subcommittee.

I am now working for a member of the Senate. In the past twelve years that I have been on Capitol Hill, staffs on both the House and Senate side have doubled. When I went to work for a New York congressman in 1967, he was allowed nine staff members. Today, he has eighteen. A comparable increase has taken place in the Senate.

To Europeans, that seems an enormous number of staff. But, of the thirty staff members who work for Senator Sarbanes, only four or five of us work on legislation, and I am the only one who works full time on foreign affairs. I have to take care of the whole world with one assistant, which does not seem to be an excessive number of staff resources compared with what we face in the executive branch. Perhaps Mr. Derrick could tell what he does with his eighteen staff members.

NELSON POLSBY, University of California, Berkeley: Reform did not begin when Cliff Hackett arrived in Washington in 1967. It was really when I came in 1958. [Laughter.] The historical basis for the current wave of reform in Congress, in my opinion, was after the 1958 election. The formation of the Democratic Study Group was the nucleus for the mobilization of the House Democratic caucus, which, in turn, was the agent in the Democratic party of virtually all the reforms that have cascaded forth in the past fifteen years.

REPRESENTATIVE DERRICK: Mr. Hackett asked me what I do with all my staff. I have seventeen staff members. Eight of them stay in my three district offices in South Carolina, and the remaining nine are in Washington. I have an administrative assistant, a lawyer, whom I pay $44,000 a year, and an office manager with twenty years of experience, whom I pay $30,000 a year. I pay three legislative assistants $25,000, $24,000, and $21,000 a year. The rest of my staff probably make an average of about $15,000 a year, and they handle casework, that is, they deal with federal agencies on behalf of the constituents.

About 250 letters or calls a day come into my office, and they all have to be answered. I get free telephone service throughout the United States, as well as stationery and various other things. I get as many trips home as I need, and I go back to my constituency about three times a month. I learned from my German counterpart here, however, that his after-tax income is $45,000, whereas my after-tax income is a little over $30,000. I therefore do not think we are overpaid.

I serve almost 500,000 constituents and run for election every two years. When I was first elected in 1974 it cost $170,000; to run the same kind of campaign now would probably cost about $300,000.

KENNETH BAKER, member, British Parliament: One aspect of the role of the backbencher, which has not been touched upon, is his capacity to be independent. This depends crucially upon the method by which he is selected.

It seems to me that the method of selection is one of the striking features in the British political system—I refer to the Conservative party, because the Labour party is a law unto itself in these matters. The Conservatives seem to be going through a phase in which a small group of activists in the constituency are trying to control the selection and nomination of candidates more tightly. One of the strengths of the Conservative members of Parliament is that if we fall afoul of our party in the House, we can turn to our party in the constituency and ask for support. Obviously, the first call is to the activists in the constituency, which with all the ward committees probably number about a hundred or so. We come up for selection before them.

If we lose that selection, we can then appeal to a much wider meeting of all the Conservative members of our association, perhaps 1,000 or 2,000 people. This has happened when certain Conservative members have fallen afoul of the leadership. In the whole period since World War II, only one Conservative backbencher has actually been unseated as a result of this process. It was over the issue of hanging and capital punishment in Bournemouth. The member there took it to a mass meeting and lost. It was a celebrated case.

One or two of my colleagues have had to face mass meetings, and it is a strength for the backbencher that he does this. It gives him a degree of independence which is inhibited in a less decentralized system of representation because the party machine has to approve. It brings us strength somewhat akin to the strength that I suspect an American congressman or an American senator receives through the primary. Not that we have anything like a primary system, but if we do fall afoul of our party, we have a process whereby we can go back to our grass roots and defend our position. And that, I believe, does allow us to be rather more independent in attitude than perhaps in a selection system that is closely tied to the party machine.

LESLIE STONE, BBC: I would like to break up this rather sinister cartel of politicians and former politicians and would-be politicians and servants of politicians and political scientists, and look at the situation from the view of the voter—George Cunningham's much maligned public, which he wants to stir up. I speak with all the authority of someone who abstained in the last election and usually will go to great lengths to disagree with anything that David Marquand says. He touched on an important point when he talked about the nature of the political power base. The trouble is that in the British system the nature of that power base for an individual is very fuzzy.

The British election is a one-shot operation. The voter is induced to have an acute fit of schizophrenia and compressed tension, because he has to choose, in one election, a prime minister and a member of Parliament. In order to get the government he wants, he may have to vote for a candidate he very much dislikes—not the candidate's personality, but his policies. The voter would be very reluctant, I think, to give additional power, through an extended committee system, to a member of Parliament for whom he is forced to vote under the British political system if he wants to elect that government. For example, it may be necessary to vote for George Cunningham or Douglas Jay or Tony Benn or Denis Skinner and give them power to frustrate the ends of the government that the voter wants. It is also very difficult under the British system to reward and punish in the way George Cunningham would like. As much as one would commend his activities and political philosophy, it is impossible, in the same election, to commend him and punish Jim Callaghan and the Labour government.

In contrast to this organizational difficulty under the British system is the rather more leisurely form of schizophrenia that sometimes exists in the United States. Here there can be a multiplicity of choices and sometimes a swing of 60,000 to 100,000 votes in the same congressional district, between the candidates for president, governor, senator, and representative. The British system seems to me to encourage a rather moribund political atmosphere in large parts of the country, where there is, in effect, only one party. It makes the Old South of the post–Civil War period seem exotic by comparison, and it makes the political scene under Mayor Daley of Chicago seem almost like a multiparty Mediterranean system in the options that are open. The danger is that in inner cities the labor organizations are ripe for takeover bids by rather unrepresentative groups, because political participation is not very great. The one-party nature of the system does not encourage people to join in active politics because the result seems to be automatic.

On the question of staff and committees, it does sometimes seem, from the sob stories one hears, that British MPs are undernourished and underfinanced. The Americans indeed seem to be overfinanced, and it is really quite alarming that even the staff have staff on Capitol Hill now. People who are not elected by anybody dominate people who are elected by at least a small proportion of the electorate.

Is the committee system supposed to encourage a smoother, more efficient form of government, or is it to provide members of parliament with a happier life and a smooth career structure? Sometimes politicians seem to want all the fringe benefits that civil servants get, with their inflation-proof pensions. Is the committee system to give active young men something to do—toys to play with—rather than to encourage better government?

Finally, I think Shirley Williams is quite right that governments have changed in their attitudes. If people want to stop a war in Vietnam, they can perfectly well do so—and not by strengthening the committee system, but by withholding money. And if enough backbenchers want to change the sitting hours of the House of Commons, they can do it by an effort of will. If normal service has been resumed, as Kenneth Baker says, it is because a majority of his colleagues actually want normal service to be resumed.

CHRISTOPHER PRICE, member, British Parliament: I think the problem of the power base is much exaggerated. British members of Parliament, of whatever party, are far too secure. They can behave in quite amazingly bizarre ways and not put their careers at any sort of risk at all, and they are not subject to any primary system. I think greater insecurity would be better. Those Labour members of Parliament who have been pushed out of their constituencies or endangered, allegedly for being too right wing with a left wing constituency, have in truth been simply very bad at personal relations. My experience is that if a member is even remotely polite and sensible, and able to look people in the eye and shake their hands once a month, he is not in the remotest danger from his constituency.

I very much agree with George Cunningham that procedural reform will not make much difference. I do not think there is a "problem" of backbench members of Parliament. The majority of British backbench MPs are perfectly happy, voting with their party, going on the odd free-loading trip, and limiting their activities to being reasonably good backup ombudsmen and social workers for their constituencies.

For those backbench members of Parliament who want to do more than that—and I place myself among them—there is no difficulty whatsoever in manipulating the media, getting on a television program, infiltrating what the Americans call public service organizations such as the National Council for Civil Liberties and getting them to lobby, using the party and a whole range of organizations to exert considerable influence (or all the influence one ought to be able to exert) on ministers and the executive, whether from the government side or from the opposition. It seems to me that the "problem" lies with a small group of backbenchers who have studied political economy at the university and are horrified to find that Parliament does not work as the textbooks say. [Laughter.] I very much agree that if one has power, it is important to use it. That is why I am rather glad the European Parliament finally plucked up the courage to use its budgetary powers for the first time. In the British Parliament, the only power that the backbencher has is to speak out. Last year, together with four colleagues, I announced the name of a secret service colonel, which the courts had tried to prevent us from doing. After we gave out the name, all the papers printed it, and an up-coming trial went the right way rather than the wrong way. In ways like that, one has to use power. But apart from this sort of constitutional power—the freedom to speak without being arrested or charged with contempt of court—the only real power a backbencher has is the power to make ministers' lives so difficult and unlivable that they finally give in a little. I think backbenchers have plenty of power in that direction.

Now that we have normal service, as Kenneth Baker calls it, with a big majority, I very much hope that we will go a bit further in trying to work up some backbench versus government majorities. We were doing this over a freedom of information bill and trying to do so over the official information bill when the government fell. We had actually worked up a majority against the government. Whether it will be possible among the Conservatives, we shall have to see. They are much more tribal in their attitudes and much more loyal, and they make this sort of cross-bench agreement much more difficult. but I live in hope.

GILES RADICE, member, British Parliament: I should like to defend the procedure committee report. We do not merely want more pleasant jobs for backbenchers, who would perhaps like something more than to be lobby fodder—though, obviously, that is part of the report's aim. We have to come to terms with three modern developments: the extension of the role of government, the more powerful party, and the growing power of interest groups. To do this, we need to develop the one thing we are extremely bad at in our Parliament, which is our investigative role.

It is possible to bring ministers and civil servants and the outside interests to some forum only by asking systematic questions, and unfortunately there is no way of doing that except by a committee system. One or two committees have been relatively successful in developing their investigative roles, and it is on the basis of their success that we are trying to extend the system to the twelve select committees. Although the standing committees, which deal with legislation, are not going to be the same as the select committees, the report says they ought to have two or three sessions in which they, too, can ask questions. The report also says, incidentally, that there should be some overlap of personnel, so that the expertise gained in the select committee is not lost but is also available—at least in part—on the standing committee.

I defend the procedure committee report because we are trying to make good the investigative role which has been lacking in our Parliament, and because we have been able to make very little impact on outside interests and on ministers and civil servants. We probably have far more to learn from, say, the Canadians or the Germans, in this respect, than from the American system. I know a bit about the Canadian system, but I would like to ask my Bundestag colleagues about their committees. Do they deal with policy as well as legislation; can they question witnesses on a systematic basis; and are they on TV and radio, as I think our select committees ought to be?

MR. RICHARDS: I will ask Klaus Daweke to answer these questions because I think it is important to have it on the record.

MR. DAWEKE: It was mentioned earlier that in the Bundestag a committee relating to each ministry is set up at the beginning of the legislative period. During the period, there might be additional committees, such as committees of inquiry. At the moment, we have nineteen committes in all, fifteen relating to the ministries. They get into action on the legislative side after the first reading, and the making of law done in these committees. It is very rare that, in the second reading in the House, there are changes which have not been announced in the committee.

The minister or, if he cannot come, the undersecretary of state appears at times to explain the long-range policies of his ministry and discuss them with the parliamentarians. We have the right to demand that civil servants appear and report. We can make decisions on long-range policy plans. We can ask the ministry to bring in figures, numbers, documents, and so forth. I think the committees are really the strong centers of politics in our Parliament.

We have public hearings, and the committee has the right to name the subject and then decide whether it is to be televised. If the stations accept the hearing, it will be on television, but the normal committee meetings, of course, are not on TV.

MR. KUNZ: Members of the second chamber can also be on the committee and have the right to speak and to be questioners.

MR. DAWEKE: But not staff members.

CHARLES WHALEN, former U.S. representative: I would like to talk from a little different perspective, that of a former backbencher in a permanent minority party. I suspect that in this conference the use of the phrase "career opportunities" in the legislative body refers to the opportunity for an individual backbencher to advance in authority, recognition, and power.

The reforms that Cliff Hackett described, which emanated from the Julia Butler Hansen committee, the arm of the Democratic caucus, have done much to enhance the career opportunities of the Democrats, the members of the permanent majority party. For example, the limitation of one subcommittee chairmanship has brought in as chairmen many individuals in their second or third term—even one first-termer. The so-called subcommittee bill of rights provides that, whenever possible, legislation will originate at that subcommittee level. It also provides adequate funding and adequate staff for subcommittees. These reforms have enhanced the power of subcommittees and thus of the individuals who chair them.

Certainly Democrats coming in for a first term can look, with some hope and expectation, to fairly rapid advancement. Since 1928, however, there have been twenty-five congressional elections in the United States, and the Republicans have won a majority in the Congress in only two of those elections, 1946 and 1952. As a consequence, Republicans have not had these career advancement opportunities to look forward to, and I do not foresee this changing in many years. This is not true of the other countries that are represented here.

We have our own shadow system in which the senior Republican on the committees or subcommittees is referred to as the ranking member. But this does not mean much, because the chairman of the committee or the subcommittee sets the agenda. The chairman has the staff at his or her disposal, has the authority, and, more important, is the focus of public attention. Whether this system is contributing to early retirement on the part of Republicans, who after three, four, five, maybe even six terms feel "there is no hope," I do not know. I would leave that to the academicians to answer.

There is, however, a very close working relationship between the subcommittee or the committee chairman, on the one hand, and the ranking member, on the other. It is a courtesy, but often it involves a cooperative parliamentary effort. The chairman will usually check with the ranking member on the bills that will receive priority on the agenda. They work very closely in the mark-up of the bills, and then usually team up as the bills follow the legislative process. I cannot recall any instance in which I have opposed the chairman of a subcommittee of which I have been the ranking member. The opposition has come from others in either party.

Regardless of the party affiliation of the congressional backbencher, that individual can have and has had an influence in shaping legislation. Three factors account for this. First, in any subcommittee meeting there will be perhaps only two or three people. Just by being there the junior member has an opportunity to make a significant contribution. Second, the individual who does his or her homework gains command of the subject and can be very influential. Third, the member of the minority party, if reasonable and not an ideologue, will be listened to and can have an impact during the subcommittee mark-up.

JEANE KIRKPATRICK, American Enterprise Institute: I have been struck by the extent to which this discussion of legislative reform has resolved itself again and again into a discussion of the power relations between leaders and followers and of intraparty relations. When seen in this way, it becomes particularly clear why, if the power of followers

—that is, of backbenchers—is to be increased, it is terribly important that they have more independent power bases in their district. This relation between the independence of tenure of the representative and his function within the legislature seems to me to be crucial.

There has been relatively little attention in the discussion so far to the relation between structural reform and policy outcomes. Is it suggested that reforms be undertaken because it will make backbenchers happier, or because it will affect positively the legislative outcomes? Does the group believe that an enhanced role for backbenchers in the British system would increase the capacity of the Parliament to perform the oversight function vis-à-vis the civil service?

BOB ECKHARDT, U.S. representative (Democrat, Texas): There are 518 members in the Bundestag, and 282 in the Canadian Parliament. I would suggest that with respect to all but the Canadian Parliament there has to be a trade-off between participation and effectiveness of the floor. I think 150 is about an optimum size. That is the size of the Texas legislature. [Laughter.] And that is 50 percent bigger than the U.S. Senate. If there are opportunities for meaningful participation in a large parliamentary body, they are to be found in the committee system. Giving more power to the committee system inevitably removes some of the power and the importance of the body as a whole.

CLIVE LANDA, political director, Tory Reform Group: As a brief rejoinder to Kenneth Baker's point about the selection of British Conservative MPs, I do not want our overseas visitors to go away with the illusion that they are encouraged to be independent. The process of their selection inhibits them from being independent. Otherwise, they are not selected.

AUSTIN RANNEY, American Enterprise Institute: My question is addressed to George Cunningham, but I want to preface it with something that may make him feel a bit better. Every academician here is familiar with the experience of sending off a book to the publisher, having it published, and thinking, by God, that will rock them—but total silence follows. [Laughter.] It is not that you expect great praise or great condemnation; I mean nothing happens. [Laughter.]

When Mr. Cunningham finished, I thought, "That will rock them, and there will be angry, heated discussions." I was wrong. By the great good fortune of my having the last question, I want to repeat Jeane Kirkpatrick's question, but in a slightly more general and open-ended context. If the people of Britain, in their majesty, rose and demanded independence and power for their backbenchers and an end to governmental tyranny, in your view, what good would result that does not now exist?

Mr. Cunningham: The House of Commons would not pass a bill such as the devolution bills—very ill-advised measures—when the judgment of a majority of the members was against it.

I would have said that if a truth drug had been administered to the 635 members of the House and they were asked, "What is your genuine opinion of the merits of these proposals?" two-thirds of the members would have voted them down. Those bills were passing through the House with some interruptions from time to time, but in the end we had to find a device to blow the damn thing up instead of voting it down in a straightforward way.

To answer Dr. Kirkpatrick's question, most of us who recommended the proposals in the procedure committee report had in mind that a tidy system of committees would have better surveillance of what the government, the machine, and the civil servants are doing. There would be the possibility of a tidier prelegislative process, because if there were a single committee on, say, transport, it could look forward to the right way to organize railways in conjunction with roads, and so on. At the moment, however, there is no committee—or, rather, there are several committees, which amounts to the same thing—which could address that kind of question.

We want better surveillance of what the executive is doing and better forms for initiating what the legislature has to do. In the end, there ought to be fewer things being passed that are contrary to the judgment of 635 people, and therefore more bills that are more in line with what the public majority wants, which, after all, is the very definition of democracy. The public should get, more or less, what it wants.

Mr. MacGuigan: The truth we are concerned with is not an abstract, theoretical kind which the great brains in the public service could formulate into a perfectly planned system. What is at issue is practical truth—whether something will work and whether it is tolerable to the people. On this kind of question, the contribution of a member of parliament or a member of Congress is likely to be of better quality than that of someone in the executive or in the administration who is more removed from the feelings of the people.

Mr. Daweke: Quite bluntly, yes, I want to be happier in parliament. Of course, that is one of my basic rights. But I think we have mixed up two things: the junior legislator who is trying to become a good legislator and the backbencher. If someone is happy to be a backbencher, that is fine, but I was talking more of the chap who wants to be a legislator. He might be a backbencher as a legislator, but he wants to become a good legislator. I want to be happier, but I also want to become a better legislator.

A second point: the American system seems to be that Congress tries to be the best administration possible. It tries to kick out the civil servants or to better them by specializing, by having more subcommittees. Therefore, it needs a large staff, of course, because it needs extra help to check the men in the ministry.

The British system seems to be to cross your fingers and hope the ministries are doing a good job, and therefore to believe in them. They just do their work at the bases.

We are in the middle in Germany—again, perhaps because of good tips after the war. But I believe that we should compromise again. We should have better staff; at times we are a working parliament, and we should be staffed better. My way to control civil service would be to concentrate on less work; that is, we should not have so many weeks in session. If the government would give us fewer legislative programs, we would have time to think more about politics. We would also be able to limit the power of civil service more than by trying to be civil servants ourselves.

Session IV

Models and Choices: What Can We Learn from Each Other?

NORMAN J. ORNSTEIN, moderator: We have come to the final session, "What Can We Learn from Each Other?" I hope that the question will have some, if not conclusive, at least interesting answers.

We have a lively and most distinguished panel with us today. There are two papers: "The Working Conditions of Members of Parliament and Congress: Changing the Tools Changes the Job," by Austin Ranney of the American Enterprise Institute, and "How to Strengthen Legislatures—Assuming That We Want to," by Anthony King of the University of Essex.

Three highly distinguished discussants will begin the discussion: the Right Honorable Francis Pym, the secretary of state for defense, Great Britain; Representative Thomas Foley of Spokane, Washington; and Gerhard Kunz, the parliamentary leader of the Christian Democrats in the Bundestag.

AUSTIN RANNEY: I tried to include in my paper as much information as I could get about how much and what kind of support members of Congress get to do their jobs, and how much support backbench members of the House of Commons get to do their jobs. Although much of this cannot be quantified, it is something in the neighborhood of $350,000 a year for a member of Congress, and certainly well under $20,000 a year for a member of the House of Commons. If, indeed, the political institutions of our two countries are converging, as we are often told, we ought to discuss how to raise the level of support for MPs and how to reduce the level of support for members of Congress. But since at least one of those two propositions will not receive serious discussion, we will not go into that.

The subtitle—"Changing the Tools Changes the Job"—suggests that we sometimes look at the subject as though we first decide the job we want our members to do, and then give them the necessary tools. Certainly, that kind of reasoning enters into it, but there are a number of other factors, not least of which is who has the power to decide what kind of tools the members will have. Do the members themselves have that power, as they do in the House of Representatives, or does some other semi-related agency such as the government have that power, as is the case in Britain? That makes a difference.

The relation between the tools and the job works both ways. If a person who is used to shooting small game is given a very large, high-powered Magnum, it may be that squirrel and rabbits will no longer satisfy him, and he may begin to think of tigers and elephants and perhaps even lions. In the House of Representatives, say, since 1970, the level of support and the size of staff have increased quite markedly. This has at least some significant relation to how the role and the activity of the House has changed. When staff has doubled and trebled in size, as it has done within the last decade or so, they have not been content to sit around in rather passive fashion, prepared to do anything that they are asked to do, but nothing more. They are intelligent, well-trained people, energetic and active. And they have quite aggressively sought additional jobs to do for their congressmen and, therefore, for the Congress as an institution.

I would suggest to people in Britain and the Federal Republic that, if the tool kit of their backbench members of parliament is significantly increased, they will use it. In considering how much additional support to give backbenchers, the people must necessarily think very hard about the kind of job they want the backbenchers to do. The tool kit does not simply reflect the size of the predetermined job; to some extent, it determines the size of the job.

The crux of this or almost any other conference on political institutions is a question on which I hope we will focus attention in this session. And that is: What difference does it make? It is all very well to talk about giving more power to select committees, or greatly expanding staff and research facilities, or cutting down the staff of congressmen, and the like. But in the end we have to decide what results we expect from any changes that we might consider, and what impact those things would have on our other values.

Geoffrey Smith, in his excellent paper, says that if, in either of our countries, things had been going well in recent years—if the economy had gone well, and inflation were low, and our foreign policies were successful—it is unlikely that we would be sitting around quite so earnestly, asking how to improve the situation. It is because we feel that neither of our governments has been having a very good win-lose record in recent years—I speak less confidently about the Federal Republic—that we have this concern.

In any event, this question of the support that the backbench MPs and members of Congress now have, and ought to have in the future, depends upon the role we want them to play and the function we want them to have. Our decision on that depends upon what difference we really think it would make to the quality of government and the nature of its output. I expect an excellent and definitive answer to this question from Anthony King.

ANTHONY KING: I will begin by making two or three points unrelated to Austin Ranney's question before proceeding to answer it. The three points are not closely related in my paper, but are subjects that have come up as we have gone along.

Let me launch the first point with an anecdote. About fifteen years ago, I found myself in the company of a distinguished former British public servant named Sir Timothy Bly, who had achieved some prominence as the private secretary to Harold Macmillan when he was prime minister. Tim Bly, talking about the relation between ministers and civil servants in Great Britain, used the metaphor of the enormous electricity pylons that disfigure the landscape of Britain and many other countries. These metal objects rise like scarecrows into the sky and carry power lines across the countryside. He described how workmen had built one on his land. First they dug an enormous hole, and into it they poured tons of concrete. And into that concrete, they put a number of very heavy metal chains. The metal chains were then raised to the surface of the earth, and the enormous ball of concrete was used to anchor the pylon, so that it would not move in the wind. The hole, with its concrete contents, was covered over, so that only the great metal pylon with the power line was visible and the enormous ball of concrete was hidden under the ground. He finished by saying, "This is the message I bring you: that ball of concrete is the civil service."

After listening to Shirley Williams, it occurred to me that it might be in the interests of the executive branch in Britain and Canada, as well as in Australia and New Zealand, to strengthen select committees. Strengthening investigative committees and enabling them to hold hearings would make it easier for ministers of the Crown and people in similar positions to force both the civil service and the interest groups to defend their positions.

One of the most striking things about British public life today is that those who hold power—states of the realm, sometimes civil servants and big companies, often trade unions—never have to give an account of themselves in public. The nearest that someone such as Alan Fisher of the National Union of Public Employees, or Mostyn Evans of the Transport and General Workers' Union, has ever been to having to set out his position and defend its consequences has been on an occasional television or radio program. I think it would be extremely useful —and I gather that Shirley Williams does too—if there were some more formal parliamentary forum in which these people had to explain their actions to the public. It might not alter their behavior, but I think it conceivably might.

My second point has to do with the fact mentioned earlier that in the House of Commons the great majority of members, especially the younger, more active members, want to be ministers. David Marquand threw out a challenge when he asked if there were anyone present who would rather be the chairman of a select committee than a parliamentary undersecretary. Nobody took up that challenge, and I think the answer is that there are almost no members of parliament who would prefer committee office to ministerial office. There may be a few, but not many.

If we want to encourage people not only to sit on the select committees, but also to take the work seriously, we might want to create two career structures within Parliament: one leading to ministerial office and one leading to select committee office. There are several problems with that, which I will not go into. But it was suggested earlier that chairmen of select committees and possibly the senior opposition member of a select committee might be paid a salary and given some staff. That sort of thing might make the job more attractive. At any rate, it is an idea worth throwing out.

My third point is connected with the educational function that Congressman Eckhardt mentioned at the beginning of this conference. At one time, there were experts—technicians, specialists, technocrats, senior civil servants, senior people in the armed forces, and so on—whose job was to know their subject thoroughly. At the other end of the continuum were laymen, who did not understand the niceties of defense policy, or education policy, or whatever. In between, acting as translators of the experts for the benefit of the laymen, were the politicians.

The word "politician" has scarcely been used in the course of this conference, but one of the jobs of the politician was to represent the aspirations, the hopes, the fears, the desires, and so on of his constituents to the experts and technicians. Another of his jobs was to simplify complicated realities so that the layman could make some sense of them. By communicating his simplifications to the people and giving them some idea of what the central choices were, a legislator was performing the educational function that Representative Eckhardt referred to. Partly as the result of the greater complexity of the world and the fact that, amazingly, we know rather more about it, but also as the result of the increase in staffs, especially in the United States, legislators have a growing desire to get involved in the details of policy. More and more politicians are moving in toward the expert end of the continuum and away from the layman end.

It seems to me that over the past fifteen years, subject after subject that I once took an interest in has been disappearing over some knowledge horizon into a world where I can no longer understand it. Defense disappeared several years ago. Social welfare and the issues connected with it disappeared three or four years ago. Although, like most of the people present, I am presumably among the top 10 percent of informed citizens in this society, I know less and less about less and less. And I wonder whether that is not a rather bad thing for the democratic process generally. The extent to which legislators are becoming policy experts worries me. That is my third point.

Let me return to Austin Ranney's question, which was, So what? If we increase staff or expand the work of select committees, does it really matter? The short answer, I think, must be, Not a great deal. It probably results, as George Cunningham said, in better public policies in some fields, and, as one of our German colleagues said, in happier legislators. But there is a longer answer that is relevant to Britain. I want change to come about in the House of Commons, not as a friend of the world's legislators, not as a political scientist interested in running an experiment in reform, but partly as a citizen of Great Britain with certain political views, which I would like the institutions of my country to promote.

I am one of the large number of people who have become slowly, but increasingly, dismayed by the phenomenon in political life called adversary politics. One side of the political fence takes up one position, often based on historic ideas that do not make much sense anymore. The other side then takes up the contrary position. The two battle it out.

This has at least two unfortunate consequences. One is that we have increasingly had unnecessary and often abrupt changes in public policy. I think it was Shirley Williams who referred to the increasing penchant of British governments for repealing the legislation of their predecessors. It cannot be a good thing for one government to do something that the next government will repeal. I would like greater stability in public policy, with people's time horizons perhaps being pushed a bit further into the future. The second consequence is that in recent years adversary politics has had the effect of causing people *not* to think pragmatically, *not* to think about what they really want to achieve and then look around for the best means of achieving it. We have suffered from an excess of ideology.

To make the point, I regard both the tribunite wing of the Labour party and what I will label the "Josephite" wing of the Conservative party as misguided and as unrepresentative of the feelings of the people of Great Britain. I would therefore be in favor of any parliamentary reform that would alter the structure of political debate. What do the select committees of the House of Commons have to do with that? Not an enormous amount, but possibly a bit. The experience of some other countries, notably Germany, suggests that if there are a number of parliamentary forums that give members of different political parties every incentive to work together, and in which the cultural norm is for people to work on a cross-party basis, this can increase the quantum of pragmatic thinking and decrease the quantum of partisan rhetoric and partisan thinking. In other countries, select committees have, to some extent, had that effect. If they had that effect in Great Britain, I would be all in favor of it. But as Jeane Kirkpatrick and Austin Ranney said earlier, in an odd way we have been talking about structure without addressing the probable consequences of changes in structure for the institutions as well as for public policy. I think that changing the institutions in Britain a little would affect public policy a little along the lines I have suggested.

THOMAS FOLEY: The American role in this meeting is not much different from what it is in other meetings where Europeans and Americans gather. We are either condemned for our excesses or we are boasting of them. Perhaps in the case of parliamentary reform, it is questionable how much either Britain or West Germany can or wants to learn from the United States. I should like to suggest, however, a few problems in the past decade or so of congressional reform that have culminated in major changes in the institution of Congress. This period extended from 1958, with the organization of the Democratic Study Group, of which Bob Eckhardt and I are former chairmen, to about 1974 and shortly thereafter, when Butler Derrick and the so-called Watergate class arrived.

By the way, it was offensive to us pathfinders of reform that the Watergate backbenchers took credit for achieving everything for which we had so carefully laid the groundwork. [Laughter.]

The American press, and political commentators in general, gave them enormous credit that properly belonged to us. There were only seventy-five of them, after all, but at least another seventy-five of us joined them in achieving the reforms.

The reform movement was not, as in Britain, a revolution against the civil service of the government or against the executive. It was a revolution, if that word can be applied, of junior or middle-ranking members against the senior established membership and leadership of the House. In the 1950s Arthur Krock of the *New York Times* called the standing committee chairmen the "Lord's Proprietors of the Congress." Indeed, Woodrow Wilson, in an earlier life as a political commentator, said, "Congress in session is Congress on exhibition; Congress in committee is Congress at work." That work, however, was directed mainly by the full committee chairmen.

My first day on the Agriculture Committee, of which I am now the chairman, was spent listening to the scriptures of the chairman, Harold Cooley of North Carolina. In the public arena of the committee room, with the press present, he told us that he hated to hear new members interrupt senior members when they were asking questions. He went on to say that we would find, if we would only remain silent, that the senior members of the committee would ask all the important questions, discuss all the relevant issues, and decide them without our interference. He added that, unfortunately, for some it would take years; other, more clever individuals might learn in months some of the basic information of the committee necessary for constructive participation. But, in the meantime, they could all help us—that is, the senior bench—by being quiet and attentive.

Pointing to a portrait on the wall, he said, "Former chairman, good Mr. Hope, ran the committee with this end of the gavel, and he just about knocked the gavel off the handle. I run it with the other end of the gavel, but I hope you have my meaning." He said, "I dislike prima donnas of any seniority rank. I *abominate* freshman prima donnas." [Laughter.]

Perhaps the most important reform came in 1972–1973, when the caucus, the meeting of all Democratic members, invoked the rule that no committee chairman could continue in that position in the next Congress without a secret ballot approving him or her. That turned the whole game around. It had been a somewhat feudal system, but suddenly the constituency of the chairman was the members of the party. Now, new members are indulged in an unbelievable way by the leadership because not only do the committee chairmen have to be elected, but also the speaker, the majority leader, the chairman of the caucus, and others have to stand for election. For example, the newest members of Congress, who came in after the November 1978 election, were given a fantastic black-tie dinner by the majority leader, who was running for his office again. The Singing Sergeants from the Air Force performed, and military bands and orchestras played. It was given on the terrace of the Rayburn building overlooking the city. The speaker gave a dinner the following night in the rotunda of the Capitol, which has been used only three times for receptions: once for Lafayette; once for

Her Majesty, Queen Elizabeth II, during the bicentennial celebration; and once for the freshmen class of House members.

If backbenchers want attention, I suggest that reform is an excellent way to approach the problem. I may sound like a mildly obese wine lover, addressing a group of emaciated, hungry, and denied individuals, by saying there is danger in overnutrition and overindulgence. Some of my own colleagues would be somewhat amazed to hear someone who is both a committee chairman and chairman of the caucus—with the extra staff and, more important, extra office space which each of these positions provides—suggest that there is a point at which committees are overstaffed and members are overindulged. But I will toss those concerns aside and give the lecture.

We have gone from being understaffed in our committees to becoming, in some cases, clearly overstaffed. When I became chairman of the Agriculture Committee in 1974, it had the smallest staff of any standing committee in the House: nineteen people, including one messenger. I have tried to hold down this number. The subcommittee chairmen, of which there are ten, have the lowest staff ratio of any committee in the House. Despite this, we now have a total of almost seventy-five staff people in the Agriculture Committee, and we are still smaller than any of the twenty-one House committees, save one.

There is even one subcommittee, on Commerce, that alone has twenty-six or twenty-eight staff persons. Representative Eckhardt has one of those Commerce subcommittees.

These congressional bureaucracies, which the British, in particular, seem to envy, are not the model of the British civil service applied to Parliament. They are—and I think quite properly so, given our situation—the result of the patronage of the committee and subcommittee chairmen and the ranking minority or opposition members. In 1974, during consideration of the Reform Act, a counterproposal known as the Hansen report was offered and carried. One of its provisions allowed every subcommittee chairman as well as up to six ranking members on each subcommittee a staff person of their own choosing. That was put in the report by an extremely clever member on the Democratic side to encourage the Republican membership to vote for the alternative report, and it succeeded admirably.

Now, almost half the House Democrats are subcommittee chairmen, and almost half the Republicans, if not more, are ranking Republicans on some committee. Each one has his own professional staff person. Of course, secretarial assistance is also required to serve the professional staff, because those people do not do typing and things like that. Thus, it proliferates. We almost have parliamentary unions. A subcommittee chairman on one committee will complain, for example, that his counterpart on another committee has four staffers to his one or two. It is fiercely competitive. In addition, staff ape each other and take on a culture of their own. I do not always talk to other members on the telephone. Instead, my staff talks to their staff.

In the Senate, senators do not often attend committee meetings. A few of them do, but normally their personal representatives attend, and they tell the other members what the senator will tolerate about a particular bill. One wonders sometimes whether the staff person is making the decision and later convincing the member, or has been instructed by the member what to say.

There is a joke in the United States about the internal—or, as the British would say, inland—revenue commissioner, who calls up the parish priest and asks if Mr. O'Malley has given $1,000 to St. Patrick's Church last year, as reported on his income tax; to which the priest replies, "If he hasn't, he will." Such is often the case when a staff member says that member X insists on a certain amendment. If he hasn't, he will, because as soon as the staff person's reputation and involvement are clearly engaged, the staff has to be backed up. Needless to say, this can lead to complications in the legislative process.

Unfortunately, we do not make the old style of patronage appointment, hiring a wife's brother-in-law, for example. Instead, we now hire Harvard Law School graduates or graduates of Berkeley and Stanford business schools. Staff positions are eagerly sought as useful appointments for a couple of years, from which it is possible to go on to either corporate or professional life with rather important experience. These staff people are bright, very hard-working, and do not think they have achieved much unless their bosses have added their own particular imprint to the bill under consideration.

That description, of course, applies to our appropriations and standing committees. Of greater interest here is the investigative role and the concept of select committees. Select committees in the United States are something quite different from what they are elsewhere. They are temporary committees, while standing committees are permanent. The whole thing is the other way around, as are some other things. To table a bill, for instance, in the United States means to kill it.

In our system the investigative or oversight role rests primarily with the standing committees; and, quite frankly, I have been disappointed in the handling of this particular aspect of committee responsibility. We have great resources at our disposal for careful, assiduous, and deliberate investigation of national problems. Further, we have no lack of staff or additional manpower. The Library of Congress, like a great monolith, is right at our finger tips. We can call on the academic community; any professor of political science, within reason, would eagerly rush down to Washington to become a special adviser to an investigative committee.

Even so, in most cases, there is almost a deadly assignation between the press and the investigating instinct. It is much easier to take a cheap shot at a government official on television than spend months and months of careful staff preparation to analyze a serious problem and write a sensible report. Perhaps the British system can overcome that tendency, but it ought to be watched, particularly if the investigative proceedings are televised. Once TV cameras are present, members suddenly have a great urge to do things such as calling for the resignation of Energy Secretary Schlesinger. A great deal of very shoddy investigative work is done in the Congress, not because we haven't the capacity, but because we haven't the will.

We have higher salaries, more staff, and advanced technological resources. Charles Rose, who is the leading figure in the technology field as chairman of the House Information Subcommittee, suggested using satellites for committee hearings so that the people testifying would not have to come to Washington but could be viewed instead on great video screens. He was not joking; that is coming. Yet, all of this has seemingly not produced happiness. I think it was George Bernard Shaw who said that there are two tragedies in life, not getting one's heart's desire and getting it. We got it. [Laughter.]

We have the staff, we have the reform, and we broke the absolute power of the committee chairmen; but we forgot about the subcommittee chairmen, of which there are now about 153 in the House. Members of the executive branch complain privately that they are continually summoned to Capitol Hill to discuss energy problems by the Committee on Agriculture, the Committee on Commerce, the committees dealing with the military, and by every subcommittee imaginable. It has become a matter of pride: no subcommittee chairman is going to settle for having a deputy assistant secretary appear when the secretary himself testified before a friend's committee. That would be an insult. Perhaps it is all right to take up the time of our executive people; they obviously have an obligation to inform. But the Congress is not doing a good job because the outcome is not so much careful investigation as it is a kind of ego satisfaction for the members.

We are losing some of our best members, not because they are not well enough paid, but because they are working harder and enjoying it less. This is in part related to the general depression of morale in the United States.

When I became a member of Congress fifteen years ago, we were still emulating the last of the British Empire. We did not have a formal empire, but the American influence extended pretty much around the world. Countries could ignore us, but they never forgot our position.

Incomes were rising in the United States at the fastest rate in the twentieth century. Prices were stable. The political consensus was that the social and economic problems of the country could be well solved merely with the application of reasonable resources and public will. Young members of Congress came in, not only happy to be in the institution, but feeling that they were about to do very productive work.

Today, after many years and many events, members feel that what they are doing is not being recognized, and, in fact, they feel grave personal doubts about how effective Congress is in solving, with the executive, the very central problems that face our society. We wanted to vote on issues, not to kill bills in secret. Now we vote by putting little IBM cards into boxes hundreds of times a year. We did not want to require a large number of people, but only a small band, to get a vote. Now almost anybody in the House can demand and get a vote, and we are faced with very difficult votes time and time again. The voting process is used as a political instrument, particularly by the opposition party. While this is perhaps the way it is supposed to be, somehow it does not seem to be as satisfying as we had hoped.

If the British moderation, discretion, and restraint, for which they are properly famous, can take the instinct for change, put some limits on it, and avoid the typical excesses of the American system, so much the better. I have one caution, however. It is sometimes easier to bring about change than to reverse it. Once a thing is done, it is not simple to undo it.

It is now generally conceded that we have too many subcommittees and too many subcommittee chairpeople, but the question is who will volunteer to give up his power base, and how do we reduce the number without, in effect, vacating those chairs and embarrassing the people who hold them? It is a very difficult problem. Everyone agrees that the organization and jurisdiction of the committees should be regularized and rationalized, but I have never, even in the Vietnam period, seen such bitter recriminations as those between members when questions of their jurisdictions were at stake. For example, one member said to another, "I will never forget that you have proposed the abolition of my subcommittee, and I will find some way, publicly or privately, to get back at you for this dastardly thing." We have embarked on another effort to rationalize the committee system, but it will probably have about as much success as it did in 1974.

I hope Michael Ryle and Kenneth Bradshaw will forgive me for saying that it strikes me as rather strange that some of my British colleagues would like to see a parliamentary version of the British civil service. If they think the civil service controls the government, why would they want to put the civil service in charge of affairs in Parliament? As an American, I do not understand, perhaps because I do not understand British institutions well enough. We are, in effect, a kind of a reverse image, one of the other. We think the civil service in our national executive branch needs strengthening, and we admire the British civil service for its reputation and capacity.

We think our own civil servants are not given enough respect and enough recognition to draw better talent into the federal service. But I would not think it compatible with free congressional or parliamentary institutions to create an independent congressional civil service of any great size, particularly if it dealt with political questions. Instead, I would suggest the model of the technically prepared political adviser.

Finally, I heartily agree with Anthony King's comment about language. Since we have had more staff and more technicians, members of Congress have started to speak a variety of languages, and the dossiers or the résumés should now say, "English, some French, also speaks social welfarese, defensese, and agriculturic."

GERHARD KUNZ: Perhaps I can add some words to what my fellow discussants have said: first, about staff. We have the same problems in Germany, but the other way around. I do not think that what Mr. Foley said is a vision for Germany in the year 2000, but I hope that we can make some progress toward having more staff than we have now.

There is only one basic mission of parliament—it has to produce good legislation, and this means it has to have a certain amount of staff. Where is equality if there is a ministry on one side and no staff on the other side? Of course, we can get help—for instance, from special interest groups—but do we really want it? Is influence exercised in this way not so strong that we lose a certain amount of independence? Therefore, one of the problems we face in Germany is to increase our staff, not to create a staff bureaucracy, but to have a staff of reasonable size, and, of course, of high quality.

My second point is that we should take care that parliaments do not atomize too much. Every parliament has to have a certain number of committees, but not too many, and especially not too many subcommittees. A typical German example is the subcommittee for disarmament problems, which thinks it is the only vital committee in the House. The members do all they can to emphasize the importance of this subcommittee. When many subcommittees have this tendency there is also a tendency toward atomization.

My third point is that there should be great emphasis on the importance of the floor. Of course, the main legislative work is done in the committees, but it is vital that the debates on the floor not be as boring as they sometimes are. For instance, in the German Parliament we all have a problem finding natural language to express what we want to say, in words that are understandable, especially to listeners from outside. Speeches should not be too long, and they should not be read from a paper, word for word, sentence for sentence, though very often it is done this way. Parliament has an obligation to find appropriate forums for discussion, and it is normal that the debate should be interrupted. Making the debates vivid is a great challenge to us all.

My fourth remark is about the role of the media. I have the feeling that the press and especially TV are sometimes of greater importance than the whole House. This tendency is not good. We can learn much from our British colleagues and from the House of Commons rule that does not permit TV broadcasts. My German colleagues will share my opinion. Whenever a member of Parliament knows that his speech is being broadcast, he immediately changes the style of his speech; it becomes more a proclamation than a contribution to a debate. Sometimes the members of Parliament are too eager to say what the press want them to say.

My fifth remark is about leadership of a political group. I share, more or less, the opinion my friend Klaus Daweke expressed, not because the happiness of legislators is a final goal, but because of the necessity for good legislation. It is a wise leadership that tries to give every member of parliament a good chance. One instrument in Germany, which is rather good, is the parliamentary reporter for each bill. We have too many bills, of course—this may be a typical German problem—but the one advantage is that we have two reporters for each bill, one from the government side—the coalition—and one from the opposition. This position of parliamentary reporter gives opportunities, influence, and power, and is especially good for a young man in Parliament because it enables him to exercise a certain influence, to play a certain role, and to contribute to good legislation.

My last remark is about the role of the opposition. I have been a member of the opposition for seven years now. I hope it will soon come to an end; nevertheless, I think the special mission of the opposition is vital. Our former foreign minister, Karl Schroeder, was once asked by Brezhnev, "What is opposition?" He answered, "The opposition is the government of tomorrow." This was the only language Brezhnev could understand. [Laughter.]

But I do not entirely agree with Schroeder. I think opposition is much more. The opposition represents the parliament, because the government is there only to present and pass the bills, and to do it quickly, without much noise. Therefore, we have to think profoundly about how to strengthen the opposition for the purpose of good legislation.

FRANCIS PYM: Comparisons between the practices in our various countries are valuable, but they do show up the differences: the job is different, the people are different, the history is different, and the circumstances are different. Although we may learn a great deal from each other, what is going to be right for the Federal Republic or Britain will not be right for the United States, and vice versa.

My first point is that we must keep in mind the interaction between the system used and the people who operate that system. The manner and the spirit in which the system is operated are very important, in Britain's case, whether we go on as we are, or have a new form of select committees, elaborate or simple. In other words, the skill and the sensitivity with which the tool is used are crucial, particularly in Britain, where nothing is written down except our procedure and our standing orders, which we are able to change whenever we like.

My second point is that it is impossible to divorce the system from the political context in which it has to work. The context of the politics does relate to the job, and in the House of Commons, in recent years and currently, the political divide between the two sides is wider than it has ever been. This may be only a temporary phenomenon. I would hope that it is, because it has led to rather extreme adversary politics, as mentioned by Anthony King. This is not good for Britain, and I would like to see that strain reduced. But political differences cannot be solved by procedural changes. The extent to which the system can be altered in order to bear upon this political divide seems to be very slight, indeed.

At the moment, the differences complicate reform and tend to become rather bitter interparty battles. As a matter of fact, historically they have been. To take but one example, very few people would say that the House of Lords is operating at its best at the moment. It could be improved in many ways. The divide comes most strikingly between one party, Labour, which at heart, I believe would like to do away with the House of Lords altogether, and the Conservative party, which would like to reform it but which is itself divided about how that should be done. At any rate, the political context is very relevant to the system.

My third point refers to the contrast between the party system in Parliament and the independence of members of Congress. They are, in fact, fundamentally different approaches to the same problem. Historically, the party system, as operated here, has been perhaps the most sophisticated method ever devised of reconciling political differences. Certainly, it is a sane and civilized way of conducting political debate when varying views exist within a party; a way of making organized, independent judgments, and at its best, very successful. The whipping system is greatly misunderstood both at home and abroad, and Anthony King has thrown a great deal of new light on it.

Austin Ranney, in his paper, says a member of Parliament has little control over his own vote and votes as his whips direct him. There is, of course, an element of truth in that, but all the argument and discussion about the various options within a party have taken place before that vote is mounted. We all take part in it. It is merely a different way of arriving at a vote. To make perhaps too simplistic a contrast, congressmen make up their own minds, and the result of the vote is whatever it may be. In our party system, the argument goes on in the party committees and among the members collectively; they reach a consensus, and then they vote. Of course, some people in each case will not go along with the party view. But it is a mistake to think that they are doing whatever they are told.

Despite the criticism of the party system and the strain under which it operates, I believe the system will survive in Britain because it is so deeply ingrained in our history. If that is true, it means that a member of Parliament requires much less backup than a member of Congress, because the party as a whole contributes to the consideration and information of a member of Parliament in a way that does not happen in Congress. Although I am sure members of Parliament ought to be in a better position than they are now, our system does not require anything comparable to the backup given in the U.S. Congress.

My next point relates to the fundamental social changes that certainly affect the operation of Parliament: greater equality, higher living standards, fewer people with independent means, and so on. They have altered the environment in which members of Parliament and the parties operate. A few decades ago the party was a collection of persons of financially independent means who combined for political purposes. If they did not like the outcome of their political debate and felt sufficiently strongly, without any penalty at all they would refuse to go along and would strike out on an independent line.

Today, most of the individual MPs depend upon a salary for everyday living and are therefore more heavily dependent upon the party. This development is inevitable in the circumstances, but it worries me because it puts a new pressure and a new influence on members and increases the power of parties and whips over members. Historically, the success of Parliament has been the independent nature of the members acting within it. I do not wish to exaggerate, but the tendency today is in a different direction.

The second important change is the expansion—even the explosion—of government activity so that it now reaches down into quite minor aspects of individual lives and businesses. In the opinion of many people, Parliament has not so far adapted itself to this development. The lack of adaptation is, of course, the reason for the proposal for a more structured and systematic arrangement of select committees.

This is necessary because of the government invasion of the lives of citizens. In parliamentary terms, it makes for a separate career structure among the select committees, which is not necessarily bad, but I would take to heart the warnings that have already been expressed about going too far.

Parliament has always evolved and changed itself rather gradually. We have got a bit behind lately and have not made enough changes since World War II. This is a change that we are now ready for, and I hope it will be put into effect. We are going to put proposals to the House of Commons in the near future, and it will be up to the House to decide whether it wants to go in this direction.

I absolutely agree that it is much easier to change than to reverse. In fact, it is impossible to reverse. If we do not like a change that is made we have to make another one. We cannot withdraw it.

If I could throw one seemingly pointless stone into the pond, the change that would be most dramatic for the House of Commons—and, in my view, it would be the healthiest change, but also the one that is impossible—would be to reduce its numbers. Cutting the membership by a third would really do more for the House of Commons than anything else that I can imagine.

There is not the slightest chance of its happening, because as far as I know, no elected assembly at any level, in any country, ever votes to reduce its own numbers. Reducing the membership would make it less parochial and would elevate it. This step would certainly change the nature of the job and would require greater backup and staff. The debate about this subject could go on forever because there is no perfect solution. Besides, circumstances change and people change. But the constant search for improvement is what is needed as long as one does not get too serious about it.

I agree that we must not be overindulgent or have too many staff people. We should not get overzealous about it. It would not do for us to become like civil servants in Parliament. That, I think, would be the ultimate disaster.

In the end, it seems to be a matter of common sense. What reform is going to work best in the circumstances depends more heavily on the people in politics than on any system. It depends on those of us who are using the system for the benefit of the people we represent.

But we also must enact reform in a way that is most appropriate and sympathetic to the circumstances of the day. We ought to move, not drastically, but firmly and reasonably, in the direction of a systematic system of select committees. In that way we can reveal to the British people much that is done in their name. As someone who is now a minister, I think it would be a healthy development. I took this view in opposition and I still take it today. It is not unhealthy at all. But let us not go to extremes; let us proceed in the normal British way of going rather gently.

RICHARD F. FENNO, JR., professor of political science, University of Rochester: My comments are mostly directed to the British, since the British seem to be wrestling at this juncture with the question of select committee scrutiny.

First, in the United States, successful legislative scrutiny of executive activity has to be connected with some retaliatory legislative power. Legislative committees need to confront executives face to face and deal with them in a more extended way than a question period, but they also have to convey some sense of legislative muscle. Many American reformers, who are discouraged with the behavior of the American Congress, sometimes think it does a poor job of legislating. They keep telling the congressmen that they really ought to be doing oversight, that they ought to give up the idea of legislating and stick to the business of scrutiny, moving somewhat toward the British system. I think that is the wrong direction to achieve any sort of legislative impact. The executive would not listen unless the legislature could convey the idea that it would retaliate in some way if the executive did not take account of what it was saying. Without that legislative law-making stick behind the door, effective scrutiny is very difficult—at least in our system.

Second, effective scrutiny takes place when it is in the career interests of the member of the legislature to conduct effective scrutiny. Representative Foley indicated some unhappiness at the lack of scrutiny or oversight on the part of American committees. I think that is largely because the members of the committees find it not in the interest of their own individual careers to conduct scrutiny. How one fits a career interest in scrutiny into the select committee process seems to me of some importance.

Third, executive scrutiny is effective when legislators are equipped to go into matters in great detail. American legislators are inductive thinkers, in my judgment. That is to say, they start with a specific, frequently constituency-related instance and get a handle on what is going on in the executive branch. They then work inductively from that very concrete, detailed event, moving outward and upward toward more general policy statements. Often it is suggested that legislators ought to deal in broad policy and leave details to the civil servants. But this suggestion would rob the legislator of precisely what he does best in the process of scrutiny, which is to grasp a detail and work out from there. I disagree when people say legislators are getting into too much detail, but that is a warning. There needs to be a balance.

Our new budget system is a legislative effort to get congressmen to think in macroeconomic terms. There has been a continual movement away from macroactivity into microanalysis of the budget item by item, which is the natural legislative style in the United States. I do not know the style in Britain, but effective scrutiny takes place in America when legislators follow their natural style toward detail.

Fourth, there is no such thing as a committee staff in the United States; it is largely a misnomer. The staff members of the committees are chosen by, and owe their allegiance to, the individual members of the committee, as Representative Foley said. For example, Senator Kennedy is said to have 100 staff members at his disposal; 50 of them are on his personal staff and work in his office; the other 50 are staff members of subcommittees and committees, but he has appointed them and their allegiance is to him. The policy result is that the individual staff member is concerned with the career of the senator or representative to whom he is attached and owes allegiance.

As Austin Ranney pointed out in his paper, every young staff member wants to earn his or her spurs by making policy, that is, by convincing the member that their ideas are good policy and should be enacted. The net result is that the explosion in the number of staff has overloaded the policy agenda of the United States, and our legislature is suffering from that at the moment.

If the select committee report betrays some longing for the American system, I, as an American listening to the discussion, long for some aspects of the British system. Whatever the British do in their reform to move toward the American system, I hope they will not give up two ingredients that our system lacks. One is their method for controlling the agenda and for dealing with legislative priorities. Our system has not been able to solve the problem of priorities and agenda overload.

The second point is that although the British may feel they suffer from an overdose of followers, I hope they keep some followers and keep whatever it is that enables leaders to find followers. We have a system without any backbenchers—or with all backbenchers, I am not sure exactly which. The problem of leadership in the Congress is that there are no followers; we have not solved the problem of how to make followers out of members of Congress with independent power bases.

MR. ORNSTEIN: Let us turn now to Ken Bradshaw, who is unique among us in many respects, but, in part, for having written a book on Parliament and the Congress.

KENNETH BRADSHAW, senior clerk, British House of Commons: David Pring was a co-author of that book and asked me to convey his regrets at not being here.

I agree with what has been said about the risks of making comparisons. In making any, it is necessary to take into account the constitutional background and history of the various legislatures. But some striking differences emerge from comparing the amount of attention that each legislature gives to various subjects. One can ask, for example, whether the British Parliament is doing enough in certain fields, such as foreign affairs, in which other parliaments are doing more.

The House of Commons has three or four major debates a year on foreign affairs. A question time comes up about once a month, and there is an occasional ministerial statement and perhaps a few short debates. Sometimes there is even an inquiry by a select committee, often over the staffing of the diplomatic service. But only on matters pertaining to the European Economic Community does the House exercise continuous and detailed coverage, and that, of course, is only since we joined the EEC. The House has a select committee to monitor legislation coming out of Brussels, and there is an equivalent body in the House of Lords. Apart from that, it is not untrue to say that Parliament confronts foreign affairs only when there is a crisis.

By contrast, in Congress, there is a committee on foreign affairs in each house, and several other committees track the work and activities and policies of the State Department very closely. I believe Dean Acheson, looking back on his period as secretary of state, once said that when Congress was sitting he had to spend one week in six either preparing for, or appearing before, a congressional committee. This may be a rather frightening statistic for British ministers who are preparing to confront House commitees of this kind.

Another area for comparison is taxation. After the House of Commons hears the chancellor present his budget, we have five or six days' debate on the budget proposals. A bill is introduced, and there are then two months of close scrutiny of the chancellor's proposal by the House and the committee. Then the House will forget about taxation until the following year, with a few important exceptions such as taxation provisions from the EEC, which come before the House in a slightly different way. Again, there is no systematic and continuing study of taxation. By contrast, Congress has standing legislative committees in both houses, which hold hearings so that the president's taxation proposal for the year can be commented on directly by all interested parties. In addition, a joint committee on internal revenue looks at taxation throughout the year and feeds the results to the finance committees of each House. The House of Commons will soon have a treasury committee and a foreign affairs committee so that I hope those gaps will be filled effectively.

Another interesting contrast is the extent to which committees sit in public. When I went to Washington in 1970, the House of Commons was rather in the lead on this. After some rather complicated calculations, we found that about 50 percent of the committees in the House of Commons were then sitting in public, compared with about 40 percent of the committees in the House of Representatives. By 1977 the picture had completely changed. Congress has now gone public with a vengeance. With very few exceptions, I think every committee now sits in public, even for executive sessions (we would call them deliberation sessions). As a member of the public, I was able to attend conferences between the two houses, which had hitherto been secret, and, perhaps even more astonishingly, to attend the Rules Committee of the House of Representatives. The equivalent in Britain would be for the weekly meeting of whips to be held in public. If we ever feel that publicity is needed in those meetings there certainly is a precedent on the American scene.

My concluding remarks concern a slight misunderstanding about bringing civil servants into the House of Commons. The proposals of the procedure committee for staffing the proposed committees were quite modest in suggesting that one administrative clerk, plus supporting executive and clerical staff and, of course, specialist advisers, could be recruited for each committee, as required. It ought to be made clear that the main staff of the House would be career staff, responsible not to the individual member, as Professor Fenno says is the case in the United States, but responsible to the committee as a whole.

A career clerk is recruited through the public service examination. But once recruited to the service of the House, he owes no allegiance whatsoever to the government of the day; he is not a civil servant in that respect. When assigned to a committee by the clerk of the House of Commons or one of his deputies, a committee clerk's allegiance is to the whole of that committee—to the chairman and every member of it. Thus he is expected to draft a report for his chairman, and also to draft amendments or a minority report for any other member of the committee who dislikes what the chairman is doing.

I agree entirely with Mr. Pym about the need to go forward slowly and to keep committees reasonably compact in the early stages. But, of course, the way in which those committees work is entirely up to the members. The powers are all there, and members can make such use of them as they like. An education committee, for example, which is proposed for the new system, would certainly look after the kind of problem that Mrs. Shirley Williams raised, because it would get wind of the pressures that associations outside the House were putting on the ministers and would itself insist on coming in on the act.

CHARLES ROSE, U.S. representative (Democrat, North Carolina): As long as we have convinced our constituents or allowed them to think that their peace of mind is in some way connected with what the government does for them, we will continue to have pressure for expanding the role of the legislature and increasing the staff to meet those expectations and to respond to the wants of our people. At some point, I hope both the United States and the parliaments that are represented here will come to grips with that problem. I have dealt with it by trying to improve the communication system in the House so that we can come a little closer to our constituents and deal more closely with each other.

I am a bit amused at the fear of television. In 1789 when the press and the public were allowed to enter the gallery of the House of Representatives, the U.S. Senate refused to go along with that move. It was feared that senators would be prima donnas, pirouetting before the press and the gallery and making long, unnecessary, and delaying arguments. The U.S. Senate gallery was therefore closed to both the press and the public until 1794.

Perhaps in Nigeria, in Germany, and in England, the television expectations of constituents are a little different from those in the United States and Canada. Perhaps in other countries elected officials do behave like fools when the camera is put on them. But the constituencies in Canada and the United States are rather sophisticated about what they see on television, and I believe they know an idiot when they see one. The television camera shows up equally well those who have something to say and those who have absolutely nothing to say. In our system, which has been in place since March 1979, if a member does not have anything to say on the floor of the House, he would be best advised to keep his mouth shut. There have been instances when slightly intoxicated members have ventured in front of the camera. I have heard rumors that the Republican congressional campaign committee is quietly circulating tapes of an incident or two and plans to make good use of them at election time. [Laughter.]

I believe that the U.S. House of Representatives copied the Canadian television system. There are 470 satellite ground stations, representing 6 million American homes, tied into the gavel-to-gavel proceedings of the House. It cannot compete with the "soaps" in the afternoon, but it reaches people who are interested in watching our proceedings. We are beginning to receive voluntary comments such as, "You are not the group of idiots the press has painted you to be. You do care about the business of the country, and you are concerned about the issues."

In closing, I would urge my European colleagues to spend a little time and effort looking at the newly developing capabilities of computers as a way to augment the research needs of parliament. Companies such as IBM, Control Data, and Honeywell are slowly developing computer systems that border on adding intelligence to our own. These computers can provide an associate memory and can be partners, in the same sense that an airplane pilot has a partnership with the navigation computer when flying across the Atlantic Ocean. We are now working with MIT on a way to marry the policy maker and the computer in a very humanizing relationship.

Isaac Asimov says that some people are afraid computers will someday take over our society. He observes that he worries more that, in the next two decades, we will not develop a computer sophisticated enough to take over the mess we have made so that we can get out of the way.

CHRISTOPHER PRICE, member, British Parliament: I would not have spoken but for Anthony King's constant reiteration that there is not a single member of Parliament who does not want to be a junior minister. I do not want to be a junior minister. I did when I was very young and first in Parliament. One or two people such as Tony Crossland had what I considered the perfect parliamentary career. They spent ten or fifteen years as a backbencher and then walked virtually straight into the Cabinet without having to go through the awfully boring, mind-bending business of being a junior minister. Colleagues of mine who were intelligent, bright backbenchers have been reduced within a couple of years to being dreadful automata without a thought in their heads, obsessed with tiny, absurd details of the Department of Employment or the Department of Health. They think the whole world revolves around the potty little argument they are having in some Cabinet committee.

I do not want that. I would quite like to be a chairman of a select committee. It worried me, however, that Mr. Bradshaw seemed to imply that the staffing of these committees is all fixed. If I were chairman of a select committee, I would want it to be run in the American manner. I would want to pick the people to run that committee, because otherwise I would have a clerks department, which is, in effect, a civil service. Although they are not civil servants, at the moment they are similar in having consensus attitudes. I learned from the clerk of the

House last summer that our clerks are drawn from an even tinier band of the social scale in Britain than are those in the administrative civil service. When we are short of clerks, we draw on former ambassadors, because they have a pension and we need not pay them very much.

My own view is that the selection of the committee must be democratic. If we are to have select committees, the chairman must be chosen by a secret ballot as he is in America. And the staffing of that committee must be at the behest of the committee and not by a vague system of consensus and government control as the clerks department of the House of Commons is at the moment.

MICHAEL MALBIN, American Enterprise Institute: One of Mr. Pym's arguments in favor of a select committee or committee reforms was that government is becoming too invasive. And Shirley Williams commented that select committees would help get the activities and perceptions of interest groups out on the public record.

In the U.S. Congress, much of the procedural reform and substantive oversight has taken place when, and because, the political interests of committee chairmen or other people active in Congress have led them to set themselves apart from, and against, the executive branch and the president. Some people see the committee system as a way of opposing government policy. But at least two people present seem to see committee reform as a way of Parliament's helping the government by having career civil servants put their opinions and reasoning on public record. If that is desired, I believe the government's interests could not be served unless the government is prepared to accept at least some potential discomfort at the hands of the committees—that is to say, as Mr. Fenno pointed out, some sanctions, whether legislative, budgetary, or otherwise, through publicity.

My question for Mr. Pym or Mrs. Williams is, Is that what the government or members of the former government hope to get out of committees, and are they willing to put up with the potential discomfort for the sake of getting that handle on the civil service and on interest groups?

MR. PYM: I think they do not want any change in the British parliamentary system that would make it so much like the American system, because the two cannot be run the same way. It would be impossible for the committee system in Britain to develop to the extent that it exists in America, because ministers are responsible, individually and collectively, to the House of Commons and must always remain so. They cannot be arraigned on the floor of the House of Commons every week and then be expected to give evidence every month upstairs to the committees. They would never be able to do any work whatsoever. One could, however, easily graft onto the British parliamentary system a select committee system that was not perhaps as extensive or as radical as Chris Price has suggested. A more limited system would be beneficial for Parliament as a further, but not an excessive, check on the government, and it would benefit the British people by throwing more light on what is done in their name. I do not see the select committee system as a way of helping the government gain better control over the career civil service.

REPRESENTATIVE FOLEY: In the United States formal oversight is done by legislative committees, which are similar to the British standing committees. Appropriations subcommittees are also effective at oversight because they have the power over money, and even a hint from the appropriations committee will produce quiet and immediate reform in the executive branch. But it is rather strange to hear Shirley Williams suggest that the committees might help the government expose and resist special interests. Our standing committees themselves are, in fact, a special interest constituency composed of the members. The people who get on the defense committee typically have an interest in defense, while those on the agriculture committee represent rural and farming areas.

It is important how the people are selected for the various committees. Will there be twelve select committees out of 600 people in the House of Commons, with perhaps one-fourth or one-fifth of the House participating? If so, how are they to be selected? If it is similar to the situation in the United States, in time, the people who are doing the select committee investigations may well be approached by outside interest groups, virtuous or otherwise, who suggest that they embarrass the government over some issue in which they have a special interest. It is a question not only of protecting the executive against special interests, but also of ensuring that the investigative committee is not used to advance special interests through the members.

REPRESENTATIVE DERRICK: Much has been said about the cost of an American legislator. I want to point out that the cost to each of my constituents is somewhat less than $1.00 a year, and I think they get a hell of a bargain.

CHARLES WHALEN, former U.S. representative: A pertinent question raised by Jeane Kirkpatrick as well as by Austin Ranney is, What has been the effect of reforms in the United States?

One effect is that, as a result of the subcommittee bill of rights, we have more people involved in the leadership process. In addition, our system today is much more open, as Kenneth Bradshaw pointed out earlier. In 1975, I think it was, the *Congressional Quarterly* found that 95 percent of the committee sessions were open; when I arrived in Congress, only 55 percent of the meetings were open. This change, of course, was brought about by the congressional reform that calls for open sessions whenever no national security issues are involved.

Also, the public now knows where the members of Congress stand on every issue. When I arrived in 1967, the amendments offered on the floor were not subject to a recorded vote but were often decided by an unrecorded teller vote. Thus, constituents did not know how their representatives stood on issues such as abortion, aid to Israel, military assistance to Turkey, and so forth. As Tom Foley has pointed out, this was changed by the rule that permits twenty people to arise and to demand that a recorded vote be taken on amendments. Largely as a result of this change, there has been a substantial increase in the House's workload. In 1969 there were 177 roll calls; in 1978 there were 944.

The recording of amendment votes, however, has given much greater power to the so-called special interest or single interest groups, for better or for worse. This fact, combined with the diffusion of power into the subcommittee areas, has certainly reduced the leadership capabilities in the House. For example, the last year that we had unrecorded teller votes, the amendment to stop funding of the SST was defeated because many members were not there to vote. Why vote when the vote is not recorded? And why vote against the leadership when it is not recorded? After this vote I heard many people indicate that they would have liked to support this amendment but did not want to oppose Jerry Ford (who was then the minority leader) or John McCormack. The next year, the same vote was subject to a recorded roll call, and despite the fact that leaders of both parties, and eighteen out of twenty-one committee chairmen, opposed this amendment to cease funding of the SST, the amendment carried. The great influence of one special interest group, the environmentalists, was apparent. It had more power then, I think, than it does today.

This phenomenon is being repeated in many other areas, reducing not only the power of the congressional leadership, but also the clout of the executive branch. Instead of being able to deal with the committee chairmen and the leadership of both parties, as was the case under the old system, today executive lobbyists have to deal with 435 House members and 100 senators, because amendments can erupt at any time from any source. It has certainly made their job infinitely more difficult.

The bottom line, then, is that the process is more open, and junior members are more involved in the leadership. But, in my opinion, bad legislation has resulted because all too often the members have looked and been responsive to the special interests, rather than to the general public interest.

MANFRED SCHULTE, member, German Bundestag: I address some questions to my American colleagues: How are subcommittees created in your Congress? Who initiates them? What majority is required? Who makes the decisions, and who decides the chairmanship? These questions seem to be important when it is decided to dissolve a committee and when one complains that there are too many subcommittees. We in Germany are confronted with the same questions, and it would be interesting to see how the development started in the United States.

REPRESENTATIVE FOLEY: The standing committees of the House, twenty-two of them, are determined by the House rules. Subcommittees are created within the committees by committee rule. That is, the members of the committee, themselves, decide how many subcommittees to have. Once a committee decides on the number of subcommittees it is to have, the subcommittee chairmanships are always held by majority party members, as full committee chairmanships are. The full committee chairmen are elected by the caucus, the whole Democratic membership. The ranking Republicans, the shadow chairmen, are elected by the Republican conference, the whole of the Republican party. General party rules require the committee members to bid for the jobs of subcommittee chairmen in the order of their seniority on each committee. Seniority is not totally dead. After they have put in their bids, the secret ballot of the Democratic members of the committee confirms or rejects those subcommittee chairmen. It is highly articulated. The rules are clear.

To give a quick comparison, in 1966 my predecessor as chairman of the Agriculture Committee created five additional subcommittees. He did it to reward returning Democrats with the little dignity and honor of being a subcommittee chairman. Of course, he could put them on as subcommittee chairmen or take them off, as he wished. At that time they had no staff, no jurisdiction, and no power except as he might determine it.

Now, there are ten subcommittees on the Agriculture Committee, a rather large number. I cannot decrease that number without the permission of the Democratic members of the committee, and the subcommittee chairmen and ranking minority members get staff.

The Agriculture Committee has, I think, twenty-seven members on the Democratic side. If I were to suggest that we reduce the subcommittees to five, the top five subcommittee chairmen and myself would constitute a minority of six. The twenty-one on the other side of the issue would say, "No, we should not reduce to five, because five of us would lose our jobs, and the other seventeen would be that much further away from a subcommittee dignity."

The only way we can now control the number of subcommittees is to go back to the full Democratic caucus and change the rules. We have taken a very tentative step by saying that members of Congress may serve on only five subcommittees, regardless of how many committees they are assigned to. Even so, we have had to make immediate exceptions for people such as Butler Derrick and Charles Rose.

MR. ORNSTEIN: I might add that in the U.S. Senate, by placing stricter limits in 1977 on the number of assignments of subcommittees to members by committee, and restrictions on the number of chairmanships, the number of subcommittees has been substantially reduced in the past two years, to 100 from 150, roughly.

BOB ECKHARDT, U.S. representative (Democrat, Texas): I should like to add to the answer to Mr. Schulte's very prescient question of how the subcommittee members are selected. When I first came to the Commerce Committee, they were selected by the chairman of the committee on the advice of the subcommittee chairmen. In that particular instance, Harley Staggers and most of the subcommittee chairmen were generally favorable to the majority position. At least on the Democratic side, they would therefore carry the bills of the government, to speak in British terms.

At present, under the reforms, they are selected in the order of their choice, the individual members being called upon in order of seniority and given the subcommittee they want. A member from, say, Texas is likely to have gotten on the Commerce Committee because the oil and gas industry wanted him there. His first choice would therefore be the Energy and Power Subcommittee. Certain others came on the full committee to please the hospital and medical interests. Their first choice would be the Health Subcommittee. The result is that the Energy and Power Subcommittee is totally controlled by the oil and gas interests. And in spite of the fact that the chairman of the Health Subcommittee is very much in favor of national medical insurance, his subcommittee is on the other side.

MARK MACGUIGAN, member, Canadian Parliament: I would like to disagree with Mr. Kunz and support Charles Rose on the televising of parliamentary proceedings. It seems to me that the objections which have so often been raised, for instance, by British parliamentarians, are based on a complete misunderstanding of television as a medium. It is a cool medium, and a grand oratorical style and florid gestures are not appropriate to it. Television has not been without its effect on the Canadian Parliament, but the effect has been to tone down proceedings and, in fact, to improve them.

Two examples will suffice. The Conservatives in opposition were the first to experiment with the effect on the public of the televised session. They sat in a group around anyone who was talking, filling all the surrounding places, thinking that this would somehow magnify the speaker. Instead, its looked very artificial, and within a week or two the practice was abandoned.

Another effect of televising has been to tone down supporting noises. Again the Conservatives lead the way. They went from the traditional desk-pounding, which sounded rather raucous, to the softer support of hand-clapping; and not only has the number of interjections decreased but also the character of interjections has changed, and other noises which were sometimes heard in the chamber have disappeared almost entirely. TV has thus civilized Parliament, and, as I suggested earlier, it has also increased the public influence of the backbencher by making his name better known across the country.

One other point: it seems to me that we have a long way to go in the parliamentary system before reaching the excesses of which Representative Foley spoke. It is not really a present worry at all. Butler Derrick told me that about 50 percent of his staff's time is spent dealing with constituency business. I have a staff of four, which is at least four times what is available to British members of Parliament, and 95 percent of my staff's time is spent in dealing with constituency business. In other words, I get almost no assistance at all in dealing with the legislative tasks of Parliament. That is where the problem lies. I do not know if 50 percent is the magic figure, but it is obvious to me that I need much more assistance with the legislative tasks. This is an indication of the distance that we have to go before the problem of which Representative Foley speaks is a real one for us.

GEOFFREY SMITH, *London Times*: In thinking of what we have to learn from each other, we are in danger of not taking into account the very different contexts in which we are operating. We are becoming alarmed by the example of the United States, with its vast staffs, the melting away of party discipline, and an executive that cannot, in any sense, control the proceedings of Congress. None of these conditions is in any danger of developing in Great Britain, and I would suspect not in Germany either.

Mr. Pym has spoken of the necessity of advancing cautiously. I think he is absolutely correct. But it might reasonably be added that there is not the slightest danger of our doing anything else—unless we decide to stand exactly still, which is a real possibility. We are rather in the position of a man with a heart condition who has been told by his doctor that it would be inadvisable to go jogging for five miles, and who has therefore concluded that it would be imprudent to stroll to the bus stop. I think we should not entirely lose sight of the bus stop.

TOM MCNALLY, member, British Parliament: After listening to Representative Foley, I felt rather like the cow reading the sign on the milk truck, which said, "pasteurized, homogenized, sterilized." The cow turned to her companion and said, "It makes you feel downright inadequate, don't it?" Having been in Parliament for five weeks, I am a little disturbed that Francis Pym now decides to get rid of a third of the seats. I want to see the third that he is going to get rid of. [Laughter.]

Two personal experiences illustrate what we have been discussing. In 1974, after I had worked nine years at the Labour party headquarters, Jim Callaghan asked me to go to the foreign office as his special adviser. When I arrived, I was met by his civil service private secretary, who conducted me to a very nice room overlooking St. James's Park and said that if I preferred a different style of furniture or if I did not like the painting, I could go down to the cellars and pick a better painting and order more modern furniture. I was told they would send up a young lady from the PA pool, and if we got on, she could be my PA, and if not, there were others. And I settled down to work in the foreign office.

About May 7, 1979, I arrived at the House of Commons as a newly elected member to find that I had a piece of pink ribbon to hang my sword on, and that was all. For three days I carried all my papers around in a suitcase. After three days, I was given the key to a locker in one of the corridors. I went to the deputy chief whip, Walter Harrison, who the *Guardian* quite rightly described as "Monitor in charge of inkwells," and asked if there were any chance of a room. "Bugger that," he said, "I have got eight Cabinet ministers who haven't got a room." [Laughter.] To this day, I do not have a telephone at the House of Commons, and I have been told very firmly that my chances of getting one before the summer recess are very scant indeed.

One reason members of Parliament continue to be served badly, as George Cunningham pointed out, is that there is not the will. I know from my period at Transport House that the party's campaign for aid to political parties was frustrated, in part, by hostility among members of Parliament. I know from my time as a special adviser that the attempt to broaden the role of the special adviser was partially frustrated by members of the House of Commons, who actually voted against the extension of that role. As an outsider for thirteen or fourteen years, I found much more emphasis on trying to prevent someone else from getting something than on working out a proper structure of staffing, and I believe that attitude still exists.

We have been talking about three different things, all of which need looking at in the British system. There is a need to work out the correct staffing for MPs, and I think Francis Pym made a valid point that we have to take account of the role of the party as a policy maker and as a research organization. Both the Labour party and the Conservative party have this role, and so do the Liberals, to a certain extent. But that point validates much more strongly the case for state aid to political parties. We should bite on that bullet—I hope in this Parliament.

We have also to look at the case for a department of the opposition. It is ridiculous that the change in power robs the front bench of all access to information and resources. And it works in both directions: There are no facilities for opposition research or opposition staffing. The Roundtree Trust made some efforts some time ago to help. As the Labour government, we made cash available to the leader of the opposition after 1974, and we now benefit from that. But the majority of frontbench spokesmen are on their own. They are doing their own research. That is another weakness in the parliamentary system. There have been proposals to put civil servants into a department of the opposition, but there is some hostility to that suggestion. It is a weakness in our system that the opposition frontbench is so inadequately staffed.

These are different parts of the same problem: how to help the individual MP and how to staff him; how to help the political party in a system such as ours; and how to give the frontbench opposition better staff and better facilities.

MICHAEL ENGLISH, member, British Parliament: David Marquand asked who would rather be a committee chairman than a junior minister. I was once asked a rather similar question by the former prime minister. Of course, any prime minister would ask it a little more subtly than David Marquand. He said, "You like being chairman of your committee, don't you?" [Laughter.]

I gave a somewhat indirect answer. I said, "Yes, I remember a man who died. As a Parliament secretary for transport, he spent half his nights answering members of Parliament who wanted some public money spent in their constituencies, and the other half of the nights he spent answering members of Parliament who did not want a road driven through their constituency. And he eventually died." Since we were discussing the question of who should be the next head of the civil service, I think I made the point sufficiently to my former prime minister.

The difference is this. Before the war, someone such as a parliamentary secretary in the foreign office was, in fact, the deputy foreign secretary for all practical purposes. He was not in theory, but in practice he was. Harold Macmillan and Harold Wilson grossly inflated the number of junior ministers. In the British Parliament they are rather like subcommittee chairmen in the United States. We have too many. And the result, of course, is to reduce their power. Previously they were, in effect, the deputies of their Cabinet ministers. The position was undoubtedly a stage on the way to the Cabinet, and it is worth being a Cabinet minister. Although the situation varies from department to department, on average, it is somewhat doubtful whether it is really worth being a junior minister now that there are so many of them.

There is a perfectly true story of a department which did not like a parliamentary secretary's decisions and simply took the same subject to one of the other five junior ministers in the same department. This can quite easily be done. Of course, they got the decision they wanted, because the other junior minister saw his power being increased and his jurisdiction somehow expanded. It is just possible that there are, as Chris Price said, now members of the British Parliament who would rather chair select committees than be one-sixth of the junior ministers in a very large department.

MANFRED VON NORDHEIM, Konrad Adenauer Stiftung: I take it that in the House of Commons there is a strong inclination to have professional staffers, that is, career personnel; whereas in the United States individual staffers are loyal to the member who appoints them and who can fire them. In Germany, we have professional staff members—career civil service people with a rather high GS rating. A chairman of a rather important German Bundestag committee once complained rather vividly that when he took over the committee he had only three or four staffers, which is very little, and could not move any of them. He could not place a man in whom he had confidence on his committee staff, and I can easily see why he did not like that at all.

It is rather interesting that Britain is considering moving in this direction. Why would a highly political body, such as Parliament, approach the staffing in a nonpolitical way? How much of an oversight and investigative function can there be when many of the people who will do the work are actually civil servants? Since they do not come and go, as legislators do, they may develop a rather cozy relation with the departments they are supposed to investigate.

CLIFFORD HACKETT, U.S. Senate staff: My point is about staff bureaucracy in Congress. There really is no staff bureaucracy, because the essence of a bureaucracy is job security, a protection of tenure. There is no protection for congressional employees. Congress is a political institution. I do not know any employee of the House or Senate who cannot be fired. That is the way it should be.

In the U.S. system there is delegation of authority—perhaps excessive sometimes—to staff. We have duplication—even chaos—but we do not have a problem of a bureaucracy. That is a problem that should concern the other two countries we have been looking at.

MICHAEL RYLE, clerk, British House of Commons: I would like to clear up one misunderstanding. It was suggested earlier that the permanent staff of select committees are in some way under the control of the government. They are independent staff serving Parliament, not the government. The committees are not debarred from recruiting at present, and under the proposals in the procedure committee they will not be debarred from recruiting their own specialist advisers.

WINFRIED STEFFANI, University of Hamburg: The topic of this session is "Models and Choices: What Can We Learn from Each Other?" Probably, we can learn to avoid many things if we listen to the problems others have. We have, however, many things in common. For instance all parliaments have, as Representative Eckhardt pointed out, a sounding-board function. But this sounding-board function can have different meanings, which can be explained by analyzing the role of the party in parliament.

In Germany, for instance, there are two concepts of responsibility, a collective and an individual one. It is necessary to strike a balance between the individual responsibility of the members of Parliament and the collective responsibility of the party. To solve this problem we should find the balance that is best for the sounding-board function of Parliament and for the interest of the whole country.

In the United States there is overemphasis on the concept of individual responsibility, because in Congress there may be 535 individual party leaders who are not much interested in forming long-lasting coalitions. Of course, there are two great party coalitions, Republicans and Democrats, but mainly for organizing the Congress, for distributing chairmanships, and so on. In the legislative process there are so many different voting patterns that it is difficult, if not impossible, to point out where, in the U.S. government, there is any collective responsibility. There are many individual responsibilities, but for the political output the voter can really call nobody, individually or collectively, to account.

At the other extreme, Great Britain lays a strong emphasis on the concept of collective responsibility: the party in government and the party in opposition. We have heard that many members of the House of Commons are frustrated if they are not a cabinet member or a leader of the governing party or of the opposition party. It seems that in Britain the concept of individual responsibility has to give way to this overemphasis on the concept of collective responsibility.

In Germany we try to develop a balance between these two extremes. Because we have a parliamentary system in our country, too, the emphasis is on the concept of collective party responsibility. But there are ways of practicing individual responsibility. Here we have been discussing mainly the possibility of the individual member to develop influence, not only in his party, but also in the committee system. Yet this is only one possibility. Another possibility is to vote on the floor against his own party. This is not, it seems, easy in the British system, because the parliamentary parties have developed the attitude that every decision on the floor is not simply a decision on a special issue, but a decision for or against their own party and their collective responsibility. Thus, every vote comes close to being a vote of confidence or no confidence for the party.

In Britain only since 1972 has there been a distinction between the vote of confidence and a vote on issues. In Germany we usually have a rather clear distinction between a vote of confidence and a vote on issues. Of course, the government is interested in declaring nearly every decision a vote of confidence, but it has not worked this way. The members as individuals can develop a great deal of influence in the party, because they have a power position. I think this is not yet the case in Great Britain. But they could develop in this direction, as we have tried to do in the past thirty years in the German Bundestag.

ROGER MOATE, member, British Parliament: I wish to state a view contrary to that expressed by Tom McNally and others, who have described the British MP as deprived of all facilities and having a pretty rough time. I think this is something of a myth. Many members enjoy disseminating this hair-shirt image, and we would actually lose an enjoyable sense of martyrdom if we gained some facilities. Tom McNally was expressing nostalgia for his days in the civil service, but in the legislature we have to look at things differently.

I do not believe there would be any qualitative improvement in output if members of the British Parliament had more office facilities and more staff. This can be demonstrated by what is available at present. Millions of pounds have been spent to provide excellent office facilities for members of Parliament, and the large proportion of members do have splendid offices. But a survey of how those offices are used while the legislature is sitting would find that 90 percent of them are empty for 90 percent of the day. In practice, members do not need a large office, and they do not need a staff. I can understand the problems of a new member's finding somewhere to locate himself, but once he has done that he will cease to use those facilities.

People fail to assess properly the immense value of the House of Commons library, which provides superb research facilities, or the expert advice available from the clerks of the House. Speaking personally, I have a very good secretary, and I regard that as sufficient. If I had a research department, I think I would regard that as a burden on my time, rather than as an asset. I think we are well served, and we would be doing a disservice to Parliament if we increased the number of research assistants and the amount of staff available to members.

JAMES LESTER, British parliamentary under secretary of state for employment: To return to Tom McNally's analogy of the cow and the milk truck, I think we have spent a great deal of time at this conference looking at the milk and deciding whether we homogenize, pasteurize, or bottle it. We have not looked at what we put in the cow to produce the milk. The type of legislation and who produces it interest me because that power is underestimated. When we come into government, clearly, the commitment to our department is to get our legislation produced with consultation. Over a five-year period in Parliament, a mass of legislation is produced within departments by the civil service, in their own forms of consultation which are, in our case, a secret. The system first comes into operation when a member of the government is confronted with a complex bill, often something of which he has no knowledge and which he had no part in producing. He is then required to master the bill and to get it through Parliament.

I would like to see more thinking done in the actual production of legislation, both to slow down the process and to widen the involvement in the process. If we do have select committees in the British Parliament, we might give them not only the power of scrutiny and investigation, but also the power to produce original legislation—particularly in controversial areas of investigation—through discussion and the involvement of all outside bodies, including interest groups, of which the civil service is only one. I think that would be a step toward looking at what we put into the cow before we actually consider how we process it.

MR. ORNSTEIN: I am glad you did not mention that a cow has more outputs than milk. Some American legislation has suggested that analogy. [Laughter.]

GEORGE CUNNINGHAM, member, British Parliament: Although I am very critical of the House of Commons (as it works), I generally do not like expressing criticisms in a multinational grouping—not because one should not wash one's dirty linen in public, but because it creates the impression that I am more dissatisfied with my own legislature than I am. I have visited other legislatures and actually studied some, and I am happier in the British House of Commons with all its faults, at the moment, than I would be in any other legislature represented here. With the modest, but very important changes that some of us want to secure in the House of Commons, it would, in my view, be the best of those legislatures.

A second point is that when there are subject committees, it is necessary to prevent outside interest groups from dominating and packing those committees. For the past year, in the European Parliament, I have been a member of the Agriculture Committee. It is absolutely packed with farmers, and if we have an Agriculture Committee in the House of Commons, as proposed, I want to make sure that it is not packed with farming interests. That means that the membership of the committee has to be decided by the House. Technically, it would be decided by the House in our system, but it has to be genuinely decided by the House to ensure that the consumer interest and the farming interests are both represented and that neither is dominant.

MR. ORNSTEIN: In the American system, one topic that has been bandied about is the rotation of committee assignments. At present people get on a committee and generally serve for their entire careers. Rotation is an alternative, which has its pros and cons, of course.

CLIVE LANDA, political director, Tory Reform Group: It is premature to talk about ensuring that select committees are not packed by outside interest groups. Such ensurance seems to me desirable, but it is about ten steps beyond where we are at the moment. We agreed that the executive branch, certainly in the British system, is influenced by outside pressure groups, many of which are not public, or on the record, or accountable. The first stage in trying to improve that situation is to make those interest groups work through a public body within Parliament, which would be the new subject committees and new select committees.

The interest groups will certainly try to pack those committees and to influence members of Parliament, as they already do. But working with the committees would at least make many of these interest groups accountable for some of their actions. It would not necessarily help members of the executive stand up to outside pressure groups, but it would at least put the arguments pro and con on the record.

It seems to me illogical in the extreme that the members of Parliament, who have designed those bodies to make interest groups accountable, should not make themselves accountable, as well. Why should the general public be excluded? I think Mr. Pym said more light should be thrown on matters for the general public in deliberations within select committees. To me, it is almost unthinkable not to televise the legislators scrutinizing and making other people accountable; otherwise, why should the interest groups feel the need to attend such committees and be made accountable? It seems to me the legislators ought to be accountable themselves. There should not be one law for the privileged and one law for the underprivileged.

DAVID ADAMS, University of Keele: I want to express surprise that I have not heard the word "federalism" in this discussion, and yet we have been comparing federal societies with a society that is nonfederal. This fundamental difference affects the nature, role, structure, and function of the national legislature. If we are concerned with what we can learn from each other, perhaps the British could learn a little something about federalism.

MR. ORNSTEIN: Professor Adams has had the last word. Thank you all for a very stimulating conference.

A Note on the Book

The typeface used for the text of this book is
Times Roman, designed by Stanley Morison.
The type was set by
Hendricks-Miller Typographic Company, of Washington.
R. R. Donnelley & Sons Company of Harrisonburg, Virginia, printed
and bound the book, using paper manufactured by the
S. D. Warren Company.
The cover and format were designed by Pat Taylor.
The manuscript was edited by Jane Carroll and Barbara Palmer, and
by Margaret Seawell of the AEI Publications staff.